Artificial Intelligence in Commercial Aviation

This book is a must read for aviation managers and all stakeholders that are interested in improving the business performance of airlines. In this book, the first of its kind on AI in Commercial Aviation, the author outlines how Machine Learning and AI are accelerating and improving the performance of airlines. Moreover, the author shares insights into many new use cases that emerging technology can deliver. He tackles all crucial functions from air navigation, flight operations, to sales, distribution, cargo, retailing, and commercial optimization. He then looks forward to blockchain and the metaverse and its opportunities.

With connected devices and the Internet of Everything (IoE), airlines can become retailers, sell, deliver, and service holistic experiences tailored to individuals in real time. This requires airlines to modernize processes and practices supported by decision intelligence (AI) that ingests sophisticated insights and executes service automation in real time. Transforming airlines from a production to a services-based execution also requires departments to be aligned along overriding customer experience and profitability goals. The book demonstrates how AI can be deployed to redesign airline organization as well.

The author also describes the next wave of business transformation around the integration of commercial functions using Composite AI at enterprise level. With his holistic understanding and experience in the airline industry, the author provides valuable insights and helps managers understand how to embrace ML and AI and contribute to future commercial aviation and cargo success.

Ricardo V. Pilon has 29 years of practical airline/aviation management and management consulting experience from line management to corporate senior management. He has worked in strategic planning, organization and governance, revenue management and pricing, business improvement, alliances, marketing, distribution, network, and product planning in both passenger services and air cargo management. He has completed over 200 projects in 98 countries with over 100 airlines and air cargo operators, industry organizations IATA and ICAO, civil aviation authorities, and aircraft manufacturers. In recent years, Ricardo has been heavily involved in creative innovation and transformation and has served as a senior executive in mid-size and large companies as an interim executive and Chief Strategy and Commercial Officer. Ricardo holds a PhD in Strategic Airline Management, an MBA in International Aviation from Concordia University in Montreal, a Master of Science in Air Transport Management from Cranfield University in the United Kingdom, a Master of Science in Applied Psychology from NTI, as well as a Bachelor of Science in International Management from the International Business School in the Netherlands. Ricardo is also the author of *Cruising to Profits*, published in 2015, and a number of airline management publications, such as *Disruptor Airline*. Since 2022, Ricardo is specializing further in the intersection of (airline) organization design, AI, and psychology and pursuing his second doctorate of applied organizational psychology in this field.

Artificial Intelligence in Commercial Aviation
Use Cases and Emerging Strategies

Ricardo V. Pilon

LONDON AND NEW YORK

Designed cover image: © Sandipkumar Patel/Getty Images

First published 2024
by Routledge
4 Park Square, Milton Park, Abingdon, Oxon OX14 4RN

and by Routledge
605 Third Avenue, New York, NY 10158

Routledge is an imprint of the Taylor & Francis Group, an informa business

© 2024 Ricardo V. Pilon

The right of Ricardo V. Pilon to be identified as author of this work has been asserted in accordance with sections 77 and 78 of the Copyright, Designs and Patents Act 1988.

All rights reserved. No part of this book may be reprinted or reproduced or utilised in any form or by any electronic, mechanical, or other means, now known or hereafter invented, including photocopying and recording, or in any information storage or retrieval system, without permission in writing from the publishers.

Trademark notice: Product or corporate names may be trademarks or registered trademarks, and are used only for identification and explanation without intent to infringe.

British Library Cataloguing-in-Publication Data
A catalogue record for this book is available from the British Library

ISBN: 9780367893620 (hbk)
ISBN: 9781032520841 (pbk)
ISBN: 9781003018810 (ebk)

DOI: 10.4324/9781003018810

Typeset in Bembo
by codeMantra

Contents

Foreword	vii
Preface	x
List of Acronyms and Abbreviations	xii
Introduction to Artificial Intelligence	1

PART 1
Applications of AI and Emerging Opportunities in Air Transport Operations — 9

1	Air Navigation and Flight Operations	10
2	Aircraft Operations and Crew	16
3	Customer, Contact, and Self-Service	26
4	Inflight and Cabin Services	35
5	Digital Cabin and Sensory Applications	43

PART 2
Applications of AI and Emerging Opportunities in Commercial Management — 53

6	Network and Schedule Planning, Aircraft Assignment	54
7	Fleet Planning and Aircraft Acquisition	65
8	Demand Forecasting, Pricing, Ancillary, and Revenue Management	72
9	Loyalty Management	81

vi *Contents*

10	Sales and Distribution	91
11	Retailing and Digital Assistants	101
12	Total Revenue Optimization (All Commercial Functions)	110
13	Brand Management, Reputation, and Social Media	119
14	Cargo Warehouse and Handling	125
15	Cargo Commercial Management	136
16	Human Resources Management	147

PART 3
Artificial Intelligence and Organization   155

17	AI and Organization Design	156
18	Enterprise, Composite AI and the Real-Time Organization	163

PART 4
Trends and Evolutions in AI   173

19	Explainable AI	174
20	Hybrid Intelligence – Addressing Deskilling, Upskilling, Reskilling	183
21	Ethical and Responsible AI (Security Privacy, Environment)	190
22	Trends and Debates in AI	198
23	AI on Blockchain, and Distributed AI with Blockchain	206
24	AI and Metaverse, Web3	217
25	Applied Psychology and AI Adoption	226

Index   233

Foreword

This book needed to be written to provide the broader context for how AI and Machine Learning is already, and will soon be, applied to the commercial aviation industry. However, it could not have been written by anyone other than creative innovation thought leader Ricardo Pilon. Ricardo has the operational experience and strategic insight in the aviation industry from decades of work helping clients to bridge the modernization of business models and novel technology to solve real business problems.

The book explains how AI can be applied across all dimensions of operating a commercial airline, so the reader can quickly focus on their area of greatest interest or take a broader approach to see how AI applied in departments and across the enterprise can help focus on the right goals, priorities, with the right insights, and the optimal recommendations.

You must of course first be able to define the business problems that can benefit from AI in aviation. A technical AI specialist would only be able to imagine conceptual applications, while Ricardo is able to explain how and why the many use cases in this book are relevant and worth solving. And, because he works with aviation professionals every day, he knows how to share insights in a very understandable way.

My main takeaway from this important book is that AI has the potential to analyze data at scale and make qualified and quantified recommendations for optimal operations such that departments can agree on common goals and stop fighting about priorities based on opinion or arguing based on data from only their own siloes.

I have been fascinated by Data Science and Artificial Intelligence for more than two decades. Both are related, but different disciplines, and both showed great promise for a long time. However, both were also slow to evolve until the past five years. I believe this slow maturing was down to missing building blocks like low-cost, extensible cloud technologies, flexible algorithm engines, and fast enough computer processors to turn around results in a reasonable timeframe.

Today, we have cloud-based data hosting and aggregation services like Snowflake that tend to be half the cost of building your own hosting environment.

viii *Foreword*

We also have exponentially more people who can ask the right questions about what the data may reveal – while at the same time, the algorithms have become smart enough to self-learn and can even figure out what to look for across terabytes of data. Furthermore, I have felt that people involved with AI for most of the past two decades were more curious about what AI might be able to do, rather than focus on use cases that maximize ROI. Today, greater business discipline, more focused business leaders, and simply more professionals that understand the technology are allowing companies to solve real business problems at scale.

The travel industry is an excellent sector to test and use AI and Machine Learning because of the massive amount of data, and the uniqueness of each business or leisure trip. People rarely travel because they like to sit in an airplane seat for 2–12 hours or deal with airport security. Fundamentally, people travel for only two reasons: (1) to communicate more effectively by being face-to-face, or (2) to expand their personal horizons by engaging with a distant culture, seeing sights in person that are more stimulating than viewing photographs, or simply to enter an environment that is different than their day-to-day routine. These are underpinnings of humanity, and the aviation industry allows people to pursue them with greater ease and less environmental harm than if the industry did not exist at all. The benefit of travel is a greater appreciation of diversity, and that is very necessary in the existing world.

Very rarely do two trips have the same objectives, involve the same people, or comprise the same modes of transportation. This is remarkable given that over 1B flights are booked each year. Given the infinite combinations involved in a trip, AI has the potential to help people achieve their goals in a more optimal way.

In this context, instead of the traveler or their travel agent "searching" around 20 to 200 alternatives, AI could do much of the analysis so the traveler can simply "choose" one of the 3–4 best alternatives presented. This has huge ramifications for search engines like Google – because intelligent agents doing the groundwork don´t engage with advertising. They just logically and rationally combine the best components and present them with no emotion involved.

For the travel companies as well, and in particular airlines, helping customers achieve their travel goals can transform their business from a company that moves large aluminum tubes from one airport to another, into a problem-solving logistics partner that builds affinity with their customers.

Of course, this would be a massive cultural change for any airline, but those who can evolve in this direction have the potential to convert themselves from a low-margin, highly cyclical, and capital-intensive business into a lifestyle brand that customers can rely on to achieve their personal goals.

Given this organization transformation, I speculate that the majority of AI investment is not in the infrastructure or algorithms, but rather in people and organizational design. It should also tear down the walls that have separated airline business units with competing agendas, so a more agile organization can work as one toward common objectives. Common agendas and collaboration at the organizational level can allow AI to work its magic – at scale – to deliver real ROI.

AI is still constrained by the quality of the data, or the quantity of the data to train algorithms. As the saying goes 'garbage in, garbage out'. Few travel companies have a problem with the quantity of data, but given the many business units in a typical travel company, getting all the right data into a single, logical repository to let AI do its job, remains elusive. Again, I believe this is more of an organizational problem than a technology problem. I believe Ricardo Pilon uncovers and tackles all these relevant areas, culminating in how applied psychology can be helpful in updating change management practices to facilitate the adoption and integration of AI and improve overall human–machine collaboration.

By Charles (Chuck) Ehredt, CEO, Currency Alliance

Preface

The idea for this book was born around 2015 after I first released my first book entitled *Cruising to Profits*. It intrigued me that airline organization and available technology could not support the evolution and execution of business models that would remove the airline industry's dependency on derived demand. And with the trend and growing importance of ancillary revenues, I conceptualized what digital giants such as Google, Amazon, or Facebook could do to spur goal-centric social commerce around individuals that are also interested in travel. This is a reversal from the practice of selling more things to people that travel. I bundled these thoughts in 'Disruptor Airline', published in early 2016 as a concept paper.

It was when I was introduced to artificial intelligence (AI) in 2017 that I realized that AI would be the key enabler to the use cases I imagined. Moreover, how AI could be used to overcome departmental barriers and silos that exist in airlines. So, I started specializing in artificial intelligence, got formal education, followed training, and started mapping solutions to use cases I wanted to pursue and introduce to clients. It was when I discovered that AI can also be used to redesign airline organizations to overcome the limitations of traditional structures that I uncovered additional human aspects around AI. This took me down a parallel path of getting another master's degree in applied organizational psychology which I completed in 2021. I realize today that these skills and disciplines are converging and leading me into a specialty of behavioral economics with deep tech to help deliver incremental business value.

I believe that the combination of capital allocation (strategy), tactical applications of AI, and organization design shapes the strategic mix necessary to modernize business model execution in airline retail transformation. This will also help evolve the industry into a true service industry, an industry which today is still constrained by operational structures and wholesale models.

Cruising to Profits gained significant popularity during the COVID-19 pandemic, when people could not travel. This book is the next level. I hope that this book inspires peers, colleagues, airline and travel companies to take a close look at the benefits that human-AI interaction can bring to elevate processes, enterprise workflows, and customer experiences to create sustainable industry profitability.

I would like to thank T&F Publishing and Routledge, in particular Amelia Bashford and Guy Loft, for the collaboration and opportunity to release this work.

List of Acronyms and Abbreviations

AI	Artificial Intelligence
B2B	Business-to-Business
B2C	Business-to-Consumer
DL	Deep Learning
DLT	Distributed Ledger Technology
F&B	Food and Beverage
GDS	Global Distribution System
MCAS	Maneuvering Characteristics Augmentation System
ML	Machine Learning
NFT	Non-Fungible Token
NLP	Natural Language Programming
OBE	Online Booking Engine
OTA	Online Travel Agent
P&L	Profit & Loss Account
TMC	Travel Management Company

Introduction to Artificial Intelligence

1.1 AI Explained

Artificial Intelligence (AI) is about taking pieces of information to create links and patterns and identify trends that combined can solve problems at the highest level of predictability. Most people today are exposed to applications of AI in everyday life, especially as consumers or customers of online platforms and services. People use search engines such as Yahoo or Google, and the popular navigation services offered by Google Maps help people save time getting to their destination or find the best itineraries by foot, train, or car even by circumventing traffic accidents or congestion in real time. We are also used to shopping online and being offered suggestions for similar and related products, even based on what other people like us seem to like. Perfecting these recommender systems is what made Amazon the success story with global and regional distribution centers employing hundreds of thousands of people worldwide.

We can group applications based on the type of technology within AI that is being used to automate the processes that make it convenient for people to use (Figure 1.1). What they have in common, is that they all work with data and can use and manipulate data to perform tasks that follow the same pattern people would with their own logic to solve problems or puzzles (Table 1.1).

In most cases, more than one technique is used to perform tasks to automate an outcome that is experienced as frictionless to a person in terms of how it was presented. For instance, if somebody types "looking for a chocolate Labrador near me" in a search engine's search field, the underlying machine learning (ML) models have to decipher many aspects, dimensions, and attributes in order to determine that we are not referring to a geographical location (for instance Newfoundland & Labrador) or a Labrador made of chocolate. Based on past search history and creating links between words in sentences, the models have to determine we are looking for a dog, that chocolate refers to the preferred color, and that the person is perhaps looking to find and purchase a Labrador near the location the person that is searching is at. In order to understand the words that the person typed, the model has to understand human language, which itself is a technique called Natural

DOI: 10.4324/9781003018810-1

2 Introduction to Artificial Intelligence

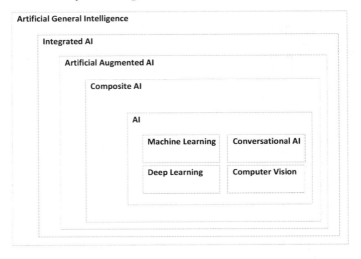

Figure I.1 Categories of artificial intelligence.

Table I.1 Different types of artificial intelligence

Type of AI Technology	Illustration
Search using Natural Language Processing	Yahoo, Google (word-based search)
	Expedia, Amazon, Kayak, Booking
	Predictive text/response (auto-reply)
Voice recognition (voice command)	Apple's Siri, Alexa
Movement sensors	Park distance control (cars)
	Surveillance
	Automated handling (warehouse)
Machine learning	Amazon (recommender system)
	Email filters (spam)
	Online games, such as chess
	Online gambling
	Predictive maintenance (jet engines)
General Narrow Intelligence	Robotics (car manufacturing, bottling)
Computer vision	Facial recognition
	Retina scans
	Fingerprint recognition
	Image recognition
	Autonomous cars

Language Programming. It must use the same technique to go through past search history to reproduce a response that, based on past searches and results, provides the highest likelihood that relevant results are displayed back to the person. ML will perform that function based on algorithms that can be built autonomously by performing billions of rounds of data mining to identify which words and attributes are most closely related and provide the best responses for different contexts. So, a separate group of ML models sifts through all results that have a high likelihood of responding accurately to the request based on physical proximity to the person's device or laptop, based on location-based services, or the location the person entered to be used as a base point.

In first generations of the deployment of search, entering "chocolate", "dog" and "Labrador" in the same sentence could have resulted in "hot dog with chocolate", which evidentially makes no sense. Or, search would not have picked up that "Labrador" is a dog, without specifying it. As such, ML also learns over time, because the models are written to keep learning from their performance and to continue perfecting themselves.

1.2 Goal of Artificial Intelligence

AI consists of many different things, techniques, and technologies but the end goal is to have general intelligence, which is defined as the ability to solve arbitrary problems like humans would, but better and faster. In practical life, the typical goals we find are:

- Reasoning (explain something)
- Knowledge presentation (display intelligence in an easy-to-interpret fashion)
- Planning better and faster
- Learning better and faster
- To understand and work with natural language (Natural Language Programming)
- Perception (interpret difficult environments)
- Ability to move and manipulate objects (robotics).

The step AI makes beyond ML is the automation of decision-making and taking action to maximize the chance of achieving a goal. Is often used to automate repetitive tasks that require many bits of information, and by incorporating insights generated from other machines. The goals are set by people, but the machine will solve the puzzle and will continue to learn as new information comes in. AI is essentially built around how humans think, analyze, and make decisions using information (neural systems). The models that are built deal with individual processes. Often multiple models are needed to solve the "end model", which is the end objective you aim to meet.

1.3 The Need for AI

The need for the use and application of AI has its origins in automating tasks that are time consuming for humans, but also to help solve problems faster than humans can. If we can automate the assembly or parts to make a car, we can save people from the physical effort and potential pain. If we can do

4 *Introduction to Artificial Intelligence*

it faster and better than humans because we may make fewer mistakes, we are increasing the quality of the product. There is also commercial interest in saving effort and selling higher volumes faster. But AI is not only driven by industrialization but also aimed at dealing with complex problems that would take humans too long to solve. For instance, it would not be possible to sift through reports or data to understand what individual people are interested in and might purchase when they shop online manually. And even if we were able to track it manually and understand it, we would not be able (nor would we have the means) to influence our product offering in a personalized manner to each potential customer. We would also not be able to compare this to what competitors are selling and at which price, and how that impacts our potential sales or likelihood to convert shoppers into customers.

So even though the application of AI started long before the internet transformed our behaviors, one of the driving forces behind the acceleration of ML and AI is that the Internet of Everything (IoE) and connectivity has increased the interactions we have with companies and each other and that this has led to an explosion in content. Marketplaces have come to life to provide a convenient shopping platform (e.g. eBay) or to simply share and compare information, such as experiences, customer reviews, and rankings, or items that are trending. In order to ensure that the experiences between sellers and buyers are convenient and relevant, it is in everybody's interest that the information is better structured and well-presented to (1) improve the customer experience, (2) create loyal customers, (3) sell more to the same and new customers, and (4) increase revenues and profits.

In sum, from the perspective of individual people as customers or companies as service providers, the key drivers of digital transformation that have necessitated the use of AI are

- Need for convenience.
- Need for speed.
- Need for mobility and mobile access.
- Need for relevancy.
- Need for control.

The transparency and abundance of information that the internet has brought have also made customers better informed and more in control of the engagement with sellers and travel providers. While initially service providers offered Apps to increase the customer experience, customers increasingly require additional functionality to drive their experiences and self-service their options and choices in real time.

The way in which customers shop and purchase online has also influenced and accelerated the digitization of processes in supply chains, in part spurred by delivering on promises of overnight delivery even across borders. This has necessitated the digitization and automation of manufacturing, sorting, dispatch, and delivery processes, all of which enabled through AI.

Introduction to Artificial Intelligence 5

But even without the speed element, the computing power required to handle all online requests, shopping, filtering, and feeding of recommender systems is such that it is beyond human capabilities in real time. Besides, there is a commercial interest to get it right and monetize digital interactions with people as much as possible. So, from a human capability perspective, the internet has resulted in a world with:

- Too much choice.
- Too much information.
- Too much content.
- Too many variables and dimensions in a complex context.
- Too many things to analyze at the same time.
- Too many decisions to make in a short time frame.
- Everything changing in real-time.
- Massive compound growth in volume and complexity of data and types.

1.5 Benefits of AI

The benefits of AI are described through the use cases that are found throughout this book as different functions with airline planning, operations, and management. For the benefit of summarizing what the benefits of using AI are in commercial aviation, Table I.2 provides an overview.

1.6 How Does AI Work

AI evolved from efforts to simulate the brain using formal logic that started in 1956. Iterative processing and use of intelligence by machines allow a system

Table I.2 Benefits of artificial intelligence

Area	Commercial Benefits
Planning, operations, management	Improves predictability
	Improves accuracy
	Improves efficiencies
	Accelerates decision making
	Improves service recovery
	Automates repetitive tasks
Problem solving	Enables more complex problem solving
	Identifies hidden patterns
	Generates options for scenario planning
	Improves what–if analysis
Customer service and experience	Improves customer service
	Enables self-service
	Powers higher volumes
Sustainability	Helps reduce emissions
	Identifies areas for improvement

6 *Introduction to Artificial Intelligence*

to interpret its environment and take action that maximizes the chance of achieving its goals. These goals are set by people. The machine then simulates how humans think by connecting the proverbial dots, i.e., by identifying which things or elements are related and how we can learn and solve problems using these observed correlations in real time or in the future. How machines draw conclusions and make predictions is within the specialized field of ML, which itself has many levels of complexity. It is based on the use of algorithms, which is explained below.

AI over time has moved into mathematical statistical ML to solve problems by predictions. How this works in practice is dependent on (1) acquiring skills and (2) learning experience through data. In other words, in order to create insights, data science is needed. Subsequently, in order to solve problems or automate task in a complex environment, data models and end models are needed and applied.

As such, a prerequisite for ML and AI is that business processes and outcomes can only be improved if data is captured. This explains why we often talk about 'digitization', 'digitalization', or 'digital transformation', as the means of using and working through electronic means allows us to use and capture new data that can help us improve business outcomes. The internet, connectivity, and mobility have as such been the clear propulsion behind the growth in ML and AI.

Data science evolved as a natural extension of analytics tools that are often referred to as Business Intelligence (BI) tools. They allow companies and users to play with data to create drill-down insights and shed light on meaningful perspectives of the business, customer segments, specific behaviors, or cause–and–effect analyses of business decisions. But in terms of data science as part of AI platforms, these are the types of methods and techniques that go into building algorithms:

- Search.
- Mathematical optimization.
- Formal logic.
- Artificial neural networks.
- Statistics.
- Probability.
- Economics.
- Computer science.
- Psychology.
- Linguistics.
- Philosophy.

To make ML and AI work, you need:

- Information (data).
- Structure.

Introduction to Artificial Intelligence   7

- Interactions between information elements.
- Correlations.
- History and activity (to learn from solved problems).

1.7 AI vs. ML

ML is a component of AI and is about the work on computer algorithms that improve automatically through experience. This can happen in one of two ways, that is (1) unsupervised learning or (2) supervised learning. In unsupervised learning, the machine can find patterns in streams of input without requiring a human to label the inputs first. In supervised learning, a human needs to structure data first to assign information to categories it belongs to (classification) and by producing a function that describes the relationship between inputs and outputs (numerical regression), to predict how outputs should change as the input changes.

Both unsupervised and supervised learning can be 'learners' and function approximators. That means that something implicit can become a category over time as the data is analyzed. A good example of this is spam email. With sufficient iterations, the characteristics of the spam emails and types of techniques used can be observed and lead to the automatic creation of filters or rules that move new spam emails into a designated mail folder.

ML essentially completes AI because it depends on the rules and outcomes that AI stipulates as the desired and optimized outcome. For instance, a person is browsing through online information about beach vacations. The AI end model that is scripted could be tasked with recommending in-house products to sell to the customer as well as additional add-on services that the customer could be interested in. The ML models will mine as much as possible about the customer and their profile (past search and past vacations) and current search context online and find the correlations that best predict the items the customer would be interested in purchasing. By feeding this through the AI pipeline, the customer may be presented with hotels at destinations the airline can serve as well as the preferred brand of sun tanning lotion that we observed for this customer, including possible taxi-ride itineraries from the known locations. The more comprehensive the offer creation, the more complex it is to build and deliver. Chapters 18 and 19 talk about layering models using deep learning to achieve this.

Advanced analytic techniques are like a microscope or magnifying glass, i.e. the help improve the effectiveness and efficiency of fraud management, thereby reducing costs. The integration of high-quality data sources and the use of new modeling techniques are transforming fraud prevention. ML is the first technique often used to speed up decision-making, improve accuracy, and reduce costs. With the rise in ML, this branch of AI has become a key technique for solving problems in very diverse areas and is recommended for complex tasks or problems involving large amounts of data and lots of variables, but no existing formula or equation. This is the case in

8 *Introduction to Artificial Intelligence*

fraud detection, where the rules of a task are constantly changing with each introduction of new tactics by fraudsters. ML models continually analyze and process incoming data, and autonomously update themselves with the new information, making ML an effective tool for detecting the most common types of fraud such as payment fraud, account takeovers (whether of customers or employees), triangulation, or loyalty currency fraud. Additionally, it improves accuracy and reduces the system's response time to new attack patterns and trends. ML also facilitates real-time decision-making by rapidly evaluating large amounts of transactional data, eliminating time-consuming manual interaction and, therefore, enabling a significant reduction in fraud management costs. Blockchain or distributed ledger technology (DLT) also promises future benefits for fraud prevention. AI on blockchain (also called "distributed AI") offers other novel use cases that are explored in Chapter 23.

1.8 Conclusions

AI is an emerging technology that is rapidly transforming industries and business models. By using data and mimicking how human solve problems, AI is helping to accelerate and automate processes with machine and deep learning. From smart search to autonomous vehicles, the combination of smart technologies is powering self-service applications and generating deep insights into patterns. These technologies unlock many efficiencies, cost savings, and new revenue potential. Moreover, AI is a powerful tool driving sustainability efforts. AI also helps to deliver better customer service and is estimated to generate over 13 trillion dollars in value each year for customers, businesses, and society.

Bibliography

C3 (2022). 'What is enterprise AI – AI suite model-driven architecture', pp. 8–12. https://c3.ai/what-is-enterprise-ai/c3-ai-suite-model-driven-architecture/

Deloitte (2022) 'State of AI in the enterprise, 2nd edition'. *Deloitte Insights*. https://www2.deloitte.com/content/dam/insights/us/articles/4780_State-of-AI-in-the-enterprise/DI_State-of-AI-in-the-enterprise-2nd-ed.pdf

McKinsey & Co. (2018) 'Notes from the AI frontier – modelling the impact of AI on the world economy'. McKinsey Global Institute (MGI). https://www.mckinsey.com/~/media/

Norvig, P. (2021) *Artificial intelligence: a modern approach*. Global edition 4th edn. London: Pearson.

Pitt, J. (2021) *Self-organising multi-agent systems: algorithmic Foundations of Cyber-anarcho-socialism*. London: World Scientific Publishing Europe (WSPE).

Poole, D. *et al.* (2017) *Artificial intelligence: foundations of computational agents*. 1st edn. Cambridge: Cambridge University Press.

Siddique, S. (2018) 'The road to enterprise artificial intelligence: a case studies driven exploration'. MIT Thesis. Cambridge: MIT.

Part 1

Applications of AI and Emerging Opportunities in Air Transport Operations

This first part of this book talks about the current applications of artificial intelligence (AI) in operations functions within air transport. It provides an overview of the early use cases and adoption in air navigation, flight operations, and aircraft operations. As part of customer-facing operations, contact center and customer service is included in the second section of this part. In addition, inflight service and cabin services that can be improved using AI are covered from a procurement and operations point of view. The last chapter looks at how connected devices (Internet of Things) can improve operations and services using sensory applications.

Part 1 is structured as follows:

Chapter 1 addresses air navigation and flight operations.
Chapter 2 speaks to aircraft operations including fuel management.
Chapter 3 talks about customer contact management and customer service.
Chapter 4 delves into inflight service management and cabin service operations.
Chapter 5 focuses on Internet of Things connected devices and sensory applications in cabins.

DOI: 10.4324/9781003018810-2

1 Air Navigation and Flight Operations

1.1 Air Navigation Explained

Air navigation is about maneuvering an aircraft from one place to another, in simple terms. It includes the process or planning, operating, and recording all steps along the way, while respecting all laws that apply to the safe operation of aircraft in the respective air space the aircraft will be flying through. Safety laws regarding operating aircraft also apply to the safety of people on the ground. Due to the speed and continuation of flight until landing, all waypoints and alternatives must be planned and filed prior to departure. This includes a review of expected weather and mitigating techniques to secure safe as well as comfortable transportation. Once in the air, constant position awareness as well as all operating conditions (such as fuel consumption) is monitored to confirm or alter initial flight plans.

There are many techniques used for navigation in the air today, and often a combination of them is used. Historically, aircraft were operated under visual flight rules (VFR) or under instrument flight rules (IFR). IFR allows pilots to use instruments and commands from air traffic control to guide aircraft to beacons, also called 'waypoints'. A more modern approach to air navigation is the use of satellite-based positioning systems, such as GPS.

Other than the technological advances that are needed, improved co-ordination and integration of air traffic control across borders is needed as well. Airlines, the International Air Transport Association (IATA) and industry stakeholders in the air transport sector have for years advocated for modernization of air traffic management systems such as the planned reform of Europe's skies under a 'Single European Sky' (SES) as put forward by the European Commissions since the early 2000s. The aim is to implement a safe, secured, and more efficient management of the airspace, with better predictive capabilities, leading to fewer delays and less fuel burned, so fewer carbon dioxide emissions for an overall smaller aviation carbon footprint. However, the delay in the implementation of this harmonized and centralized system has been the requirement for all EU states and their air navigation service providers (ANSPs) to ratify the agreement and move forward.

DOI: 10.4324/9781003018810-3

Air Navigation and Flight Operations 11

IATA has argued that the Single European Sky (SES) is vital for a safe, sustainable, and efficient European air transport industry and that among its benefits are[1]:

- An improvement in safety performance by a factor of ten.
- Greater capacity and fewer delays, giving a EUR 245 billion boost to Europe's GDP and a million extra jobs annually from 2035.
- A 10% cut in EU aviation emissions, supporting the European Green Deal.

The airline industry has argued that crises, such as COVID-19, make efficiency gains ever more critical but that the climate crisis is an urgent driver for required change to immediately reduce the environmental impact of aviation. There are no technological barriers to implementing a single air traffic management system. And before 2019, the discussion on the modernization of this infrastructure does not even refer to the possibility of driving additional efficiencies through the adoption of machine learning and artificial intelligence in flight operations through Europe's skies and between Europe's airports. More recently, NATS (National Air Traffic Services), the ANSP in the UK, has been publicizing the need for artificial intelligence (AI) in air navigation. NATS even have a Chief Solutions Officer, Digital Towers (Andy Taylor).

1.2 AI in Air Navigation

AI platforms in air navigation can augment the quality, speed, and precision of human decision-makers in air traffic management and the need to adopt it is increasingly apparent. AI has started to complement and enhance the capabilities of humans, reducing their involvement in repetitive or low-value tasks, and freeing up more time for more critical tasks, where human intervention is crucial.

Aviation is being reshaped by several powerful forces that are also fundamentally impacting the Air Traffic Management sector. This is not only because we can continue to expect growth in air transport and the expansion of traditional aircraft fleets but also because the composition of different aircraft and new types of flying vehicles navigating the skies will rapidly change. We are already witnessing small-scale deployment of drones for small parcel and cargo deliveries. But by 2025, we can expect the first small electric vertical take-off and landing (eVTOL) aircraft with the capacity to carry 4–6 people to be certified for commercial operation.[2] This means that air transport management (ATM) and new technologies in airspace management need to support and manage increased complexity in different types of flight operations and vehicles and include a new set of airfields or eVTOL pads or vertiports around urban areas.

12 Uses of AI and Emerging Opportunities in Air Transport Operations

Safe and secure airspace management in this new era will require modern systems that can handle increased volumes and alleviate the many repetitive tasks that air traffic controllers perform, including the hand-over of vehicles throughout different stages in flight. AI-enabled platforms and machine learning are playing a role in transforming ATM in a number of ways.

The ANSPs in several countries are upgrading their infrastructure to centralize the coordination of multiple sites, harmonize practices, and improve efficiency while safeguarding safety using new ATM capabilities. For instance, by incorporating improved predictions and weather updates into ATM systems using AI, different sets of likely scenarios can be predicted with higher accuracy, that will allow the system to recommend rerouting of aircraft or otherwise find other ways to reduce fuel burn.

Eurocontrol, the ANSP for the EU, has revealed gains of between 20% and 30% in terms of predictability and efficiency from the use of AI. AI has been a vital part of the European Commission's digital single market strategy since 2017 and the program was supported by €1.5 billion funding under the Horizon 2020 program from 2018 to 2020.[3] This was followed by a roadmap and establishment of the European AI Alliance in 2018 to put Europe firmly on the path to becoming a leader in the AI revolution.

Once machine learning models can train on repetitive tasks (daily operations), they can help rectify or mitigate irregular operations (IRROPS). This is because it will understand the correlation between factors and learn how to optimize operations. It can also recommend the best way to ramp up operations to minimize delays and expedite service recovery in the air as well as on runways and the ramp.

Improved forecasts can be incorporated not only for the flight portion but also for all other expected movements and predictable maneuvers and potential delays based on situational awareness at airports. For instance, gate and ramp operations can be monitored through the airport operations control center (AOCC) and any incidents or unexpected changes can be fed digitally to Air Traffic Control or ATM systems. The ATM systems will in turn use the data and insights and couple them with runway operations and use automated support to stage, slow down or accelerate and alter aircraft approaches to optimize the overall flow of traffic to and around an airport. No human could look at all these aspects from an airport system's perspective and simultaneously calculate the likely outcomes of possible scenarios to make decisions in real time.

The new generation of automated systems increases the efficiency of ATM, but humans will always be part of the process to oversee their functioning, supervise the learning of models based on experience the AI models have not yet learned and allow them to have the final decision on critical events or situations. Human interaction is one of ultimate supervision and quality control as we cannot expect an automated system to run and manage all vehicles in the air without any mechanism to overrule the decisions that are made. The way humans interact with machines is also critical in this area, as further explored in Chapter 20 on Hybrid Intelligence.

Air Navigation and Flight Operations 13

Managing risk is even more critical if we start incorporating unmanned aerial vehicles (UAVs), for which parameters need to be set within ATM to alert and intervene in case the software of UAVs makes dangerous decisions or takes actions that are against the safety protocols and standard operating procedures (SOPs) agreed to by the airport authorities and civil aviation authorities. With a more dynamic environment with a more diverse set of craft in the air, smart decision-making solutions will be required.

1.3 Alaska Airlines

Alaska Airlines uses Flyways, a platform that uses AI and machine learning developed by Airspace Intelligence. Founder of Airspace Intelligence Phillip Buckendorf was a researcher in his early career and had started other companies before in smart commerce and robotics. He approached Alaska Airlines in 2018 with an idea about improving flight planning and dispatch. The goal was to assist dispatchers by providing them with automated insights for flight operations that could make it more efficient and sustainable by using existing and available information that is updated in real time. This would optimize routes and improve the predictability of airline traffic. This in turn could be used to improve the flow of the airline's traffic over the network and thus improve completion factors, on-time performance, and connectivity while reducing fuel burn.

> You have this incredibly dynamic environment where you want to predict; where are you going to be in the airspace? And what does the environment look like? And how do you optimize for that?
> (Phillip Buckendorf, Founder & former CEO of Flyways)

Following a few trials in 2020 that lasted almost six months, Alaska Airlines signed a multi-year contract with Airspace Intelligence, based in Silicon Valley. The software, Flyways, looks at all the scheduled and active flights across the USA. While it needs to look at each flight individually, it takes a systems look to scan overall air traffic volumes and particularities it can cluster in patterns. It can constantly and dynamically analyze and interpret the overall system of all moving objects. It then uses information from a number of real-time digital data sources to help flight dispatchers by advising them on the best ways to fly or operate each mission from its origin to its destination. Flyways tap into weather systems, capture insights, and interpret potential problems using AI and run these learnings through an end model that re-optimizes the flight plan for each mission. The AI software creates the prediction models of useable and best airspace to use while taking into consideration all possible and realistic constraints, including no-fly zones and other restrictions that are known or acquired in real time from ATC. One way of looking at this is by comparing the solution to how Google Maps provides re-routing recommendations based on actual and predicted delays caused by heavy traffic, accidents, or road obstacles.

14 *Uses of AI and Emerging Opportunities in Air Transport Operations*

Flyways have enabled Alaska Airlines to streamline its flight operations and traffic flows. It allowed the airline to reduce fuel burn in 64% of its flights during the six-month trial that started in early 2020.[4] The reduction in fuel burn has beneficial effects on the reduction of carbon dioxide emissions, but the overall improved flight completion factors, on-time performance, and crew efficiency have also benefited air travelers in improved service levels.

1.4 Conclusions

AI-powered applications in flight planning and dispatch, like Flyways deployed at Alaska Airlines, can significantly improve flight completion factors, and reduce fuel burn. At scale, AI can improve air traffic management for ANSPs by automating the ingestion of more and deeper insights into contextual factors, dimensions, and risk into their workflow. The significance of this regarding a more sustainable air transport industry as well as related efficiencies is beyond estimation. It is expected that deep learning and AI will transform air traffic management as well as how aircraft operate and navigate in real time.

Notes

1 IATA (2021) 'Now or never for Single European Sky'. Press release. https://www.iata.org/en/pressroom/pr/2021-04-20-02.
2 Nevans, J. (2022) 'Lilium extends eVTOL type certification timeline to 2025'. *Vertical.* Blog. https://verticalmag.com/news/lilium-extends-evtol-type-certification-timeline-2025/#:~:text=Estimated%20reading%20time%205%20minutes,the%20Lilium%20Jet%20eVTOL%20aircraft.
3 Eurocontrol (2022) 'Why artificial intelligence is highly relevant to air traffic control'. https://www.eurocontrol.int/article/why-artificial-intelligence-highly-relevant-air-traffic-control.
4 Semuels, A. (2021) 'Travel is coming back, and artificial intelligence may be planning your next flight'. *TIME Magazine.* https://time.com/6050921/artificial-intelligence-air-travel.

Bibliography

Degas, A. *et al.* (2022) 'A survey on artificial intelligence (AI) and eXplainable AI in air traffic management: current trends and development with future research trajectory', *Applied Sciences*, 12(3), p. 1295.
Fayyaz, R. (2022) 'Artificial intelligence for cybersecurity in air traffic control'. *SkyRadar.* https://www.skyradar.com/blog/artificial-intelligence-for-cybersecurity-in-air-traffic-control
IBM (2022) 'Co-creating the future of air traffic management'. https://www.ibm.com/case-studies/luftfartsverket/
NATS (2019) 'Embracing artificial intelligence in aviation and air traffic management'. Blog. https://nats.aero/blog/2019/06/embracing-artificial-intelligence-in-aviation-and-air-traffic-management/

Taylor, A. (2022) 'Digital towers, artificial intelligence, and the next generation of airport air traffic management'. *International Airport Review.* https://www.internationalairportreview.com/article/178144/digital-towers-artificial-intelligence-air-traffic-management/

ThinkML (2021) 'How air traffic can be optimized using artificial intelligence'. https://thinkml.ai/how-air-traffic-can-be-optimized-using-artificial-intelligence/

2 Aircraft Operations and Crew

2.1 Aircraft Operations Explained

Aircraft operations are those that are related to operating aircraft in the air, including all support functions that ensure the aircraft is legally serviceable, meets all the technical and service requirements, and is in optimal condition to operate missions without expected interruptions or avoidable incremental costs.

There is a significant amount of work that goes into planning a flight. In this chapter, we focus on operating flights that have already been scheduled. In Part 2 of this book, where we discuss commercial airline planning, the topics of network, route planning and fleet assignment will be explored separately.

Before looking at each separate aspect of flight operations, it is important to highlight that modern airlines take a total mission optimization (TMO) approach. This means that even though separate solutions manage flight planning, fuel efficiency programs, crew management, and maintenance, there is increased communication between functions and systems in real time. Interfaces allow processes to be aligned for planning but also to solve problems that happen in real time and require collaboration from all functions. Whether the solutions are all provided by a single vendor or not, the trend is to integrate the communication between them and to use artificial intelligence to analyze and solve problems based on predictive analytics in real time. This also means that the approach of a network perspective is taken to consider the context of individual flights and the impact they have on passenger journeys as well as crew and their needs.

2.2 AI in Aircraft Operations

Most of the benefits derived from artificial intelligence lie in (a) combining large and new sources of data, and (b) using a higher granularity of specific information that determines the extent of the impact new optimization techniques will have. For instance, aircraft engines (even when they are new) have particular performance deviations. But as aircraft age, the performance

DOI: 10.4324/9781003018810-4

degradation is not symmetrical or linear. All parts of the aircraft will show distinct patterns of degradation that all impact, for instance, fuel efficiency. Even a dirty fuselage does, so how often an aircraft is cleaned can be shown to be related to fuel efficiency.

Tracking all the moving parts and (over)consumption of liquids and other wear all goes into large calculations that ultimately help airlines plan and operate better. With artificial intelligence, more dimensions with unlimited data can be used to improve this with surgical precision. And tracking aircraft performance is not only about efficiency, but more fundamentally about reliability and safety.

2.2.1 Fuel Optimization and Emissions Reduction

With fuel typically being the largest single cost component of an airline (22–28% of total operating costs) and the largest variable cost in operating aircraft, airlines typically have a constant search for initiatives that can help them save fuel costs, because they have a direct impact on the bottom line. This is particularly the case within a given schedule where airlines look at cost-saving opportunities with the existing fleet.

By leveraging AI in aircraft operations during flight, airlines can also reduce their greenhouse emissions (NO_x and CO_2) significantly. Air France started looking at ways to reduce emissions by combining and optimizing data from multiple sources in 2018.[1] It started by using the information from the plane's black boxes and then combining all the aircraft's operational data with the data from communication systems and flight plans. So, plans were laid out against real-time data about the flight itself. The algorithm can generate a deep analysis of the efficiency of fuel utilization on any flight. Air France can then utilize this data to make recommendations on how to reduce fuel consumption and reduce emissions by overlaying recommended practices and flight operations for future flights. The results indicated that Air France had already slashed its emissions in 2020 by half.[2]

The program implemented by Air France is called 'SkyBreathe' and was designed by OpenAirlines.[3] It is currently also used by Norwegian, Go Air, and Malaysian Airlines, among others. OpenAirlines is an international software company based in Toulouse, with offices in Hong Kong and Miami and has, since launched in 2006, been "on a mission to help airlines save 2–5% of their fuel consumption, without any modification on the aircraft". According to OpenAirlines, the program had already saved the airlines over USD 150 million in fuel costs while reducing carbon emissions by nearly 600 tonnes in 2020 alone.[4]

More specifically individual aircraft performance monitoring is important to gain insights into the actual performance of individual aircraft. Airlines such as Cebu Pacific, SpiceJet, and Ukraine International Airlines have set up fuel efficiency programs this way and use a large data set of specific data to create actionable insights (OpenAirlines, 2022). What they do helps to identify the accurate fuel factor of each specific 'tail' (aircraft with fin number) and link that to the Flight Management System (FMS) and flight planning system used by the aircraft. In this manner, the amount of fuel necessary to fly a particular mission can be computed based on meteorological circumstances, expected traffic, and air navigation for each specific aircraft. Not using an accurate fuel factor can lead to problems when too much fuel is carried because the performance was better than assumed (additional fuel weight also increases fuel burn and emissions). Conversely, it could lead to a situation when not enough fuel was carried because the performance of the aircraft is worse than known or assumed. Using algorithms to solve the calculation based on rich aircraft and contextual data while incorporating the use of the cost of fuel weight in terms of dollars burned or tons of carbon dioxide allows airlines to get it right. Each time the aircraft is operating a mission. Also, the performance of the model is monitored and enhanced through machine learning, but it is also updated with updates on aircraft performance monitoring itself. In this fashion, all inputs the algorithms depend on are near real-time in terms of continuous improvement.

A good case study of how a fuel efficiency program was built from the ground up is SpiceJet, one of the fastest growing airlines in India. With over 100 aircraft and a serious cargo operation, it added 30 aircraft in three weeks in 2019, just before the Covid-19 pandemic hit. The fuel efficiency team recognized the importance of liaising with key stakeholders who are directly or indirectly impacted by the program and also have a key contribution to make in its success, both in design as well as execution. These relevant departments are the finance team, engineering and maintenance division, flight dispatch department, and the pilots. The team knew that AI would be an enabler but that the right type, amount, and quality of data was required to build an application that could solve real-life cases well. Their focus was on these priorities:

- Obtain the right representation of the data by gathering correct data on fuel consumption (for each operated flight and specific aircraft).
- Capture all the relevant real-world parameters that are directly related to this consumption (including passengers, bags, route, weather, flight plans, and navigational constraints).
- Compare the planned against actual parameters and identify root causes for deviations (including original flight plan and pilot-driven decisions or deviations).
- Compare auto-pilot against hand-flying overrides and best practices to gain insights.

Data is the first priority in a fuel efficiency program and that data can be useful in training plus the data science team can conduct data modelling; depending on the strength of data gathered, forecasts can be made and patterns identified.

(Nittin Gulati, GM, IT – SpiceJet)[5]

Regarding collecting the right data, there is significant room for error or influence. There are processes and human interventions that can interfere with capturing the data correctly. For instance, dispatchers have discretion over recommending the amount of fuel to carry based on the parameters they look at, but so do pilots have the power to add discretionary fuel as they see fit in a particular instance. To what extent additional fuel is carried for safety or for bunkering purposes can be influenced by the CFO's team, as they look at the economics of doing the latter. Also, due to the degradation in aircraft performance known to maintenance and engineering, they as well can have a say in how throttle settings are used or set and what that means for fuel consumption. What matters most, is capturing the technical details as well as the specific context or reason attached to them. This is the part that is written in algorithms and learned from with regard to identifying patterns and finding optimal solutions using the correlations identified in the data.

The reason SpiceJet engaged with a firm to automate the data preparation and science is that it faced too many challenges in cleansing the data before it could experiment with it. Data integrity and availability are often a challenge, particularly when data comes from different sources and is extracted in different or difficult-to-use formats. According to some data quality firms, this can represent 60–80% of the time-consuming work in data science.

Modern AI-based solutions that are used in fuel efficiency programs also offer a mobile App for pilots, such as the 'MyFuelCoach' mobile App offered by SkyBreathe. It allows pilots to monitor how they are doing, and how much fuel and costs they have saved on each flight, or in the past month, for instance. This is also helping pilots see the results of the improvements they make having learned from the insights fed to them thanks to the solution. The success of the solution is in no small part thanks to the participation and direction of pilots. By the same token, pilots have embraced how this technology can further fine-tune operations in even the smallest of areas where this role is best performed by automated systems in real time. It becomes a data-driven or digital assistant, and that is the best way to look at the positive contribution of AI to commercial aviation.

All in all, typical implementation timeframes for these solutions are anywhere between two to five months, depending on the size and composition of the fleet as well as the availability of data from the various systems. But ROIs are reported to be positive within four months, with 30 to 50% reductions in fuel and emissions, similar to what Air France reported.

2.2.2 Weight & Balance: Payload Optimization, Trim and Fuel Efficiency

Reducing fuel costs by carrying the optimal amount of fuel or cleaning the aircraft is not the only way. How the aircraft is loaded with passengers, bags, and cargo impact on the amount of trim around the center of gravity (CG) during flight. For this, payload management solutions are available, otherwise known as 'weight and balance' (W&B) management systems. These systems can lead to savings of between 0.5% and 1.5% per flight due to optimized trim and increased staff productivity. Often, they even lead to increased revenues owing to the ability to carry more payload.

An aircraft Weight and Balance System (W&B) is a critical component of the Departure Control System (DCS) of an airline. It essentially ensures that the aircraft is loaded correctly to fly safely and efficiently. It is therefore important to follow load control requirements as they can help prevent air accidents. Conversely, even if it is safe to operate, an aircraft that is overloaded or imbalanced will require more power and consequently burn more fuel.

Payload optimization systems help plan the work of a Load Master, i.e., the load controller who oversees how the aircraft is loaded to meet safety as well as CG rules. This includes managing the loading and unloading process. The contributions made by artificial intelligence center on insights created by transparency in data in process-oriented management, a streamlined workflow that integrates and automates complex or time-consuming tasks, and problem-solving around exception management.

Modern payload optimization solutions incorporate AI for the representation of the load information in an easy-to-interpret visual way, while providing configuration options and full automation of the planning process. One of the great advances has been the integration of data in a visual way, so that Load Masters can drag and drop 'boxes' (the containers) on a location on their screen, sending instructions to the handheld devices to the ground handling staff managing the maneuvering of the containers on the tarmac. Any irregularities are caught as well, and solutions provided in real time, such as the reallocation of container locations on board.

There are at least 50 vendors that offer payload optimization systems, such as Lufthansa Systems, Collins Aerospace, CHAMP Cargosystems, Sabre, Jeppesen, Avionica, APG, and Amadeus. Most have in recent years redesigned and modernized their solutions. These are some of the key functions and features they offer:

- Consolidate relevant load parameters:
  - Regulations
  - Technical data
  - Passenger data
  - Baggage data
  - Cargo data
  - Mail data
  - Operational flight plan
  - Flight dispatch information
- Calculate the optimum weight and trim conditions.
- Estimate turnaround time (payload specific).
- Generate load/unload instructions and sequencing.
- Optimize fuel uptake and last-minute adjustments.

Aircraft Operations and Crew   21

- Run/rerun scenarios based on payload deviations or weather changes.
- Manage resources, supervisor, and flight leg distribution to load controllers.

Most of the advances that are driven by AI are not obvious to the regular user's eye. But they facilitate the convenience of viewing processes and the click of a button that triggers the execution of a process that sends new instructions. These are all based on the coded algorithms and rules that determine how information is to work together to solve problems and notify people. Perhaps the most visible element is when a load controller uses the handheld device and moves containers around, triggering instructions or alert messages about operations or safety violations when decisions exceed parameters. The convenience and speed of the inner workings are what facilitates the adoption of these tools.

2.2.3 Crew Management

Airlines need to staff their aircraft with pilots and flight attendants to operate their flights. The management of crews is a complex undertaking. It must consider the roles and responsibilities, seniority levels, certified training levels by aircraft type, base locations, spoken languages, schedules, and personal preferences, to name only a few factors. Nonetheless, it is imperative that an airline can generate a feasible and efficient crew roster as it is the key to safe and smooth operations. It is also key to ensure business continuity when things go wrong enroute or due to other unforeseen circumstances.

Crew management throughout an airline's network is a complex task involving pairing construction, duty assignments during rostering, and crew tracking while considering legal and training requirements and robust reserves for contingencies. The objectives of crew management include reducing costs, improving crew productivity, and managing short-term operational changes or disruptions.

One of the key areas in optimizing crew management is efficiency through productivity. The goal is to minimize crew slack time and remove waiting times beyond regular crew rest periods. By using artificial intelligence, some airlines have been able to reduce crew slack time between 5% and 10% using modern crew rostering solutions,[6] such as those offered by Jeppesen, Infogain, and Lufthansa Systems.

In a closed environment, an optimizer can take a crew pool and related parameters and run it against a given flight schedule. It will find the most optimal crew assignment and roster to operate for that month. But rarely does everything go exactly according to plan. There can be weather conditions that disrupt operations, cause flight cancelations, or necessitate flight consolidations. Staff can get ill and not present themselves for duty. There are also incidents, misconnects, or even crew that become 'illegal' to carry out

22　*Uses of AI and Emerging Opportunities in Air Transport Operations*

their duties because they would exceed the maximum permittable number of working hours on a given day.

The approach to using AI in crew management is around data collection of all core data (schedules, crew) and parameters (rules) as well as contextual determinants (conditions) that impact continuity. Then, while an AI optimizer can run the dry optimization, the learning part kicks in when the actual operations can be compared to the planned schedule and roster. Manual interventions are tracked so that the solution can learn and automate future interventions in real time.

Modern use of crew management using AI now also offers:

- Embedding communication functions – notify individual crew members of changes to their paring or roster.
- Crew evaluation scenario planning – calculate and compare costs of different scenarios, e.g., hotel accommodation and productivity.
- Mapping crew rosters directly onto flight schedules to assess how flights could be staffed sufficiently, or how to re-assign rosters to fit schedule operability.
- Integrated crew member request processing allows crew members to request pairings and dynamically trigger new pairings and rosters only where there is an impact.
- Crew access: Permit 'accept/reject' suggestions to individual staff members and run new rosters upon the actions taken by staff when they review their roster, or indicate preferred vacation days (through their own login and online access).
- Crew exchange: Allows individual crew members to trade blocks once the rosters have been released.
- Dashboards of previous, current, and traded rosters with all statistics around duty times, trips, hours, distances.
- Offer real-time information from check-in to arrival at home or check-in at hotel, including the management of service interruptions (alternate hotels) and surface transportation, through handheld devices.
- A monitoring function provides advance notification and information about disruptions to flight operations or logistics and triggers the activation of standby crews to mitigate irregularities.

One of the latest innovations in crew management is around fatigue risk management. While there is some work in setting up the configurations and indicating the contextual factors impacting on crew fatigue, crew trackers can evaluate and detect the risk of fatigue throughout the entire crew management and flight operations process. This is done by tagging duties associated with flights in combination with the length of flight and the number of time zones that are crossed. By calculating accumulated fatigue from individual flights, rotations, pairings and specific rosters, crew alertness and fatigue can be predicted. This risk is then visualized in a Gantt chart and can be sent as an alert to a crew scheduling manager. By the same token, this fatigue risk manager can be run in conjunction with a disruption in rosters caused by irregular operations (IRROPS). It essentially cancels out or otherwise produces an exception report about scenarios that are not recommended. In the future, fatigue risk management could be enhanced by allowing individual crew members to assess, report and rank fatigue levels related to specific flights. Artificial intelligence could then incorporate these well-being indicators in the machine-learning component of the optimizer to recommend better pairings within rosters, perhaps even at individual crew member level.

While there are 'within-system' applications of AI in crew management, it is evident that in today's world with high-volume traffic, various systems need to communicate with each other in real time to trigger re-optimization processes. This can be at the central Operations Control Center (OCC) level (e.g., aircraft goes mechanical) or at an airport level (e.g., airport shuts down due to inclement weather), or a specific flight crew can misconnect or run over duty hours. In order to automate the communication, and more importantly coordinate the interdependencies, AI is used to create smart processes that increase transparency, create room for maneuver and enable proactive decision-making in real time. Composite AI on Enterprise AI, as discussed in Chapter 18, is often seen as the approach to make this a reality.

2.2.4 Aircraft and Engine Maintenance

Predictive maintenance and preventative maintenance of airframes and engines is possible with the help of artificial intelligence. It helps predict maintenance failures and prevents unscheduled Aircraft on Ground (AOG) situations. This reduces costs by avoiding or reducing the likelihood of deteriorating damage and by eliminating flight delays and cancellations. The application of AI has, according to SP's Aviation (2019) led to a reduction in engine failures by one-third. The foundation for AI in aircraft systems and engine maintenance lies in the use of digital twins, as explained below.

These are some of the applications of AI in aircraft and engine maintenance:

* Creation of digital twins backed by Internet-of-Things (connected) sensors to create a virtual copy of the engine that operates in the real world. By doing so, real-time visibility is created in all aspects and moving parts related to engine performance. This allows machine learning models to learn with real data and AI to deploy recommendations based on the vast experience in the data.
* Computer vision and AI-based metallurgic analytics help identify airframe metal fatigue and cracks before the human eye can. These technologies allow for obtaining images of real-world objects, processing, and analyzing them, and then using data and end models to solve applied problems. Combined with machine learning, AI models can recommend preventive maintenance to aircraft skin and airframes.

24 *Uses of AI and Emerging Opportunities in Air Transport Operations*

2.2.5 Operations Control Center

The central operations control center (OCC) of an airline oversees and co-ordinates all flight operations in real time. It can also be used to generate data to learn from to improve network, scheduling, and even taxiing and gate operations. Airlines like KLM Royal Dutch Airlines have invested in an artificial intelligence-based solution in partnership with Boston Consulting Group (BCG). Due to the success, they have now commercialized and sold it to other airlines like Virgin Atlantic. The solution helps improve airline operations worldwide by streamlining operations to meet the growing demands of today's travelers. The decision support platform helps with making informed trade-offs between aircraft utilization, costs, and customer service impacts. It has helped reduce delays, cancelations, and missed connections while increasing customer satisfaction. KLM reported a 20–30% reduction in non-performance-related costs and a 2–5% increase in fleet utilization. There was also a 30% reduction in average delay minutes.[7]

2.3 Conclusions

This chapter explored the emergence of artificial intelligence in modern applications related to aircraft operations, aircraft maintenance, and engine maintenance. The predictive capabilities that the combined technologies allow also improve fuel efficiency, reduce emissions, enhance dispatch as well as airline crew efficacy, and prevent maintenance on aircraft and engines. The chapter also shared examples, for instance, Rolls-Royce prevented one-third of engine maintenance failures thanks to the use of digital twins and artificial intelligence in maintenance technologies.

Notes

1 Air France, Annual Report, 2019.
2 Analytics India Magazine, 2020. https://analyticsindiamag.com/how-airlines-use-ai-to-streamline-operations-save-fuel/.
3 Air France (2020) *Air France chooses SkyBreathe® eco-flying solution to reduce fuel burn and CO_2 emissions.* Paris: Corporate Air France Press Release. https://corporate.airfrance.com/en/press-release/air-france-chooses-skybreather-eco-flying-solution-reduce-fuel-burn-and-co2-emissions.
4 https://www.openairlines.com.
5 Aircraft IT (2021) 'Saving fuel, reducing emissions and a culture of improvement at SpiceJet'. https://www.aircraftit.com/articles/saving-fuel-reducing-emissions-and-a-culture-of-improvement-at-spicejet/.
6 Infogain (2021) 'Artificial intelligence: transforming airline crew management'. https://www.infogain.com/blog/artificial-intelligence-transforming-airline-crew-management/.
7 BCG (2020) 'Optimizing and digitizing airline operations with artificial intelligence'. https://www.bcg.com/industries/travel-tourism/airline-industry/optimizing-digitizing-airline-operations.

Bibliography

Caswell, M. (2020) 'Air France to use artificial intelligence to reduce CO2 emissions'. *Business Traveller.* https://www.businesstraveller.com/business-travel/2020/07/15/air-france-to-use-artificial-intelligence-to-reduce-co2-emissions/

England, R. (2020) 'Air France uses 'Sky Breathe' AI to slash fuel costs and reduce emissions'. *AI Business.* https://aibusiness.com/document.asp?doc_id=762446

Kontakt.io (2020) 'Digital twins in aviation and 8 ways they can transform workflows'. https://kontakt.io/blog/digital-twins-in-aviation-and-8-ways-they-can-transform-workflows/

Pratt & Whitney (2017) 'P&WC to deliver predictive and preventive maintenance to PT6A engine-powered Beechcraft King Air customers through Fast™ Prognostics Solution'. https://www.pwc.ca/en/company/news-and-events/news-details/pwc-to-deliver-predictive-and-preventive-main?id=123030

Rolls-Royce (2022) 'How digital twin technology can enhance aviation'. https://www.rolls-royce.com/media/our-stories/discover/2019/how-digital-twin-technology-can-enhance-aviation.aspx

Sabre (2021) 'Movement manager technology increases China Airlines' network efficiency and productivity'. https://www.sabre.com/insights/releases/sabres-movement-manager-technology-increases-china-airlines-network-efficiency-and-productivity/

SP's Aviation (2019) 'GE brings AI into preventive maintenance to reduce jet engine failure by one third'. https://www.sps-aviation.com/story/?id=2646&h=GE-brings-AI-into-preventive-maintenance-to-reduce-jet-engine-failure-by-one-third

Yaakoubi, Y. *et al.* (2020) 'Machine learning in airline crew pairing to construct initial clusters for dynamic constraint aggregation', *EURO Journal on Transportation and Logistics*, 9(4), pp. 1–14.

3 Customer, Contact, and Self-Service

3.1 Passenger Communications

There is abundant research on consumer behavior and expectations regarding customer service and contact centers. And companies that are active in contact center management within the airline industry can share meaningful insights into how customer behavior has changed and how intolerance has grown. For instance, according to communications firm Comnica, 53% of customers are ready to switch brands due to poor customer experience.[1] No less than 32% of customers are only willing to wait 5 minutes or less for a response from customer service. In addition, people are no longer willing to be constrained to the business hours of the company's location and demand 24/7 availability. And while improvements have been made using interactive voice recognition (IVR), the often resulting maze of options and loops has angered customers, undermining its effectiveness in accelerating service.

3.2 Artificial Intelligence in Passenger Communications and Social Service

Airlines have been facing several challenges in recent years when it comes to passenger communications. On the one hand, social media (such as Facebook, Twitter, WhatsApp, and Instagram) provided airlines with a tool to have direct, and personal dialogue with customers. On the other hand, various media is requiring agents to look at multiple channels. And over 90% of the customers surveyed by Comnica indicate they demand consistent interactions across all channels. This is a challenge because beyond responses such as text replies, integration is needed with other passenger service systems via the contact center system. Conversely, when companies handle the interaction across channels well, it can increase retention rates nine-fold, Comnica found. Research conducted at Harvard Business School confirms these findings (Dixon, 2017).

So, the challenges that have led airlines to consider automation in passenger communications around call centers and other channels have been driven by:

1   The volume of calls, particularly during disruptions and the COVID-19 pandemic.

DOI: 10.4324/9781003018810-5

2 The increase in number of channels.
3 The need for coherent insights (why, what, who, and history).
4 The need for quick problem resolution.

These pain points became more and more pressing as customers increasingly booked online and became conditioned to higher levels of self-service in other industries, such as online retailing. Therefore, airlines started looking at ways not only to improve the overall experience but also be able to handle increasing volumes of requests and calls better. Most of them started to invest in this around 2011, with KLM being one of the first. Others, like Qantas,[2] Singapore[3] Airlines, Cathay Pacific,[4] Lufthansa,[5] and British Airways[6] soon followed suit. They set in motion a trend to:

- Respond better.
- Respond faster.
- Not waste time (remove duplication, transfers, re-entry of info).
- Solve problems on the spot (be better prepared with information about the file).
- Solve problems pro-actively (anticipate problems such as required itinerary changes).
- Monetize customer contact when engaged.

KLM was one of the first to have a new 'no forms' policy, whereby customers would be able to type in their request in a chatbot, Twitter, or WhatsApp. Issues like lost luggage or change requests were handled within the channel. This was, in fact, one of KLM's other policies, which is to never redirect a customer to another agent or channel.

Over the years and by 2017, most airlines had adopted chatbots, but most were simply redirecting customers to a website where information or the 'what to do' could be found by posting a link in the chatbox. This was no longer considered enough by 2019. The expectations of customers had gone up and passengers demanded higher standards. These are particular expectations in modern times:

- Control over journey and changes (be self-reliant).
- More convenience (remove more friction).
- Speed (never make me wait).
- Transparency ('show me what you see').
- Relevance (only provide what I need and want).
- Real time (it must be completed now).

As we approach another big crisis for the airline industry, this time coronavirus, we can look back on those incidents and learn from them but passengers' expectations have also evolved, they expect a lot more

28 *Uses of AI and Emerging Opportunities in Air Transport Operations*

> information in real time, a lot more detailed information and accurate information. Back in 2009 with the Ash Cloud it was completely different.
> (Nicholas Key, CEO, 15below)[7]

This also pushed airlines like KLM to go further. KLM's dedicated team of 250 social media service agents was handling over 30,000 conversations per week by 2017.[8] It was at that time still sifting through 130,000 mentions via social media per week, with staff looking for opportunities to surprise people with the gift based on the profile and gate information they could pick up. But it could not sustain delivering on its commitment to, what it called, "social service" and maintain quality of service. The volumes had increased, and KLM had found a solution to deliver on its promises.

KLM realized it was more important to shift attention to automation for the handling of calls, complaint resolution, and resolving more complex ticket items. In 2019, it partnered with artificial intelligence (AI) frontrunner DigitalGenius, a UK-based company. The initial aim was to add automated answers to general repetitive questions from customers without the intervention of a human service agent. This would give KLM agents more time to focus on questions in conversations with customers that require a hands-on approach to problem resolution.

The way it works is as follows. DigitalGenius adds a layer to the contact center application and learns from observing the workflow. It learns from the agents' actions and understands which action resolves which problem. Over time, it is able to recognize requests and recommend the 'next best action', which is the term used for the proposed solution. Initially, agents would have to review the recommendation in a pop-up window, which also carried an indicated percentage of the likelihood it would solve the problem. The agent would then click on 'accept' or 'no', or 'personalize' the response. In the beginning, KLM was able to support up to 50% of the inquiries within months, but it has improved over time and now supports around 87% of all common tasks. The automated tool also understands and responds in ten different languages (Dutch, English, German, Spanish, Portuguese, French, Chinese, Japanese, Korean, and Italian).

Following the success of the Human+AI customer service platform that DigitalGenius integrated at KLM, the airline added other services, such as 'BB', it's BlueBot. The BB can help customers book a ticket on Messenger and pack your bag on Google Home. Mobile payment in-channel was also added, making it even more convenient.

The benefits of automation in customer contact and communications are evident in that it increases the quality and efficiency of customer service and supports conversations across all communication channels. But it also allows agents to work with richer information. For instance, by adding additional layers of machine learning and AI, smart processes can be designed to harmonize the view of the customers based on all the information and profile the airline has about the customer. By pulling up the reservation, and by reading through previous reservations, or issues during journeys captured in their profiles and frequent flier program membership, they have a single version of the truth. Machine learning can then propose more suitable, personal solutions to recognize individuals. Below is a quote of what Singapore Airlines said when their solution (1Point) was announced in partnership with SalesForce Service Cloud and Mulesoft Anypoint Platform:

> Service agents will have access to the relevant information, including those related to each customer's previous interactions, at every step. This facilitates quicker decision-making, and allows them to pre-empt a customer's needs more efficiently.
>
> (Singapore Airlines (2021))[9]

With the new system, SIA's service agents will no longer need to switch between multiple systems to retrieve customer data. The agents will be able to pull all up-to-date information not only on previous customer journeys, products, and services but also on all commercial policies and procedures to resolve issues without handovers to other staff. The guided workflows are supported by Singapore Airlines' own AI and machine learning capabilities.

Table 3.1 summarizes key applications and use cases of machine learning and AI in this area.

3.3 AI Versus Human Touch

People still want personalized answers. They understand an automated process to guide them along general inquiries, but ultimately, they want to feel a human touch in their experience. So, not all functions will be automated even though the ML model could do more. For instance, dealing with compliments is hard for an AI system. For a response to sound authentic, a human can always improve this experience and add a flavor of the day tone. It cannot

Table 3.1 Overview of technologies and use cases of AI in call centers

Technology Used	Use Case
Chatbot using Natural Language Processing	Customer self-service for Q&A
Digital assistant in call center using ML	System-recommended ticket resolution with 'next-best action', workflow, and deep customer insights
Computer vision, optical character reading, and AI	Eye-recognition and passport reader-based self-service kiosk
AI-based process automation	Integration of voice command with ticket reservation and mobile payment, such as Google Home or Amazon Alexa
Natural Language Processing	Listening to social media chatter to recommend and provide personalized service

become too robotic, at least, that is what KLM indicates in the media. Nonetheless, AI quickly enabled the airline to increase the speed of replies by 20%. The more repetitive tasks and queries are 90% automated.

> We do not see [AI] as a substitute for human interaction, just a way to improve it.
>
> (Tjalling Smit, SVP of Digital, KLM)

3.4 Self-Service

The push for self-service in aviation is driven by a general trend reflecting customers' desire to have more control over their daily lives, from planning, booking, to experiencing activities. Across industries, 81% of all customers attempt to take care of matters themselves before reaching out to a live representative (Dixon *et al.*, 2017). In aviation, there were other motivations to push for automation. Long queues at airport for check-in, baggage drop, and tagging became problematic during peak times because of the increasing volumes of passengers and lack of check-in counter space and staff. Security and passenger screening became a stranglehold, especially after 9/11. Therefore, airlines quickly rolled out online check-in facilities, and later airport check-in kiosks and self-tagging capabilities to print luggage tags. These systems form part of self-service technologies (SSTs). They are now also commonly used by immigration and naturalization authorities at airports before people are cleared to enter. They also capture data in a more structured manner.

Self-service kiosks are interactive computer terminals that give customers access to information, such as inventory availability, menus, queuing, travel plans, and more. Prior to kiosk technology becoming widely adopted, cost-conscious businesses had to choose between a faster check-in or fewer employees working the counters and floors. Now kiosks make it possible for handling agents and airlines to do both without sacrificing service.

These new capabilities required development and included the application of AI. Self-check-in initially worked as follows:

- Enter your identification number (or PNR) you have provided while booking the tickets or passport number.
- Enter your personal information if asked.
- Once the verification is done, you can view your flight details on the screen.
- Confirm your flight details.
- Select, modify, or upgrade seats.
- Enter luggage details.
- Answer security questions.
- Confirm and print boarding pass.

Customer, Contact, and Self-Service   31

To speed up this process, passport readers were added. This required computer vision for image recognition and machine learning to link passport details with the information on record. Once confirmed, the process would be the same. Further, the function to enter checked bag information (number of items) was added but required additional checks against the luggage allowance related to the type of ticket purchased. These cross-checks are made through business rules. But it can be improved by AI. For instance, if the customer does not have an allowance for a free bag, the process halts until the passenger uses a credit card through the reader to make the necessary payment. Only then will the departure control system allow a luggage tag to be printed.

Another use case is to drive recommended upgrade fees for business class travel that are optimized based on the likelihood that the identified customer will purchase it.

In this process, there are many processes that are enabled by AI. But companies like Delta Airlines went even further in 2018. They installed cameras in the self-check-in kiosks that would identify passengers through face recognition. Images are captured and compared with those on file and linked to passport and reservation data. By 2021, Delta was setting a new standard for the industry as the first airline to build a dedicated bag drop space for TSA PreCheck customers. It also meant that facial recognition was used to get through security, so the process was seamless throughout. The facial recognition option became more popular during the COVID-19 pandemic when touchless travel was promoted wherever possible. The trend is now to use SSTs more for automated border control and security and to develop standards across nations and airports worldwide.

> We want to give our customers more time to enjoy travel by unlocking simplified, seamless and efficient experiences from end to end.
> (Byron Merritt, Vice President of Brand
> Experience Design, Delta Airlines)[10]

Clearly, kiosks are popular in that they give customers a sense of control. They can also help remove inefficiencies in the overall process and reduce human errors. But they do rely on a customer's self-concept (am I competent to do this myself?), and learning curves as initially, first-time users take up more time than if an agent would have processed check-in.[11]

There are cost aspects, too. Kiosks are expensive and need to be able to withstand abuse, floods, liquid spills, and extremely high usage. But once installed, the cost of a customer doing things themselves is measured in pennies, while the costs associated with a live customer service agent can be $7 in hospitality, whether it be by email, phone, or webchat. These costs have increased from $7 to approximately $10 or more recently, according to Harvard Business School research. In addition, more complex matters are now predominantly resolved with human assistance. There have been reports of overwhelmed staff by complex requests, pressure, and lack of information system support. This has pushed employee turnover rates to levels of over 25% (Dixon *et al.*, 2017).

Also, at the airport, kiosks do not replace workers, but it gives the handling agent or airline the flexibility to redistribute labor to other job codes on the floor and add a human touch while they roam around. Kiosks mean some tasks can be handled quickly but people need to be there to ensure a pleasant flow. Therefore, kiosk technology can be leveraged to optimize labor not by replacing employees, but by lightening their workload. Kiosks can become especially helpful during peak hours when staff is overwhelmed.

More recently, the US released its Mobile Passport Control (MPC), which is an app that allows customers to submit their passport details and customs declaration through the app on their smartphone. The AI application behind the interface performs all the necessary background checks and applies all the rules before issuing the preclearance pass (US CBP, 2022).

3.5 Self-Service, Upselling, Data

Millennials and technology fans will flock to technology every time they are presented a choice. An interesting finding is that self-order kiosks in food and beverage increase the average ticket size for orders compared to those taken by staff. This is in part because consumers take more time and feel less pressured. But this is also because recommender systems can entice customers to upsell/-cross-sell on every screen and every transaction with incentives. Automating the prompting of offers encourages passengers to try new add-on items they usually would not order. And this is becoming important in self-service on board.

The move to self-service on board is possible with order management functions added to inflight entertainment (IFE) systems, and it will increase revenues, optimize labor and enhance customer experience. Passengers can customize their order and take their time to browse. This is different than presenting passenger options and making them decide on the spot. As a result, average ticket purchases go up by 15–20% because people order more.[12] In the case of kiosks and apps, the sense of anonymity also allows customers the freedom to make choices, do things, or order items without worrying about judgment or shaming. This aspect will become more and more important in personalizing travel and experiences, notably private or luxurious activities.

Finally, the move to kiosks and apps generates powerful data from which important and monetizable insight can be inferred. Information about customer buying habits, shopping behavior, likes and dislikes and offer relevancy can be obtained. This will help to improve sales as well as customer centricity.

3.6 Customer Journey and Passenger Engagement

While customer contact can be improved when passengers need the help of agents in call centers, the IoT and use of smartphones allow passengers to interact with everybody and every company or store around them or elsewhere. This also means that through location-based marketing, passengers will be sold to by other companies offering their products and services, for instance in airport terminals or at destination, often using social media.

This also means that passengers want to be able to contact their airlines in-transit or during the journey for any unexpected issues, changes, or new reservations. Airlines must strike a balance between sales-related and other meaningful communications but must anticipate that customers can respond to it personally, or broadcast their opinions in public.

The concept of constant engagement and kiosks can also be extended to airline Super Apps. Tired travelers appreciate having a kiosk at an airport or hotel to simplify the check-in process. But these terminals also function as a concierge and can help guests order room service, book a spa treatment, or find local attractions. There is no reason that airlines cannot extend the scope of their services, remain engaged at destination or any location with their customers, and offer relevant products and services. How this is executed depends on the commercial and servicing model, including the ecosystem of partners that will deliver the services onsite. This can include hotels, adventure, and inbound tour operators, or content aggregators that have relationships with the operators to deliver service.

As airlines move all their customer data from different touch points and functions into a customer data platform (CDP) and use a date lakehouse for DevOps of end models, more and more products and services can be offered by mining the data and writing models in machine learning that solve how and when these offers are made, and then automate this 'pop-up and transact' feature for passengers while they are at destination. The use of deep learning models and process automation using end models will become more the norm.

3.7 Conclusions

This chapter addressed the field of passenger communication and customer services. It highlights how the internet, social media, and rising volumes of customer service requests have spurred the investment in smart technology (AI) in call centers and SST like kiosks. The application of machine learning has enabled the automation of repetitive Q&A call center tasks through self-service using chatbots, whereas the application of deep learning and AI has allowed service agents to work with smart workflows that provide them with a 360-degree view of the customer. These solutions have reduced call center workloads and improved customer service in a cost-effective manner.

Notes

1 Brauer, B., 'Passenger communication trends', Comnica webinar, 17 February 2022.
2 ITnews (2022) 'Qantas looks to tech platforms to reduce call centre wait times'. https://www.itnews.com.au/news/qantas-looks-to-tech-platforms-to-reduce-call-centre-wait-times-578456.

34 *Uses of AI and Emerging Opportunities in Air Transport Operations*

3 Channel News Asia (2021) 'Singapore Airlines to move to new customer case system to raise service standards'. https://www.channelnewsasia.com/business/singapore-airlines-move-new-customer-case-system-raise-service-standards-198986.

4 QualtricsXM (2019) 'How Cathay Pacific focuses on passenger feedback to soar above the competition'. https://www.qualtrics.com/blog/passenger-feedback/.

5 Cision PR Newswire (2019) 'IBM Watson helps Lufthansa group optimize its customer service'. https://www.prnewswire.com/news-releases/ibm-watson-helps-lufthansa-group-optimize-its-customer-service-300947053.html.

6 AnalyticsInsight (2019) 'British Airways employs AI technology for better air travel experiences'.https://www.analyticsinsight.net/british-airways-employs-ai-technology-better-air-travel-experiences/.

7 Fox, L. "Keeping communication channels open is critical for airlines during a crisis", Phocuswire. https://www.phocuswire.com/15Below-airlines-coronavirus.

8 KLM, press release 19 December 2017, and Annual Report 2017.

9 Singapore Airlines (2021) Annual Report.

10 Delta Airlines (2021) 'Newsroom'. https://news.delta.com/delta-reveals-first-ever-dedicated-tsa-precheckr-lobby-bag-drop.

11 Atkinson, J. (2014) *Consumer psychology: buyer perceptions and self concept*. Nunawading: Persuasionworks.

12 Touchdynamic.com (2019) 'Everything you need to know about self-service kiosks'. https://www.touchdynamic.com/everything-you-need-to-know-about-self-service-kiosks/.

Bibliography

Antwi, C.O. *et al.* (2021) 'Airport self-service technologies, passenger self-concept, and behavior: an attributional view', *Sustainability*, 13(6), p. 3134. https://www.mdpi.com/2071-1050/13/6/3134/pdf

Dixon, M., Ponomareff, L., Turner, S., and DeLisi, R. (2017) 'Kick-Ass customer service consumers want results—not sympathy'. *Harvard Business Review*, January–February, 2017.

Ueda, K., and Kurahashi, S. (2018) 'Agent-based self-service technology adoption model for air-travelers: exploring best operational practices', *Frontiers in Physics*, 6(5). https://ui.adsabs.harvard.edu/abs/2018FrP.....6....5U/abstract

US CBP (2022) 'Mobile passport control'. https://www.cbp.gov/travel/us-citizens/mobile-passport-control

4 Inflight and Cabin Services

4.1 Inflight Services Explained

Inflight services refer to all the equipment and service items that are used and offered to passengers during their flight. It includes the provisioning of the planes with meals and beverages, for-sale meals and snacks, and duty-free items. It also includes onboard inflight entertainment (IFE) and in-seat ordering but this is treated as a separate subject in Chapter 5. Due to the complexity and increasing attention on digital cabins and using mobile connectivity to engage and sell to customers while they are in their seats in real time, a dedicated section is provided on this area in Chapter 5. From a commercial perspective, smart retailing using artificial intelligence (AI) is also explored in detail in Chapter 11.

There are several important preparations that go into the provisioning of aircraft so that they are ready for flight from a passenger perspective. In this chapter, we focus on operating flights that have already been cleared by maintenance and engineering as fully serviceable since Chapter 2 already discussed this topic. In Part 2 of this book, when we discuss commercial airline planning from a more holistic perspective, which has an impact on the fine-tuning of cabin services in a digitally connected context.

4.2 AI for Inflight and Cabin Services

Most of the benefits derived from AI lie in (a) combining large and new sources of data, and (b) using a higher granularity of specific information to optimize the planning and delivery of inflight service and related items. Key objectives are not only to plan the right number of meals to satisfy customer needs and preferences but also to avoid waste. But there are other areas in which AI improves customer service and increases revenues, for instance as it relates to planning the right number and types of movies for the IFE systems depending on the mix of passengers, the destination, or the type of flight (e.g., day or night, eastbound or westbound). The differences in passenger behavior about these dimensions do exist, so they can be measured and used.

DOI: 10.4324/9781003018810-6

36 Uses of AI and Emerging Opportunities in Air Transport Operations

By using data from the manifest of the passengers and their loyalty status, automated recommendations can be made to personalize offers to passengers such as upgrades for purchase. Simply recognizing people with the help of information about them in real time can assist in conversations between cabin staff and customers.

4.2.1 Meals and Beverages Provisioning

The inflight meal provisioning process involves producing meals in an airport kitchen by a caterer and delivering them to a plane for consumption by passengers inflight. At several subsequent decision points prior to the departure of a flight, the caterer may adjust the meal quantity to be delivered to the plane. The overall process consists of a meal production part as well as the adjustment part all the way to the last decision point. The planning of this, including the opportunity to use AI, is around capturing, and analyzing data and write scripts for how an airline wants to optimize this process around key objectives.

Air Canada is an airline that tackled the integration of functions around meals and beverage provisioning by combining the key areas of (1) catering scheduling, (2) invoicing, and (3) galley stowage. These are all pieces that need to communicate with each other. Also, to enable these individual functions to perform well, they each rely on communications from other systems through processes that send data in real or near-real time. In most airlines, prior to the automation in this area, older and standalone systems were used that did not integrate well, requiring manual intervention and manipulation of information so that instructions could be dispatched. Vietnam Airlines, like Air Canada, also worked with Sabre[1] to provide the validations of cost-benefit studies regarding creating smart processes and automation.[2] Vendors can provide a comprehensive solution that spans all aspects of service planning, meal ordering, forecasting, operations, materials management, financial controls, and reporting. Following the implementation of the automation, Air Canada indicated to save over $1 million per year in efficiencies, including saving time for improved turnarounds. Other airlines, such as Etihad, claimed to save even more.

> The enhanced control means we should make savings in excess of $5 million per annum, while continuing to provide a world-class and award-winning guest experience on board.[3]
>
> (Etihad Airways)

The objectives of meals and beverages provisioning are as follows:

- Minimize waste
- Minimize the cost but at the desired service levels
- Maximize customer service levels

Inflight and Cabin Services 37

Table 4.1 Inflight food and beverage provisioning objectives

Objectives	Sample Minimum Service Level Criteria
Ensure that all special meals that have been requested are available	Meet expectation
Achieve the highest likelihood that meal preferences stored in loyalty members' profiles can be provided to each loyalty member	Deliver with >80% accuracy
Generate a list of people and their priority of whom to serve first	Desired, may exceed expectations
Ensure there is sufficient choice among other travelers	40% of passengers will have choice between two meals
Minimize loss of customer goodwill	<5% did not get their meal choice

The impact on customer service levels of food and beverage (F&B)-related aircraft provisioning depends on meeting the objectives in Table 4.1. Criteria can be set based on the metrics that airline managers want to see. But first they need to be collected, which is difficult to capture when flight attendants are not involved in collecting the data. In the future, other digital mechanisms and order management flows can be used to collect this behavioral data.

The costs related to losing customer goodwill are more difficult to quantify, but they are clearly higher on long-haul flights compared to short flights. While the outcomes can more easily be described, the calculations that go into solving the problem are multi-faceted. They must also include a model to derive an efficient frontier and investigate trade-offs between having too few and too many meals on a flight. This model can include a 'value-distracting' item as in potentially being detrimental to customer satisfaction or loyalty. The dollar value impact of under-delivering or wasting food is increasingly used in AI models that improve food ordering by incorporating better business rules.

Caterers determine the number of meals to produce well in advance based on the historical data provided by airlines. In most cases, historical data is complemented with a passenger load forecast at the time the caterer does their overall planning and schedule for the days and weeks ahead. But even while the caterer prepares or already has prepared the meals for a flight, there are several subsequent updates based on modified forecasts all the way until an hour before departure. As the trucks on the tarmac are on their way and load the galleys of the aircraft, no further changes can be made. Even though in many cases, the actual people on board do not correspond with the manifest used for check-in. This is because passenger no-show and misconnect or are removed by the captain as not fit to fly, which happens in a few rare cases. Some of these misconnects are groups of people from other flights and it can amount to quite a few people. Yet, production and delivery costs are significant and vary over time with unscheduled deliveries very close to departure, which are more costly.

Even before the age of AI, operations research was used to develop a decision-making framework for this meal provisioning process. Today, and by using more data sources to feed the decision-making model, cost-based algorithms can be combined with improved and updated forecasts of the final order quantity based on accumulated data. The airline acts as a broker of information and an AI model needs to combine historical data with updated forecasts as well as information from the loyalty program and reservations about passenger preferences. A machine learning component assesses to what extent the model has performed and what it has learned to make better predictions to meet the AI model's goals. Another layer can come from flight operations (dispatch) regarding irregular operations, and delays, which can trickle passenger-rebooking functions in other AI-enabled processes for the reservation system. These updates on affected passengers are fed to the meals provisioning model to manage the last-minute updates for the final trolley dispatches on the delivery trucks. The latter is tricky because they occur after the original batch of meals has already left the kitchen area. Furthermore, in some circumstances, an additional van is dispatched to the plane and a driver can be seen entering the aircraft or walking through the aisle with a few additional meals. This inconveniences passengers and represents costly practices.

The core components of using AI in meals and beverage provisioning to create an automated optimizer are therefore those listed in Table 4.2 below.

A spin-off of this process is the generation and electronic receipt of a meal-service delivery sequence for flight attendants on board. Cabin staff in many airlines, such as KLM Royal Dutch Airlines, use tablets as digital assistants for customer service-related purposes, as discussed in the next section. But they can also receive a meal service priority list by individual passenger name/seat number. This helps to ensure the passengers in the top tier of the loyalty program obtain the meal they prefer (in economy or economy comfort) class, as indicated in their loyalty member profile or reservation. In some cases, special attention can be given to a passenger that usually flies in business class, or for whatever reason had a service hiccup in the past. This is stored and can trigger a recommended perk to be provided inflight.

4.2.2 Passenger Customer Service Inflight

Bringing information and technology onboard for flight attendants is another way in which AI is starting to enhance customer service onboard

Table 4.2 AI components in smart food and beverage planning

AI Components in Smart F&B Planning
Company policies and guidelines (hard-coded business rules in algorithm)
Forecasts and real-time updates on expected individuals and preferences
Cost information (meals, cost of wastage, delivery times, time savings)
Customer service (estimated financial impact of non-compliance)
Generation of meal preparation and delivery list
Real-time modifications and loading instructions

Inflight and Cabin Services 39

and inflight. In 2015, KLM Royal Dutch Airlines started issuing iPads to around 5,000 pilots, senior cabin service directors, and flight attendants. The tablets were issued to digitize flight activities as well as improve customer service. This was the result of a pilot project that was initiated by a firm in the USA.

The application that was built by MI Airline[4] helped crew organize and assist passengers during the flight. It provides information not only in real-time about passengers before a trip but also as they board and during the flight. It is used to resolve seating issues when somebody would like to move, and it does so by recognizing the individual and their status with the airline. It means that personalized upgrades can be provided or sold on the spot.

The application also works to resolve operational changes, by working out the best way to help travelers when connections are about to or known to be missed, due to delays. Instead of having to resort to ground staff at a connecting airport, this can be automated while the passenger is still in the air. It removes stress and provides the comfort knowing that connections are secured ahead of time and that their luggage will follow as well.

> Innovation is high on KLM's agenda. Via this project we are investing in our customers and crew. We also feel it is our responsibility to keep innovating in the area of sustainability. Ultimately, when the iPad replaces all the documentation that crew bring along on board, this will reduce weight and therefore fuel consumption.[5]
>
> (Peter Hartman, Former CEO, KLM)

There are other applications for using this technology. For instance:

- Enrolling a customer as a new member in the frequent flier program.
- Issuing instant credit vouchers or promotional offers by email when a service item is missing, broken, or something disappoints the traveler (e.g. the seat is broken or the IFE system in that seat does not function).
- Granting a passenger a free Wi-Fi code or upgrading them on their connecting flight while issuing a new electronic boarding pass to their email address or by text.

In order to enable the delivery of these services, AI works as a glue in the middle connecting these electronic processes. The application pulls information and real-time updates are used in an optimization process (algorithms) to provide recommendations on actions that can be taken. Once selected, the AI acts again as a glue to distribute the commands to the various underlying systems and applications to ensure the cabin attendant and customer receive confirmation. All other systems are updated and keep a record of the changes that were made, such as the reservation, seat and boarding pass, and note in the frequent flier program.

4.2.3 Duty-Free

Duty-free shopping refers to the articles and products people can purchase at airports or on flights free of taxes. Often, sales taxes or other duties such as excise tax on tobacco or alcohol can easily increase prices by 20–40%. The concept of stimulating sales of products in duty-free zones at airports (passed security) originated at Shannon Airport in 1947.[6] Goods that tend to be taxed higher are popular among travelers, and airports such as Amsterdam Airport Schiphol even built Airport City shopping, retailing, and entertainment villages around the traffic that airline hubs generate. Originally, duty-free stores were available for departing passengers, but in the last two decades, countries started allowing airports to open duty-free shop areas for arriving passengers as well.

Airlines were quick to jump on the bandwagon by carrying duty-free articles onboard flights. The shopping experience was typically promoted through separate brochures or duty-free magazines that were placed in the seat pockets. In recent years, there have been trends to modernize duty-free although others, like Qantas Airways,[7] have decided to abandon the service due to lack of inflight sales and to remove the additional weight of carrying items on board. Removing the service also alleviates the burden on staff.

According to SimpleFlying, total duty-free sales onboard aircraft totaled USD 3 billion in 2020. The overall duty-free market around travel is estimated to be USD 127 billion by 2027 according to Bloomberg.[8] During the Covid-19 related fallout in travel, some duty-free companies were even offering free 60 minutes flights out of Seoul, South Korea to allow passengers to shop at the airport, during their brief flight and upon return having briefly flown into Japanese airspace.

But there are divergent trends in this area. Notwithstanding, digitization and AI are potentially facilitating a different revival in this business. Carrying paper duty-free magazines adds labor-intensive time, increases weight to the aircraft, and thereby results in additional fuel burn. However, duty-free magazines, much like inflight magazines were often spun-off activities handled by an external firm that would raise funds from advertising money. They were as such revenue-contributing, just by sitting in the in-seat pocket. But it does not fit airlines striving to be more sustainable by reducing emissions.

Moving from paper to digital processes, but also the opportunity to offer and deliver the service without having to carry the products on board, is a new trend. Some developments include offering passengers to[9]:

- Purchase duty-free articles online before they travel (Emirates Airline).
- Purchase duty-free articles within 30 days of having traveled (Singapore Airlines KrisShop).
- Have articles delivered at the gate, in the plane, or during your return flight (Air Transat).

- Have goods delivered to your home (free of charge over GBP 60 on British Airways), or otherwise depending on the eligibility (Cathay Pacific, EVA Air, Finnair, Hong Kong Airlines, KLM, Malaysia Airlines, Saudi Arabian Airlines, and Virgin Atlantic).
- Redeem points to use as a duty-free boutique certificate onboard (order online), like Air Canada Aeroplan.
- Use your FFP points on board for full or partial payment through the flight attendant's iPad application (KLM).[10]

Some airlines offer home delivery of items beyond the duty-free catalogue. Items sold through the duty-free or online stores are not always without duties and levies. This depends on the rules and regulations. Nonetheless, selling duty-free fits again within the retailing trend that the airline industry is displaying. It is clear that AI is enabling a convenient shopping experience by allowing customers to log in, review personalized offers, and choose a delivery method that meets their needs. Much of how this comes together is again based on (a) analyzing data from all relevant sources, (b) creating relationships between data elements to drive recommendations, and (c) integrating and automating the tasks and functions between customers browsing through content, transacting to make purchases, and operational delivery aspects. In the process, machine learning learns from what customers look at, buy, and improves what else can be offered to travelers to increase sales. The more details we know about individual people, the more machine learning will be able to tailor individual offers to each person. This creates a true customer-centric experience.

4.3 Conclusions

This chapter highlighted how personalized passenger services and customer experiences can be improved with the help of AI. It described how F&B planning gains from the application of AI and how smarter processes will also reduce wastage. The chapter further illustrated that the digitization of customer service processes can improve customer recognition and personalized service deliveries, including prioritizing individuals that display the highest levels of loyalty to airlines. This chapter concludes by explaining how retailing, such as digital duty-free boutiques, can be re-energized owing to the technical advances of AI.

Notes

1 Sabre (2022) 'In-flight management'. https://www.sabre.com/page/as-product-dictionary/opr-plt-in-flight-management/.
2 Travel Daily Media (2019) 'Somethings cooking: Vietnam Airlines "optimises" its onboard catering'. https://www.traveldailymedia.com/vietnam-airlines-sabre-onboard-catering/.
3 Sabre (2022) https://www.sabre.com/products/in-flight/.

4 PhocusWire (2014) 'KLM backs cabin crew technology startup MI airline with Euro 1–2 million round' https://www.phocuswire.com/KLM-backs-cabin-crew-technology-startup-MI-Airline-with-Euro-1-2-million-round.

5 KLM Royal Dutch Airlines (2015) Annual Report.

6 SimpleFlying (2020) 'Duty free sales' https://simpleflying.com/duty-free-sales/.

7 Qantas Airways (2017) 'Inflight duty free' https://www.qantas.com/ca/en/-qantas-experience/onboard/inflight-duty-free.html.

8 Bloomberg (2021) 'People are flying to nowhere just to shop duty free during covid' https://www.bloomberg.com/news/articles/2021-05-11/people-are-flying-to-nowhere-just-to-shop-duty-free-during-covid.

9 Shoppair (2021) https://www.shoppair.com/.

10 All information was obtained from the airlines' websites directly during May 2022.

Bibliography

Avram, B. (2016) 'Ancillaries in the aviation industry. Importance, trends, going digital', *Expert Journal of Marketing*, 5(2), pp. 53–65.

Brochado, A. *et al.* (2019) 'Airline passengers' perceptions of service quality: themes in online reviews', *International Journal of Contemporary Hospitality Management*, 31(-2), pp. 855–873. https://doi.org/10.1108/IJCHM-09-2017-0572

Goto, J.H., Lewis, M.E., and Puterman, M.L. (2002) *A Markov decision process model for airline meal provisioning*. New York: Cornell University. https://people.orie.cornell.edu/melewis/pubs/canadian_air.pdf

Hawk, E. (2018) 'Dynamic airline in-flight entertainment systems using predictive analysis'. Master's thesis, Bibliothek, Hochschule Anhalt: Bernburg, Germany. https://opendata.unihalle.de/bitstream/1981185920/12361/1/Masterarbeit%20Elena%20Hawk.pdf

5 Digital Cabin and Sensory Applications

5.1 Introduction of Digital Cabin

Since the early 2000s, airline websites have improved, and with the advent of the iPhone in 2007, smartphones have redefined convenience and personal control. Airlines are also seeing that being a traveler's digital assistant starts on the ground but must evolve and find its place inside the cabin in-flight and do more. And continue onwards. This is the journey to airline next-generation retailing and merchandising, although it starts with digitizing the cabin through connected devices, such as sensors, and systems.

Over the years, the use of electronics in cabins has increased, both using portable or mobile devices as well as the through the latest technology for Inflight Entertainment (IFE). The equipment is heavy at 5–7 pounds per seat and can add 2,000–3,000 pounds to a Boeing 777s weight.[1] Also, the wiring can heat up the cabin, requiring more energy consumption for air conditioning on board and thus fuel consumption as bleed air is taken from the turbines. But cabins are also increasingly connected and driving other benefits that make up for their costs. In both incremental fuel savings as well as customer service.

But especially since COVID-19, the adoption of contactless and self-service technologies (SST) is much faster. And it is not becoming personal, because we can blend in technology and physical contact when we need to see somebody, e.g. in the cabin, lounge, airport, or hotel. We can make contact with people more relevant and instantly gratifying because all the information and context are there. We know what customers are looking at, purchasing, and what they do next.

The digital cabin that some airlines are looking at is connecting a series of little next-gen black boxes to Wireless Avionics Intra-Communications (WAIC).[2] This connectivity platform can also host self-sufficient sensors and transmit data over short distances through Li-Fi.[3] It allows radio communication between two or more points on a single aircraft, through integrated wireless or installed components of the aircraft. It is part of a closed, exclusive network that is also required for the operation of the aircraft, although only used for safety-related applications. The short-range technology (Li-Fi)

DOI: 10.4324/9781003018810-7

44 *Uses of AI and Emerging Opportunities in Air Transport Operations*

works within 100 meters only and has power levels of only 10 mW for low rate and 50 mW for high-rate applications.[4]

WAIC (also known as wireless sensor networks) will allow the airline industry to realize benefits of wireless technologies to increase safety across all functions and aircraft systems. One of the key and overall benefits is the removal of aging wiring and associated cable weight, which also has environmental benefits. It further reduces the life-cycle costs of airplane rewiring and provides dissimilar redundancy thereby improving safety. Fewer wires mean a reduction in connector pins and potential failure points. In addition, there are things you can measure with sensors and communicate through wireless technology that you could never capture otherwise, especially when it comes to monitoring movement and surfaces in a cabin.

But there are other immediate benefits in reducing aircraft weight as well. For example, on an Airbus A380–800, the total wire count is around 100,000 with a total length of 470 kilometers. The weight of all wires combined is 5,700 kg, excluding around another 30% (2,000 kg) of weight to fix the harness to the airframe structure.[5] Almost one-third of all these wires can be removed using WAIC. This represents immense savings in fuel and emissions.

Nonetheless, its goal is further to unlock operational efficiencies and benefit from better integration between on-the-ground and in-flight data during flight. Using machine learning, existing (on-the-ground) insights can be enriched with flown data and encapsulate more dimensions and contexts to identify better linkages between cause and effect (weather related, energy consumption related, in-flight service related, the use of galleys, lavatories, and seats). Once deep insights into how things behave in-flight are better integrated with what we already know on the ground (e.g. maintenance of seats), we can better predict how to prevent or limit the extent of damage, wear, and tear and design sustainable ways to reduce weight, waste, and pollution.

For instance, in discussing opportunities at Garuda Indonesia Airlines with its CEO Irfan Setiaputra in March 2022, we identified ways of minimizing the waste of meals in First and Business Class by capturing which meals were not touched, or partially consumed, and using novel insights and metrics to better steer the flight kitchen for meal forecasts, by route, length of haul, direction, and even flight number (time of day). We could not ask flight attendants to collect and store this information (how, and in what format?). The catering companies also do not look at this when they take the trolleys off a plane at the end of their flight. Meals are destroyed, and thus wasted. There is nothing in this workflow that can be altered today, because it does not fit into the process. Therefore, we recommended the use of artificial intelligence (AI) cameras supported by algorithms that can identify meal types through computer vision and measure to what extent these meals should be offered. We demonstrated that defining the goal well could enable data scientists to write the end model that could provide better predictions for the catering company.

But even taking the aircraft as a vehicle perspective, there are promising uses and applications of sensors and wireless communication. It will reduce

Digital Cabin and Sensory Applications 45

weight, increase safety, and lead to related benefits due to better insights into relationships between events around aircraft systems. Airbus already has this black box of interconnected systems and built a solution around it (Skywise), as described in Chapters 1 and 2. Research from the Aerospace Vehicle Systems Institute (AVSI) indicated several potential WAIC applications.[6] This was released already back in 2014. The AVSI listed applications for low data range, interior as well as outside applications. In addition, it presented a list of applications for high data range for interior and outside applications, as listed in Table 5.1.

The table above demonstrates that these applications are all possible today and relevant for safety-related purposes. Adding sensors in seats, table trays, and movement detectors that measure and interpret cabin behaviors will generate use cases for applications that result in passenger services and benefit customers. This is considered the next stage of sensory applications. The need for higher data range applications will arise as we measure more complex onboard activities beyond what is listed in Table 5.2.

Table 5.1 Low data range applications of wireless avionics intra-communications

Low Data Range – Interior Applications (LI)	*Low Data Range – Outside Applications (LO)*
Sensors: • Cabin pressure • Smoke detection • Fuel tank/line • Proximity temperature • EMI incident detection • Structural health monitoring • Humidity/corrosion detection Controls: • Emergency lighting • Cabin functions	Sensors: • Ice detection • Landing gear position feedback • Brake • Temperature • Tire pressure • Wheel speed • Steering feedback • Flight controls position feedback

Table 5.2 High data range applications of wireless avionics intra-communications

High Data Range – Interior Applications (HI)	*Hi Data Range – Outside Applications (HO)*
Sensors: • Air data • Engine prognostic • Flight deck/cabin crew images/video Comms: • Avionics communications bus • FADEC aircraft interface • Flight Deck/Cabin Crew Audio/Video (safety-related) • High Data Rate	Sensors: • Structural health monitoring • Door sensors • Engine sensors – structural sensors Controls: • Active vibration control

46 *Uses of AI and Emerging Opportunities in Air Transport Operations*

Most of the above-mentioned sensors allow better control of a coordinate system and operation. Connecting them to the ground (first in batch and also in real time) will generate incremental benefits through safe and sustainable operations.

5.2 Customer Service Use Cases

There are many use cases for sensory devices and AI applications in a digital cabin. There are applications when you connect seat sensors that measure how the seat is used, how often it is reclined, or predict when it needs maintenance. Your seat or IFE breaks down? The F/A receives an alert, will come see you, and can instantly grant a credit or voucher on your PED in-flight. Flight attendants get alerts through their tablet App based on sensors that measure which passengers are restless or dehydrated and recommends what they want so they can prepare and bring it.

This platform can host all sorts of other Apps and will collectively drive a better and tailored customer experience while making customers purchase things they want. App-2-App (A2A) interfaces, such as IFE's ability to connect to your phone through Bluetooth also allow an improved, personalized experience while giving the customer a sense of control. More importantly, all digital behaviors can be analyzed and trends observed. This is also how airlines such as KLM or Emirates learn which movies to load in which 'top recommended' lists based on what viewers chose. This differs by flight, distance, and even direction (east vs west, or daytime vs nighttime flights). These insights become valuable when new products and services need to be presented to customers, notably if it involves a fee that airlines want to charge.

5.3 Inflight Entertainment

IFE in air travel has evolved as rapidly as the technology to offer personal TV screens and self-service made it technically feasible and economically viable. It has evolved from watching loops of films on a few channels that ran concurrently to menus allowing customers to browse through and select any of the over 4,500 channels of entertainment on demand, like on Emirates Airline. Not only is it possible to enjoy movies, but other content has been added to these platforms. People can play around with live maps, flight tracking, or browse through the duty-free catalogue and promotions.

Now airlines want to become influencers, too, and they can sell many relevant things. But they must be discovered in a global marketplace for travel-related experiences. And that requires a lot to keep track of, if they want to turn insights into personalized offerings. Virgin Atlantic Airways, Air New Zealand, Japan Airlines, Norwegian, Qantas, and Eva Airways are visionary pioneers whose data-driven product and retailing strategy will improve customer experience and help achieve commercial goals. Further, and through collaboration with Airbus, Boeing, and joint ventures between engineering

Digital Cabin and Sensory Applications 47

and electronics firms like Lufthansa Technik, LG, and Panasonic, the IoE and AI will be a powerful combination for airlines that want to unlock the commercial value of digital cabins in retailing, including duty free.

For instance, the weather forecast says rain at the destination. The AI platform is automatically sending instructions to the system to recommend the purchase of umbrellas by passengers. They appear on a list of recommendations on their IFT screen and mobile payment makes it easy to pay. The umbrellas will be waiting at the end of the jet bridge at the destination airport. With predictive insights, the commercial platform can even predict who will purchase them, based on deep analytics of the travelers and their profiles using deep learning.

The above opportunities are described in further detail in Chapter 11 on retailing and digital assistants.

5.4 Other Sensory Applications

TAP Air Portugal uses sensors to give insights into seat use, when and how often the seatbelts are fastened, how the tray table is used, and how often the seat is reclined.[7] They can even sense when people are thirsty. They do this to fold new insights into digital information. This data can then be used and ultimately ingested into an AI strategy to what and when to sell relevant personalized services.

The approach to using sensory applications has five levels:

1 Functional purpose, e.g., determining customer satisfaction or customer needs
2 Measurement of values, e.g., whether customer feels safe, comfortable, or is stressed
3 Customer outcome, i.e., the decision that the customer makes (purchase, abandon)
4 Object-related processes, e.g., context, information that is provided, navigation
5 Physical objects, i.e., personnel, cabin materials, equipment and digital tools, Apps.

In aircraft, airlines are not only concerned with detecting passengers' emotional state but also with activity detection. The activity detection, in turn, needs to be interpreted so that activity features can be extracted. In other words, we need to understand how people feel and be able to read why people move about the cabin, or in their seat/bed, and how this information can become actionable for flight attendants and digital tools that can recommend services to them. Regarding air quality, using sensors is also how hygiene and comfort can be captured and improved.[8]

In the online world, emotional analytics are feasible through remote user-testing software. Facial emotions and eye-tracking are fed into AI-based

48 *Uses of AI and Emerging Opportunities in Air Transport Operations*

software that helps to draw attention to what is being measured. For instance, it can indicate where negative emotions or stress are triggered in the travel booking process, or at which step in the mortgage application process with a bank the customer gets most anxious. Facial emotion can be tracked through facial coding technology. It is used to understand the subconscious actions of online consumers, which determine most of their buying decisions. The challenge for airlines will be to adapt this technology like the surveillance industry has done but for different purposes. With permission, cameras and sensors in the cabin can be used to enhance passenger services this way.

The cameras and sensors can be installed and used as follows:

- Sensors in seats measure movement, discomfort, and restlessness
- Sensors in tray tables measure functional performance and predict maintenance
- Aircraft cabin environment sensor (ACES)[9] throughout the cabin measuring air quality to assess the performance of HALO[10] filters
- Above-head sensors measure atmosphere and body heat and help regulate ventilation
- Sensors in the cabin floor help manage and timing of overall traffic
- Sensors in armrests to evaluate and improve their use and position
- Sensors in lavatories to help predict timely servicing inflight.

In sum, the multi-purpose sensor and communication systems serve a range of capabilities, ranging from passenger convenience communication services, over crew member devices, to maintenance planning.

5.5 Digital Assistant and Marketplace

And once we start using on-the-ground data about customers with what happens onboard, a truly frictionless experience can continue inflight to deliver and sell more experiences related to the purpose of each person's trip. Chapter 11 describes how a digital assistant on an experience marketplace can maximize the potential of customer intimacy by better positioning the airline industry as a service industry using modern technology. Solving problems and making customers' lives easier should be the end goal and finding meaningful ways to deliver propositions in a non-intrusive way will be key.

The path to deliver incremental benefits that start with the operational flight-based approach today could include the following:

- Ultra high-speed Wi-Fi enabling streaming with personal devices (PDA) inflight.
- Improved airline App with additional features and uses cases.
- Enabling control of the in-seat IFE through Bluetooth on PDA.
- Integration of in-cabin digital billboards and promotions with phones (pop-up).

Digital Cabin and Sensory Applications

- Integration of VR on IFE and phone for augmented experiences (metaverse).
- Enabling control of seat surfaces and aircraft window blinds using PDA.
- Integration of mobile payment for on-board ordering.
- Enhanced retail marketplace supported by personal digital assistant for customers.
- Further integration and servicing of travel-related and other retailing experiences on the ground.

What these opportunities bring will also necessitate more sophisticated sales and revenue optimization techniques. Not only in the presentation of content to individual groups (billboards) or customers (in-seat screen or personal device) but in integrating sales optimization of digital services and perishable in-cabin food products. An optimization of this kind would require Edge AI applications (refer to Chapter 22) and bringing revenue management platforms onboard aircraft. The concept of this is illustrated below in Figure 5.1 and further elaborated on in Chapter 11 on digital cabins and real-time retailing.

A lot of the possibilities that will exist on the ground will drive future experiences on board. To that extent, the possibilities are limitless and depend on how the market will adopt SuperApps, and how we structure and present relevant content to individual customers in each context as they move around. As a case in point, the purchase of Uber by Grab in Singapore signals how SuperApps are integrating urban mobility, and what this will look like with electric vertical take-off and landing vehicles (eVTOLs).

5.6 Conclusions

This chapter discussed the opportunities the digital cabin brings in terms of systems as well as passenger service operations. Given the connected aircraft

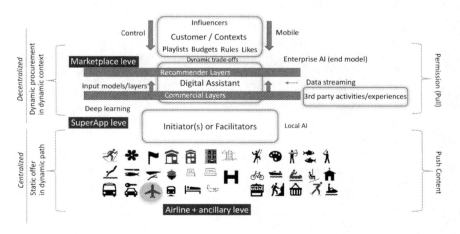

Figure 5.1 Inflight cabin digital and physical assets revenue management concept.

50 *Uses of AI and Emerging Opportunities in Air Transport Operations*

cabin, the deployment of digitized and interconnected sensors, devices, and the capture of passenger behaviors provide valuable and comprehensive data about the state of and emotions in the cabin. AI lays a pivotal role in modelling the insights and deploying automated services that enhance customer service regarding cabin services, climate, as well as entertainment and convenience-related services. Joint communication and sensing radio systems, such as WAIC and LiFi, within the connected aircraft cabin, will enable these services.

Notes

1 Boeing (2022) https://www.boeing.com.
2 ICAO (2014) https://www.icao.int/APAC/Meetings/2014%20RPGWRC15/SP05_Boeing-J.%20Cramer_Wireless%20Avionics.pdf.
3 LiFi is a game-changing innovation that can transmit enormous amounts of data through LEDs (Light Emitting Diodes). Source: LiFi (2022) 'What is light fidelity technology'. https://lifi.co/what-is-light-fidelity-technology/.
4 TrustedReviews (2022) 'What is Li-Fi? The fast wireless technology explained'. https://www.trustedreviews.com/explainer/what-is-lifi-2932109#:~:text=One%20major%20disadvantage%20to%20Li,unable%20to%20pass%20through%20walls.
5 Airbus (2020) 'Aircraft characteristics – airport and maintenance planning' https://www.airbus.com/sites/g/files/jlcbta136/files/2021-11/Airbus-Aircraft-AC-A380.pdf.
6 AVSI (2011) 'Wireless Avionics Intra-Communications (WAIC). https://waic.avsi.aero/wp-content/uploads/sites/3/2015/05/WAIC_Overview_and_Application_Examples.pdf.
7 APEX (2019) 'TAP Begins Flying With Sensor-Equipped Recaro iSeats'. https://apex.aero/articles/tap-begins-flying-sensor-equipped-recaro-iseats/#:~:text=The%20sensors%20gather%20data%20on,whether%20the%20seatbelt%20is%20fastened.
8 Aircraft Interiors International (2021) 'Aircraft cabin environment sensor certified for A320'. https://www.aircraftinteriorsinternational.com/news/passenger-health-safety/aircraft-cabin-environment-sensor-certified-for-a320.html.
9 Teledyne Technologies (2021) 'Teledyne controls' aircraft cabin environment sensor (ACES) now certified for Airbus A320 aircraft series'. https://www.teledyne.com/en-us/news/Pages/teledyne-controls-aircraft-cabin-environment-sensor-now-certified-for-airbus-a320-aircraft-series.aspx.
10 Boeing (2020) 'Cabin air filtration'. https://www.boeing.com/confident-travel/cabin-air.html.

Bibliography

Airbus (2022) 'Skywise'. https://aircraft.airbus.com/en/services/enhance/skywise
Aviation Today (2022) 'Development of wireless avionics & intra communications'. http://interactive.aviationtoday.com/development-of-wireless-avionics-intra-communications/
AVSI-Aerospace Vehicle Systems Institute (2014) 'Update and Status on implementing of a regulatory framework for WAIC'. ICAO Regional WRC-15 Preparatory Workshop, Pattaya, Thailand. Agenda Item 1.17 2014. https://www.icao.

int/APAC/Meetings/2014%20RPGWRC15/SP05_Boeing-J.%20Cramer_Wireless%20Avionics.pdf

Emirates Airline (2022) 'Inflight entertainment'. https://www.emirates.com/ca/english/experience/inflight-entertainment/

Ninnemann, J. (2022) 'Multipath-assisted radio sensing and state detection for the connected aircraft cabin', *Sensors*, 2, p. 2859. https://doi.org/10.3390/s22082859

Part 2

Applications of AI and Emerging Opportunities in Commercial Management

Part 2 of this book reviews the current applications of artificial intelligence (AI) in commercial functions within air transport. It looks at initial use cases and adoption of AI in both the passenger and air cargo business. The first chapters concentrate on the passenger side and focus on functions from network planning, fleet planning, finance, to demand forecasting, pricing, and revenue management but also loyalty, sales and distribution, and retailing. It also elaborates on more novel concepts such as total revenue management. The last two chapters of this part of the book are dedicated to air cargo, handling, and cargo warehouse management and the role AI increasingly plays and can play in this area.

Part 2 is structured as follows:

Chapter 6 addresses network planning.
Chapter 7 speaks to fleet planning and the use of AI in aircraft finance.
Chapter 8 talks about AI in demand forecasting, dynamic pricing and revenue optimization.
Chapter 9 delves into loyalty management and its evolving scope.
Chapter 10 focuses on sales, corporate contracts, and distribution management.
Chapter 11 introduces AI in potential applications of dynamic retailing and procurement.
Chapter 12 provides insights into new opportunities of total revenue management.
Chapter 13 rounds up this part by showcasing how brand management benefits from AI.
Chapter 14 elaborates on AI use cases in cargo handling and warehouse management.
Chapter 15 discusses AI and its opportunities in cargo commercial management.
Chapter 16 talks about the benefits of AI in human resource management.

DOI: 10.4324/9781003018810-8

6 Network and Schedule Planning, Aircraft Assignment

6.1 Network Planning Described

Almost no other function within an airline integrates as many divisions as airline network planning. It is often also referred to as route planning, although routes can sometimes be seen as individual mini businesses for which business cases are built. In the context of network planning, it is meant as the more holistic planning function of the overall network of markets served, either directly (non-stop or through connections) or indirectly with the help of commercial agreements with other airlines through marketing, or alliance agreements. In most cases, the initial scope of this is air transport only. However, when airlines study market opportunities, markets are also defined as catchment areas from which to draw potential customers and, in addition, markets to serve from other existing markets. There are several dimensions to it, which include but are not limited to the catchment around:

- Primary airports.
- Secondary airports.
- Regional airports.
- Quality of service of the airport and handling facilities (for the carrier).
- Airport restrictions (such as noise or curfews).
- Quality of service of the airport itself (for the traveller).
- Mobility around airports (ease of getting to/from the airport).
- Parallel markets (airports that are alternatives for travellers based on geographical proximity).
- Online connectivity or other potential connectivity.
- Market response to non-stop or transit requirements.

This covers only the physical aspect of transport. While important, it is a means to an end in network planning. The market opportunity itself is the initial and main consideration for airlines and evidently, it is related to the airport infrastructure.

DOI: 10.4324/9781003018810-9

Network and Schedule Planning, Aircraft Assignment 55

Opportunities for network changes arise due to the following factors:

- Market demand: population and economic growth are the principal drivers of growing market demand, but ultra-low fares by ULCCs are also attracting travellers that could not afford to travel before. This stimulation effect can often allow low-cost airlines to start completely new routes with single-aisle aircraft in short-haul markets.
- Competitive market: airlines start up, fail, merge, or withdraw from routes. Capacity fluctuates in a dynamic environment, as does pricing.
- Technology: new aircraft allow new missions or allow other missions to become economically feasible, such as the Boeing 787 connecting secondary city-pairs like Denver to Tokyo.

The network planning function is complex. It requires the airline to get many critical pieces in place to get it right and to make money. There are also many information needs for which data needs to be collected, structured, and modeled. Network planning is generally a function that caters to the long term and is sequentially broken down into shorter time frames. But there are three distinct perspectives within the network planning framework. Between them, adjustments are always made as discussed later. The three stages are

1 Long term (typically beyond six months).
2 Medium term (typically between two and six months).
3 Short term (typically one week to one month with daily ad-hoc rotational changes).

The long-term process is concerned with the development of a fleet plan, the overall network, routes, and the structure of the network. Its goal is to allow the carrier to extract as much value out of the markets as possible, based on its business model, using the existing and planned fleet, and maximizing the multiplier effect of connectivity, reach, density, and frequency. This long-term process takes into consideration all macro-economic, political, and legal factors to identify threats and opportunities. One of the key aspects of modern aviation is the migration of growth centers across continents and within regions due to shifting labor forces. For instance, the engines of manufacturing and supply chains have been shifting not only within China but also to Vietnam, Cambodia, and Thailand. Investments made by large corporations and airline groups based in the Middle East are also investing heavily in the African continent, driving the need for more air transportation. What this means is that airlines and alliance groups that can tap into regions with above-average growth and improving yields will attempt to structure their networks along these shifts.

To fulfill the information needs of long-term network planning, airline specialists amass large sets of internal airline data, external industry data, and other economic, financial, and behavioral trends. Network planners then

56 *Uses of AI and Emerging Opportunities in Commercial Management*

forecast market opportunities not only in general but also around a specific existing or planned network and business model. The launch of each new route is treated as a business case, not only with each of their own predicted performance criteria but also in the context of the overall network contribution. There is often a time element to that meaning that there are short-term, medium-term, and long-term expectations the business case must address and meet.

In building the network planning model, each variable or assumption has to be explicitly identified and tested. For instance, the model must allow planners to evaluate the impact of expected changes in demand, the composition of demand, competition and market capacity, connectivity, frequency, and so forth. Given that it is a model with inputs and outputs that drive other decisions, it is a good candidate for the use of artificial intelligence.

The typical output of the long-term network plan is the basic structure of a network, the list of routes, and the initial level of frequencies. In a second iteration, the timings of flights are established representing a typical month and week. In the next step, adjustments are made to reflect specific events, national holidays, moving statutory holidays, and other recognizable factors that influence demand in specific weeks and days. Additional validations are made to see if aircraft type and aircraft rotations work across the schedule. It is at this point that the schedule is sent to various departments for input, to cross-check what extent it is fit for purpose from a corporate sales, partnerships, maintenance, and engineering perspective. Senior station managers at key airports typically have a say as well. Once the schedule is published and in-season, adaptations are made. This is referred to as the medium and short-term cycle of network planning.

In the medium term, network planning is about evaluating the performance of the network to identify opportunities for improvement, or to identify the root causes of disappointing performance. This is a difficult task as many variables are related and dynamically move concurrently. Nonetheless, business analytics assist network planners, route, and revenue managers in exposing relationships between data elements that are not so obvious to the human eye. The output of this process is therefore used to fine-tune network planning in the long term, and the analytics can be used to code algorithms that drive artificial intelligence in long-term network planning. In some cases, an airline needs to restructure its operating model using banks (or 'waves') of flights at its main hub because of changes in its alliance network. For instance, by signing an agreement with another carrier, or when a new carrier enters a global alliance group, the networks must be re-aligned to ensure optimal connectivity and improve the network multiplier that creates economies of scope, economies of density, and economies of market dominance. Since global alliance groups compete at this level, this element or network adjustment is of crucial importance, as it allows travelers to connect better while reducing transit times. This is what enables end-to-end markets and a higher number of seamless ODs (Origin-Destination combinations).

Network and Schedule Planning, Aircraft Assignment 57

Lastly, the short term is about the schedule that is planned or being operated in the current season. From an execution standpoint, it is carrying out what was planned at higher levels before. From a day-to-day perspective, short-term network planning (or schedule management), is about fine-tuning, addressing unforeseen circumstances such as cancelations, mechanical aircraft-on-ground (AOG) instances, consolidations of flights, as well as up-gauging or downgauging capacity due to unexpected short-term spikes or troughs in demand. The latter could be the case in times of war or in regions being hit by natural disasters, such as a tsunami or volcano eruptions. The short term does permit tactical changes to the schedule, but it must be done without interrupting the overall network strategy that underpins the business model. This means that any aircraft or aircraft type change cannot have carry-forward negative effects, such as bad ripple effect in following rotations. The change cannot lead to an unwanted interruption that undermines the business elsewhere. It is for this reason that carriers build in some spare capacity or room to manoeuvre across the bases of their aircraft. In the schedule itself, there is usually also a bit of time flexibility after several rotations, allowing some agility for service recovery or ad-hoc rescue missions. But no airline wants to have aircraft sitting on the ground, and therefore this is kept to an acceptable level.

The overall process has traditionally been manually intensive, despite the use of planning software. For a large full-service airline, the development cycle of a full network could take up between one to three, in some cases six months. This is because all the data needs to be collected and considered, and also due to the number of iterations in ironing out all coordination between the different departments, i.e., network planning, maintenance, scheduling, revenue management, crew planning, and dispatch.

6.2 Aircraft Assignment

The aircraft assignment process is one that completes the network planning exercise. While it is also part of fleet planning (at aircraft type level), in aircraft assignment, specific tail numbers are assigned to operate missions, which are a set of take-offs and landings on city pairs that rotate the aircraft back to their base after several cycles. This applies mainly to narrow-body aircraft that fly short domestic or transborder missions.

Each individual aircraft (also called 'tail' or 'fin' number) has specific characteristics. Even for a given fleet of Airbus A330s, each aircraft and its engines will perform differently. There are also slight variations in maximum take-off weight. The engines also burn fuel at different rates. But more importantly, the configurations inside the cabin (or in the cargo hold) are not always identical. Some aircraft have been acquired as used aircraft and went into service without a full like-for-like cabin. Others are operated in different regions and have different cabin configurations in terms of the number of business class versus economy class aircraft. This is what Air Canada used to

58 *Uses of AI and Emerging Opportunities in Commercial Management*

do with its Boeing 767s across the Pacific Ocean. Also, some of Air Canada's Boeing 777s are configured in a high–density layout, which adds 109 seats in economy class. That's a total of 458 seats instead of 349. It is using these aircraft on the Montreal-Paris route, for instance.[1]

When aircraft perform or are configured differently, it becomes important to ensure they are mapped to meet the requirements of the market they serve. Not only in terms of completing the mission economically but also in terms of the service product on board. As such, when the fleet of aircraft has been assigned to regions, another process re-optimizes the aircraft assignment with specific tail numbers. At that point, the schedule for dispatch, operations, and maintenance, is updated with each individual aircraft assigned to specific flights per day and week of the year.

6.3 Impact of COVID-19 Pandemic

Before the COVID-19 pandemic hit the travel world, airlines had their own network planning process. In most cases, when airlines go through their network planning exercise, they start off with the existing schedule. This traditional approach minimizes complexity and allows the team to work off a base scenario. However, since the pandemic wiped out demand and presented a very unpredictable and unstable market, demand looked very different and became challenging to forecast. And while the situation was dramatic, whether airlines surmised that this was the new normal or 'business as usual' much depended on the extent to which airlines had modernized their network planning tools with more capable technology.

The new capability to build a network from scratch (also referred to as the 'cleansheet approach') was needed by airlines that were more manual and less agile. And even though most of the old data inputs remained largely the same, others had and continued to change and became almost unpredictable variables. To illustrate, flight times between points A and B remained the same, but in some markets the flight time was less due to less congestion. The traffic levels were significantly lower and air navigation service providers (ANSPs) were allowing pilots to fly shorter routes and narrower airport approaches with fewer holding patterns. Likewise, while boarding times were similar, check-in, security, and airport connection times were not, due to sanitary checks, increased physical separation, and additional screen time across airport facilities. People also moved slower through airports in the sense that they were disoriented by closed areas, routing changes, and other distracting and situational factors, even for those that travel frequently. In addition, aircraft turnaround times were longer. Aircraft had to be cleansed differently, had to be disinfected, and this meant that aircraft rotations and connecting slots were different. Lastly, usable aircraft capacity became uncertain as it was not known which regulatory policy would be in place for physical separation on board, such as the blocking of middle seats.

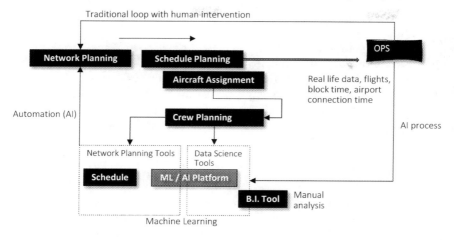

Figure 6.1 Network planning flow supported by ML/AI.

Due to the new complexity of additional and moving variables in schedule planning, some airlines even considered reducing connections in order to focus on point-to-point operations first. Airlines were looking at which old inputs could be used, had to be updated, and which new inputs had to be included in the giant puzzle of generating a schedule for the network. It is for this reason that airlines that already used network planning technology based on machine learning and artificial intelligence had a significant advantage. Others had to build many new scenarios and go through the whole process in a more time-consuming way.

Figure 6.1 outlines a simplified flow of the traditional versus the AI-powered process where machine learning is used to learn from real-life flight operations to enhance network planning.

6.4 Artificial Intelligence in Network Planning

The benefits that the use of artificial intelligence in network planning brings are not only around processing more data with more computational power but also the opportunity to run multiple optimization tasks at the same time. It means the technology can consider more variables and factors, such as crew scheduling, operational constraints in schedule planning, and alliance partner schedules. For illustration, the factors that could be built into the network and schedule development cycle include:

- The economics of the network from a passenger volume perspective, including the markets, demand trends, demand composition, and prevailing fares.
- Competitive schedules, including seat capacity and weekly frequencies.
- Demand data including ingested insights of propensity to travel data.

60   *Uses of AI and Emerging Opportunities in Commercial Management*

- Economic data that influence the nature and velocity of demand, such as foreign exchange.
- Resource constraints such as fleet, fleet type, operational constraints of aircraft, airport gates, and airport slots.
- Geographical characteristics, such as block times, airport opening or curfew hours, congestion around banks of flight, seasonal weather patterns, and disruption risk.
- Partner/alliance reliability, such as flight completion factor, and on-time performance (OTP).
- Near real-time processes update all input data and how they impact the variables.

By running these processes at the same time there are significant time savings compared to following sequential steps. It also means there is less need to go back and forth with trial and error to what fits or does not work. In addition, because machine learning will improve each time it is trying to optimize the puzzle, the forecasts are more accurate. The added benefit of this is that there is sufficient 'brain power' for the machine to calibrate itself without manual intervention and make updates in real time.

In the configuration of a network planning optimizer, the user interface is such that network planners can still intuitively follow the logic, or neural path, of the model. This helps not only for training purposes but also for user adoption when it is first implemented. Network planners that were used to other tools and a more manual approach will have a natural reluctance to allow the machine to run these processes. But with time, they see that their jobs become more strategic as they can think of other factors and scenarios that will help their airline generate incremental revenues.

Network and schedule planning has evolved a great deal in recent years. New technology, new computing power, and the application of machine learning and artificial intelligence have greatly contributed to the agility and effectiveness of this function. What has changed more recently is that additional data sets from both internal sources and external market sources can be added to what is already used in a lakehouse of an artificial intelligence platform. There, new scenarios can be created with different outlooks of demand and other commercials or constraints as sets of rules in the machine learning models. They are then stacked for the end model to produce a recommended and optimized network and schedule given everything that is known and anticipated. Using feeds with data obtained from other systems in the ecosystem, such as revenue management, the machine learning model can learn and recommend further improvements. To illustrate this, revenue management collects and can feed short-term booking data and computes how trends are changing. When patterns are detected and can be generalized to all flights, the pro-rata reduction in demand can be predicted forward for the immediate future. The machine learning component within RM can then also update itself as it is picking up an increase in demand and travel.

Internally, airlines already had the capability through analytics-based MarTech (demand analysis, campaign ROI) to evaluate and assess market demand by observing demand based on a trip search using their online booking engine, the loyalty app, or by tracking call center activity. The new data that is now available from external sources includes shopping information extracted from search engines. People look at trips or travel on search engines, such as Google, or on websites of online travel agents. But further information is obtained through the Global Distribution Systems' (GDS) conventional travel agents. With all this in hand, airlines found new ways in using it and that is what matters.

The artificial intelligence that is built into network planning tools such as SkySuite of Amadeus allows airlines to do more with fewer people, which came in handy during the pandemic. But it also allowed people to do even more work than they did before. The additional work stemmed from integrating new data sets, such as turnaround time rules and aircraft cleaning constraints. These had to be added in the set of algorithms. This is because there were new data sets to integrated, higher volumes of data, and more rules and constraints to add in the algorithm. The fact that the pandemic was a moving obstacle in different regions of the world meant that airlines were required to work with multiple scenarios simultaneously. This would have been almost impossible without the automation and intelligence that the solutions can provide in real time.

Looking further, the potential exists to build MarTech ingested insights into a set of layers or deep learning algorithms that, through convolution algorithms, will run complex optimization processes that can automated recommended network decisions. This is shown in Figure 6.2 in an overly simplified fashion.

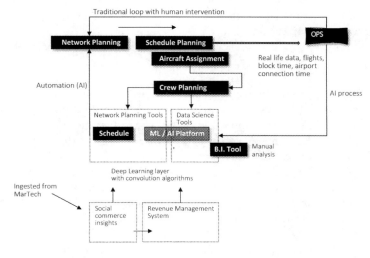

Figure 6.2 Augmented network optimization process with AI.

62 *Uses of AI and Emerging Opportunities in Commercial Management*

6.5 Network Planning as AI Process

Much of what has been written so far in this book about the systematic process of exploring and adopting machine learning and artificial intelligence in production applies to network planning as well. If an airline is a first-adopter, it needs to (1) design the enterprise workflow, (2) define its data strategy and sources, (3) conceive and write the models and end model, and (4) use predictions and real-time feedback to allow machine learning to optimize the recommendations on a continuous basis. Whether the airline has a dedicated data science team in network planning or not, it can also rely on vendors to implement and update the solutions when new rules must be built in, or data must be updated.

The long-term network planning process is run once all data (or a sufficient subset thereof) is collected and infused into the model and all factors in the consideration set of rules are activated. The output will be an optimized recommended schedule with passenger numbers, aircraft rotations, take-off and landings, and block hours, all broken down by aircraft type by week. Based on the yield and cost inputs, the schedule will have a total revenue number attached to it, even a forecast operating profit figure. For different scenarios, based on the consideration set and change in configuration of parameters, the network optimizer will

- Reschedule and retime the entire network for a better passenger flow.
- Evaluate the impact of different frequencies or flight additions/deletions.
- Allocate capacity to maximize passenger demand and meet operational requirements.
- Optimal aircraft routes considering, crew and route-based maintenance.

The tools will enable us to offer more to our customers through better network planning and uncovering new ways to continue growing our network in a meaningful way.

(Adam Decaire, Vice President
Network Planning, Southwest Airlines)[2]

One of the bigger contributions of automation underpinned by artificial intelligence is that it allows what-if analyses in a matter of minutes. This is very helpful in times of uncertainty, or to test a few scenarios and assumptions for insights and learning. According to Amadeus, airlines that use their tools have been able to report a total profit increase of up to 12.5% on a weekly basis, against revenue gains of 3.3%. Most of the revenue gains were from improved connectivity (up 6.5%) compared to originating traffic (0.7%). The increase in captured demand in passenger numbers can be up to 2.7%, driven by the increase in the number of connecting itineraries.

Artificial intelligence is also helping airlines in other ways. The technology that is supported by AI can elude network planners to potential problems. It can display alerts when:

- Flights appear to be bottlenecks that could lead to an erosion in OTP.
- Blocks need extra time in order to secure or have more certainty of a good OTP.
- Flights will likely be delayed, and to what extent and how often.
- Flights cause delay propagation, i.e., cause a ripple effect of delays through the network.

The solutions can also optimize duty times by swapping routes. In some cases, changing the rotations can reduce the number of duties. This is because aircraft differ in their crewing requirements and optimizing the pool of cabin crew by juggling aircraft rotations produces a different mix of staff across the flights.

The US Federal Aviation Administration tracks flight delays and calculates the estimated costs for airlines and passengers related to delays. It estimates the operating cost as \$57 per delay minute and the passenger cost as \$67 per delay minute. That is almost \$120 per delay minute for an aircraft with 150 seats.[3] And evidence-based research by Amadeus shows that modern technology in network and scheduling solutions can improve OTP by an average of 3% with little to no impact on schedule profitability. As more and more data can be obtained and used, the process can continue to improve provided the data is relevant to the task at hand. The integration of flight operations and flight dispatch, today also using AI, is an example of how very short-term schedule adjustments could be improved even further. These workflows can be aligned so that the intersections between these functions can be automated using Enterprise AI applications (the topic of Chapter 18).

Modern scheduling solutions automatically factor in commercial viability. This is because it is also based on customer travel preferences, itinerary, or even airport preferences. As such, customer choice and estimates of price elasticities are built in and can be adjusted over time. This further requires competitive schedule and frequency monitoring, which, combined with competitive fare analysis can be incorporated in the future to further align with revenue management functions.

With all the advances in computing and automation, modern solutions in network and schedule planning allow schedulers to highlight any violation and click the quick fix button to invoke a micro-optimizer to best resolve the violation. This means that any new data that is relevant to the chain of events that can be obtained in a digital format can potentially be included. This is already the case with weather, anticipated de-icing, and surface congestion. But it could potentially include events such as strikes, security threats, and other updates that are provided in real time. If the data can be captured, it can be modeled. And it can be made to be part of the consideration set that machine learning can learn from. Artificial intelligence will again act as the glue to automate the functions in a frictionless manner smartly.

6.6 Conclusions

This chapter is about the functions that are responsible for network and scheduling planning and aircraft assignment. It describes the main tasks in these functions and highlights how global market disruptions, such as pandemics, accelerate the need for smart automation around inter-dependent planning tasks and workflows. It shows that due to the information requirements and computational power that is required, this area is a prime candidate for machine learning and smart automation using AI. It also allows airlines to plan for just-in-case situations faster and resolve ad-hoc disruptions in a matter of minutes, instead of hours or days.

Notes

1 Wingborn (2014). 'Inflight review: Air Canada 777, high density economy'. https://www.wingborn.com/inflight-review-air-canada-777-high-density-economy/.
2 Amadeus (2022) 'Seven breakthroughs with airline flight scheduling'. Blog. https://amadeus.com/en/insights/blog/seven-breakthroughs-airline-flight-scheduling#modal-1294471558.
3 FAA (2019) https://www.faa.gov/data_research/aviation_data_statistics/media/cost_delay_estimates.pdf.

Bibliography

Amadeus (2022) https://amadeus.com/en/insights/blog/seven-breakthroughs-airline-flight-scheduling#modal-1294471558

Clarke, M. *et al.* (2012) 'Impact of operations research on the evolution of the Airline industry', *Journal of Aircraft*, 41(1), pp. 62–81.

Franke, M. (2021) *Managing airline networks.* London: Routledge.

Ogunsina, K. *et al.* (2021) 'Enabling integration and interaction for decentralized artificial intelligence in airline disruption management', *Engineering Applications of Artificial Intelligence,* 109. https://doi.org/10.1016/j.engappai.2021.104600

Sukhorukov, A. *et al.* (2020) 'Digital transformation of Airline management as the basis of innovative development'. In Z. Popovic, A. Manakov, and V. Breskich (Eds.), *Advances in intelligent systems and computing,* pp. 845–854, vol. 1115. Cham: Springer.

7 Fleet Planning and Aircraft Acquisition

7.1 Fleet Planning Described

To build on the previous chapter, fleet planning is a function with a longer perspective than network planning. It is mainly concerned with determining future fleet requirements as per the airline's overall longer-term plan and business goals. Not only the number and the types of aircraft are important, the timing of aircraft acquisitions, how they are financed, and when they are integrated into the operation are equally critical. Therefore, not only the airline's overall objectives but also its operating constraints and financial position matter.

There are many factors that airline operators must consider when selecting a new or replacement fleet of aircraft:

- Macro-economic demand trends.
- Alliance group, alliance activity, and own airline's alliance plans.
- Availability of airport slots (and/or slot trading market).
- Technological advancements in aircraft performance.
- Capacity characteristics of to-be-developed or released aircraft.
- Aircraft payload/range capabilities.
- The value of revenue-generating physical and digital assets or aircraft.
- The optimum number of fleet types.
- Fleet commonality (at least in medium-term).
- Aircraft take-off performance and airfield requirements.
- Relative fuel consumption characteristics.
- Alternative fuel options or acceptance levels.
- Maintenance cost and other engineering requirements.
- Cargo capacity.
- Old versus new trade-offs.
- Cabin configuration and compatibility.
- Aircraft values and lease market trends.
- Aircraft buy versus lease trade-offs.
- Aircraft sale and leaseback market.
- Availability and affordability of financing.

DOI: 10.4324/9781003018810-10

66 *Uses of AI and Emerging Opportunities in Commercial Management*

- Trends in financial structures, such as special purpose vehicles (SPV).
- The value of passenger comfort.
- Relative revenue driven by seat count.

It is imperative that airport slots, as a strategic asset and resource for the airline's network and thus its revenue multiplier, are considered in fleet planning. Political/legal aspects around slots are abound in the field, and airport slot trading is a market that can be of strategic importance to tap into. Today, artificial intelligence (AI) plays a minor role in this. But that can change.

New aircraft can have a material impact on the incremental revenue they generate per passenger. This is not only because the latest updates and technology can be incorporated in the cabin, business class seats, and inflight connectivity, but also because of passenger comfort, such as onboard climate, noise cancellation technology, and the overall appeal of the aircraft. In addition, future trends toward allowing passengers and merchants access to a digital marketplace platform on board will transform retailing, as discussed in Chapter 11.

Nonetheless, there is an extra amount of effort and work that goes into forecasting the revenue per passenger, per flight, per block hour, and on an annualized basis. The reason for this is that increasingly, and due to trends in airline pricing, airlines offer passengers more choices in selecting and choosing individual products and services. Airlines allow customers more choice in choosing only those services they want to pay for, such as seat selection, a checked bag, a carry-on bag, lounge access, or better meals or Wi-Fi onboard. This trend will continue with the digital cabin and modern ancillaries as discussed earlier in this book. All these line items require forecasts by aircraft type and customers, and the routes they will be operated on. This also requires assumptions on the traffic mix and likelihood of passengers buying different services, even on board. It even incorporates the commissions airlines will generate from selling affiliate companies' products and services. As such, this process has become more complex and requires new approaches.

Since fleet planning is a large exercise that (at major fleet overhaul level) is only done once every few years with minor periodic adjustments, many airlines outsource this specialist work. The required skill sets and evaluation of alternatives using specialist tools are often acquired from an external firm. Nonetheless, the airlines are specializing more in these areas due to special revenue-generating capabilities of modern aircraft that can be customized along the airline's product marketing and customer service strategy.

There are often lists of criteria and performance measures and ultimately one needs to use a balanced score method to rank alternatives against four main criteria: (1) financially, (2) operationally, (3) customer experience, and (4) sustainability. An aircraft type that wins on some of the above factors will lose on others and there are often other considerations that can swing a decision, such as relationships, national interests (manufacturer is based in the nation), and an overall cultural fit. Not all decisions can be 100% rational.

Fleet planning is not necessarily a function that is currently automated using machine learning or AI at most airlines. For instance, British Airways (still part of IAG) still relies on in-house tools and operations research (OR) methods, supported by manual work and specialist insights. That is mainly because the process is not repeated often enough.[1] But it is also because there are many data elements that are both quantifiable and qualifiable, making it more difficult to mathematically write a model that considers softer aspects. This is where fleet acquisition models have traditionally relied heavily on OR models to determine the optimal number of aircraft given the input of a future network, demand, and other operational factors. A multi-stage process then considers other aspects that include customer satisfaction goals, financial evaluations of the aircraft values as well as the financing options available. It is important to note that some aircraft can be an operational fit, but more difficult to acquire financially. This is often related to the forecast value and serviceability (and thus marketability) of the aircraft. Aircraft lessors are also concerned with mitigating risk and being able to place aircraft elsewhere in case of repossession or airline bankruptcies. This is reflected in their lease rates.

7.2 Artificial Intelligence in Fleet Planning

Not many airlines use machine learning and AI for fleet planning. But some airlines, such as Southwest Airlines, who already use sophisticated tools (Amadeus SkySuite) for network planning have extended it into fleet planning. In this context, the managers can consider new and different fleet types when doing fleet assignments thus ensuring a fleet mix study is always in the context of a specific schedule. This can then be augmented by overlayering a future schedule based on the output provided by network planning. In this exercise, existing slots and outstanding slot requests (pending approval) can be incorporated. In some cases, the functionality goes as far as signaling issues with existing or missing but required slots. This helps managers with the planning of slot requests.

While fleet planning is a long-term process, there are many variables in the optimization mix that change, as highlighted before. This necessitates constant monitoring of changing market conditions so that opportunities to add or replace aircraft are evaluated, while respecting the integrity of the network and related requirements. Changes in the financial market make it financially attractive to sell and lease back aircraft. Changes in the capital market can also make it more interesting to upgrade or modernize aging fleet at a different time than originally anticipated. In some cases, as happened during the Covid-19 pandemic, governments provided financial support under the condition they update their fleet with more fuel-efficient aircraft. This is precisely what KLM Royal Dutch as well as the Air France KLM Group did, by ordering a new fleet of Airbus A220s, A320s, and Airbus A350s to replace aging Boeing 737s and A330s. It also ordered 4 A350 freighters to start phasing out the Boeing 747 freighters and reduce costs per available mile.[2]

7.3 Integrated Fleet Planning as AI Process

The concept of integrated and automated fleet planning essentially combines all areas around the network, schedule, fleet, as well as crewing together. Its objective is to support both the long-term planning function and fleet evaluations but optimize the daily processes as well, including all maintenance-related requirements and irregular operations. It optimizes all functions within the chain, manages the coordination between individual tasks, and pre-empts potential conflict or integrity issues. It also means that predictive maintenance is updated in real time and trickles down to make adjustments in dispatch, including pilots and cabin crewing changes related to aircraft types. This is all possible, and almost the reality today. At least, the digital information flows are such that information and alerts are provided early on, allowing people to act. And oversight will remain important, as systems can break down and connectivity can be at risk (e.g., cyber-attacks).

An integrated system will make all processes in the business far more efficient and allow for improved, proactive fleet management and maintenance. This means more efficient communication and savings in the form of lower operating costs, a reduction of unexpected repairs, and, overall, improved fleet management capabilities.

Integrated, automated solutions are a combination of various harmonized components that deliver end-to-end assistance in supervising the fleet, flight, crew, and all related resources. They will also include employee time and productivity tracking, as we will increasingly be able to track people as well. Not only for security and safety purposes but also for efficiency purposes and to streamline operations related to flight operations and resource planning.

With a view toward the long term, integrated and automated network planning will even produce recommendations on the number of pilots and their type ratings that will be required. It will feed into pilot training programs and track KPIs as to meeting the fleet and network requirements of the future. It will even indicate where the staff should be based, to what extent they can commute, and how far they can commute to solidify operational integrity. And all this can be updated, tracked, and re-optimized in real time.

The workflows can be further aligned if airlines move from functional-level processes supported by machine learning and AI to harmonization and optimization of effort at enterprise level. For illustrative purposes, this is shown in Figure 7.1 below. It also highlights how enterprise processes can be extended from network planning to fleet planning, acquisition, and even airport slot request management. This would enable real-life, real-time scenario evaluations that avoid tremendous repetitive work but would also assist in ad-hoc and very near-term crises around fleets, slots, and networks, such as in times of pandemics.

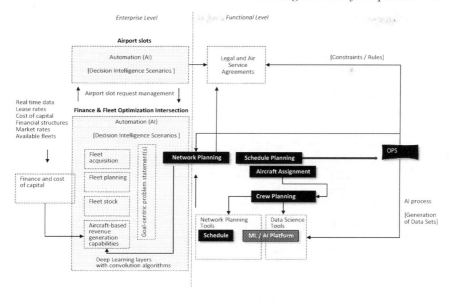

Figure 7.1 Illustration of airport slot and fleet planning at enterprise level.

7.4 Fleet Acquisition, Aircraft Finance, and AI

Artificial intelligence is heavily used in the finance world. AI is used to extract and analyze contractual provisions in legal documents. This can provide valuable time and cost savings when contracts are reviewed. Legal professionals use machine learning tools (such as Kira) in a litigation context for discovery purposes.[3] This can assist in due diligence for mergers and acquisition (M&A) assessments but could also be applied to aviation transactions.

AI is also used in forecasting interest rates or currency exchange markets, but it is also used to build, evaluate, and recommend investments, hedge opportunities and automate other decision-making processes. The three most common schemes for financing commercial aircraft are secured lending, operating leasing, and finance leasing. However, there are other ways to pay for the aircraft, and there are many debt financing or SPV structure that can be used, some even through specific countries like Japan.

Using AI in fleet planning and aircraft financing will depend on how the goals are defined. For instance, are the goals defined in terms of finding the best financing option for a particular aircraft with all available inputs and parameters? Or will it be used to simulate different scenarios and outcomes, such as different revenue generation models based on aircraft configurations, including projected asset values across economic life cycles depending on how the aircraft will be used (which is based on cycles and number of landings)?

Critical in any use of AI is defining the goal, breaking it down into problems that need to be answered (solved), and identifying the source, quality,

70 Uses of AI and Emerging Opportunities in Commercial Management

and quantity of the relevant data required to solve the problems. The crux of the problem in using AI in aircraft financing is not on the financing side, because that largely exists in investment banking. There, almost 70% of financial firms use some extent of machine learning to predict cash flow events, adjust credit scores and detect fraud (Columbus, 2020).

Currently, machine learning and AI is used in finance for the following popular purposes although there are many more on the consumer side as well:

- Risk assessment: Banks are using ML algorithms to determine a person's loan eligibility and provide personalized options.[4]
- Risk management: Machine learning can help identify trends and risks and support better planning.[5]
- Fraud detection and prevention: Artificial intelligence helps in analyzing a corporate customer's transactions to flag potential fraud and help prevent it.
- Credit decisions: Based on available data (including loan and payment behavior), decisions on credit levels are supported by insights obtained from machine learning.
- Financial advisory services: Artificial intelligence can analyze large chunks of data to guide a company in investment decisions in assets or acquisitions.

The main potential of AI in aircraft financing is in creating realistic simulations between existing, new, and potential data streams and automating linkages between cash flows. AI can be used to predict the revenue-generating capabilities of a particular aircraft (by context or deployment in specific markets), and include expected onboard purchases, digital retailing, and commission revenues. This may also make one particular configuration more interesting than another, depending on who will spend the most onboard.

Once new revenue-generating streams have been incorporated into the overall (base) revenue-generating capabilities of an aircraft, they can be tied to the cash outflows related to different financing mechanisms, and even investment flows, where AI can be used to predict the likely residual value of an aircraft. This creates a holistic enterprise-level view of an aircraft, and basically, the entire business case, P&L as well as the net cash flow (operating/financing/ investment) by aircraft type. This may, arguably, be the best way to discriminate between aircraft and base all decisions on facts and clean data. It may also result in a more expensive aircraft purchase if the overall net profit-generating capabilities of that aircraft are better, based on better insights. And this could be the difference between a Boeing 787 or Airbus A350 when, for other intents and purposes, one or the other seemed preferred. Small insights can have large impacts.

In the above-described approach, composite AI using convolution algorithms means that all repetitive work can be removed, and any scenario can be run to generate new predictions, insights, and decision recommendations.

Fleet Planning and Aircraft Acquisition 71

This requires a lot of thinking and designing, particularly the neural network. But with the right set of high-quality data, the benefits are immense and currently beyond estimation. And once it runs, it can be updated with new goals or real-time data in minutes, not months of work.

7.5 Conclusions

This chapter described how AI is helping to improve and accelerate fleet planning and aircraft acquisition by automating processes using rich data. It first described how fleet planning works and how real-time insights can drive decisions that have long-term ramifications for improved profitability and sustainability. It further touched on how machine learning is used in automated reviews of provisions in legal documents and what the valuable use cases are for AI in aircraft finance. Finally, it showed how AI enables new practices at enterprise level based on revenue-generating capabilities of aircraft by using multiple dimensions of that asset in holistic workflows.

Notes

1 Based on conversations with British Airways in February 2022, for which the source had to remain confidential.
2 https://www.airfranceklm.com/en/air-france-klm-orders-100-airbus-a320neo-family-aircraft-purchase-rights-additional-60-aircraft-klm.
3 Herbert Smith Freehills (2021) 'The case for technology solutions in aviation finance transactions: will they take flight? https://hsfnotes.com/aviationfinance/2021/01/11/the-case-for-technology-solutions-in-aviation-finance-transactions-will-they-take-flight/.
4 https://towardsdatascience.com/the-growing-impact-of-ai-in-financial-services-six-examples-da386c0301b2.
5 https://builtin.com/artificial-intelligence/ai-finance-banking-applications-companies.

Bibliography

Amadeus (2022) 'Seven breakthroughs in airline flight scheduling'. https://amadeus.com/en/insights/blog/seven-breakthroughs-airline-flight-scheduling#modal-1294471558

Assets America (2022) 'Airline finance – guide to financing a commercial fleet' https://assetsamerica.com/airline-finance/

Bazargan, M. (2010) *Airline operations and scheduling.* 2nd ed. Farnham: Ashgate.

Belobaba, P. *et al.* (2009) *The global airline industry.* London: John Wiley & Sons.

Butler, G. *et al.* (2000) *Handbook of airline operations.* 1st ed. New York: McGraw-Hill.

Columbus, L. (2020) 'The state of AI adoption in financial services'. *Forbes,* Investing Digest.https://www.forbes.com/sites/louiscolumbus/2020/10/31/the-state-of-ai-adoption-in-financial-services/?sh=6e529bba2aac

Dempsey, P. (1997) *Airline management: strategies for the 21st century.* Chandler, AZ: Coast Aire Publications.

Morrell, P. (2021) *Airline finance.* 5th ed. London: Routledge.

8 Demand Forecasting, Pricing, Ancillary, and Revenue Management

8.1 Revenue Management Described

Revenue management (RM) combined with the pricing function has traditionally been aimed at charging the right price to the right customer at the right time. It has been the phrase used by vendors to indicate that the principles of RM are around demand segmentation, differential pricing, and capacity controls. Differential pricing is aimed at identifying price points that fall within the frame of reference of segmented customers based on perceived benefits and sacrifices. Traditionally, these sacrifices were represented by 'fences', or barriers that would prevent customers that had a higher willingness to pay from purchasing lower fares. With the advent of low-cost carriers that were initially not concerned with business travelers, the first come-first served pricing model was used. It meant that prices would go up as the booking load factor of future flights went up. It fits the simplicity and lower-cost way of operating and managing these carriers. However, as airlines such as Southwest Airlines, Ryanair, EasyJet, and later on Wizz Jet and the like grew, there was a twofold trend. On the one hand, they started to attract business travelers due to their extensive and competitive network. On the other, they were starting to see some market saturation. As such, they started enhancing their service product to attract a different clientele and steal more market share away from more traditional full-service carriers through loyalty programs and even offered lounges. Canada's WestJet is an example of an airline that grew from a regional point-to-point LCC to an airline offering connections, to operating international long-haul routes using Boeing 787 from Canada to the UK by April 2019.[1]

The term RM and yield management are often used inter-changeably. The same applies to RM, revenue maximization, revenue optimization, or profit optimization. RM systems, though, rarely operate on the basis of pure margin per ticket sold. This is because many of the (incremental) costs cannot realistically be broken down to the individual passenger level. Many of the incremental costs, such as fuel burn, are negligible if you take the view of adding one passenger and one meal. Furthermore, how the passenger books and through which distribution channel does carry differing costs, but it is

DOI: 10.4324/9781003018810-11

Demand Forecasting, Pricing, Ancillary and Revenue Management   73

not known to RM systems. Channel and payment costs are typically added by pricing through the application of a GDS or credit card fee.

RM systems are based on the expected demand and willingness to pay for seats. Historically, the basis for analyzing how strong the demand was depended on comparing current demand with data from previous years for the same flight or date (with slight seasonal adjustments). This would allow the calculation of bid prices that a booking request for a point-to-point or connecting flight had to exceed in order to be confirmed as a booking, within the filed fares in fare classes. The opening and closing of these fare classes were managed by the RM system.

RM, therefore, traditionally has had several components. There is often a workbench module where analysts can review flights, both historically and future flights. They can sift through analytics of the flight's booking profile as well as how flights behave by day of the week, during specific seasons, or around holidays and special events. There are also more technical functions to set up configurations and parameters for automated processes. There is a demand forecast function, and there is an inventory management function with built-in optimization logic at point-to-point (e.g. Paris – New York) level, or origin and destination level (e.g. Hamburg – Paris – New York). The first example is an illustration of a 'local market', or 'nonstop OD' with special characteristics of demand and willingness to pay. The second is an example of an 'OD' with connection. Since pricing in the airline industry is very loosely based on distance flown and more on market competition, airline networks compete for connecting traffic to create traffic density and economies of scope (combining flight missions) by offering attractive fares. In long-haul markets, connecting flights are often cheaper than those that originate at large hubs with large catchment areas like London or Paris.

Pricing is separate from inventory control within RM, but the traditional way in which airlines managed their seat inventory involved fare classes, also referred to as 'buckets'. Since different distribution channels or groups (such as corporate travel, travel management companies, and other specially negotiated rates) need access to the flight, there is a need to map the value of those customer groups in the overall value map (nesting). This was largely done manually in the configurations, but it has evolved into more sophisticated automation using group sales modules. Companies such as PROS, Amadeus, RTS, and Accelya offer these solutions.

Revenue managers' primary job is to enable profitable revenue growth. They do not actually sell anything. To do this, they undertake a range of analytical tasks such as financial analyses (revenue, variance analysis), sales and product mix management (fare classes/fare bundles), price volume and supply elasticities as well as promotional pricing and new product pricing campaigns. While the latter part is generally orchestrated by marketing, revenue managers can alert management to situations where a flight is predicted to underperform. The departments then work together to find creative ways to stimulate demand through campaigns, attractive pricing, and/or by releasing

74   *Uses of AI and Emerging Opportunities in Commercial Management*

more seat inventory in lower fare classes to attract a higher share of the demand in the market.

In recent years, the role of the RM function has evolved. RM teams use analytics generated outside the RM system as well, obtained from other marketing and sales tools used in the business. This helps revenue managers design new pricing strategies. When fare bundles were first introduced by Air Canada in 2004, RM had to re-engineer the pricing architecture. Branded fares (also called fare bundles or families) entail grouping fares together that share the same characteristics but can still vary within their fare product's bucket. These characteristics are, for example, permitted changes for free or at a fee, or refundable vs. non-refundable fares, baggage allowance or at a fee, seat selection (none, paid, or free), no mileage accrual or single/double the miles, in-flight meals, and priority airport services for boarding and check-in. Some of these service attributes are only available when they are attached to a seat in a different cabin, such as premium economy or business class. An obvious example of that is priority check-in and lounge access.

8.2 Impact of COVID-19 on RM

The COVID-19 pandemic had a devastating impact on the travel and airline industry. With such dramatic drops in demand and the ongoing uncertainty that ensued, airlines saw themselves unable to use their traditional methods and tools to complete their planning processes. As discussed in the network planning chapter, airlines could no longer use their historical data and had no reliable insights as to how to adjust whatever data they had. They were forced to create a new planning process around ad-hoc information, shorter planning cycles, and near real-time information and management controls. This also required the use of new key performance indicators (KPIs) that reflected the new market.

In a practical sense, revenue managers worked with vendors to modify historical data in order to make use of it. By observing the actual market demand, they would apply a ratio of the observed demand compared with 2018 or 2019 traffic numbers. Often, this led to a 70–80% reduction in the total numbers. They would then manually work out the segmentation profile of flights and assign an expected booking curve. By creating scenarios, they could track the performance and save different demand forecasts in the system. These forecasts would improve again as new data came in, meaning the model would learn and improve. Nonetheless, with repeated new outbreaks and national governments issuing new travel restrictions, this exercise proved very laborious and time-consuming during a time that some airlines had cut the staff in each department between 20% and 60%, including RM. More had to be done, with fewer people.

> In a post-COVID-19 world it is anticipated that airline business processes will transform to be nimbler and more proactive in making timely decisions at a greater velocity.
>
> (Ben Vinod, former senior executive at Sabre Corp)[2]

The disruption in the market as well as within airline organizations has often been referred to as a 'new normal'. During 2019 and deep into 2022, the industry witnessed many route cuts. First, due to the pandemic. Later, due to staff shortages. By Summer 2022, overall scheduled capacity between Europe and North America was still 11.5% below 2019 levels while recovery was well underway.[3] In addition, soaring inflation and fuel prices that had gone up over 100% between 2021 and 2022 were creating havoc. The average rise in airfare between January and April 2022 was also found to be 40%.[4] Pilot shortages, aircraft delivery delays, and even airport security staff shortages caused many problems at airports such as Amsterdam Airport Schiphol.

Airlines started to look for solutions to key challenges such as

- How could they predict changes to demand more accurately in the turbulent market?
- Do current practices in pricing and fare rules hinder or help sales and RM?
- How could they overcome the constraints of conventional RM methods and systems?
- How could they incorporate new technology in the organization to improve insights?

This led to changes in RM, its scope, and the design of future solutions.

8.3 Modifying RM during Crises

The Covid-19 pandemic spurred a movement by airlines to start looking into the collection and use of near real-time data that could generate insights into the propensity of people and potential travelers to book flights. As such, efforts focused on tapping into the online search data, both on websites outside of the airline's direct reach as well as their own website booking engines.

Online search had become an issue for both travelers and travel providers. With customers confused about flight cancelations, uncertainty about schedules, travel restrictions, and closed borders, many took to the internet for answers. However, with so much content online, travelers can easily be overwhelmed by the amount of information and often question what was presented to them. Also, global distribution systems, such as Amadeus, saw the look-to-book ratio (the number of search queries compared with an actual booking) went up to 1,600, a record level. Compared with the early 2000 when the internet was more commonly used, that number went up almost eight-fold from 200 to 250 per conversion.[5]

8.4 Artificial Intelligence in Revenue Management

The use of artificial intelligence (AI) as defined today is relatively new in RM. Although from a philosophical and academic standpoint, older techniques in decision sciences are grouped into the evolution of AI since the

76 *Uses of AI and Emerging Opportunities in Commercial Management*

1950s. For instance, operations research (OR), linear programming (LP), and time series analyses were traditionally at the heart of RM. In OR, problems are broken down into basic components and then solved in defined steps by mathematical analysis. Three essential characteristics of OR are a systems orientation, the use of interdisciplinary teams, and the application of scientific method to the conditions under which the research is conducted.

LP is an analytical method of problem-solving and decision-making that is useful in the management of organizations. LP is the mathematical technique for the best allocation of scarce resources, such as labor, material, machine, capital, and energy. This helps to manage revenue from several activities by coordinating how many items to produce, what the quantity of required resources are, and how to plan jobs, equipment, and projects. In essence, it is how network planning tools were built in the past.

One of the biggest changes in RM is the ability to use analytics to optimize pricing with automation. Previously, airline pricing was largely a manual task performed using competitive rate monitoring tools. The RM systems would then optimize inventory controls given the fare structure but using demand forecasts to control how many seats were sold within each fare class or 'bucket'. Machine learning can not only optimize this through dynamic pricing within a fare class (continuous pricing) but also recommend fare differentials between the fare classes to maintain a 'spread'.

The real question is whether fare classes (which are based on legacy distribution and simplified segmentation, not customers) should be maintained when we can use AI to automate them with a simplified approach with more sophistication. For instance, airlines could sell only one fare at a time per aircraft cabin (economy, economy plus, business class, first class) which dynamically moves in real time as per the market value of 'real estate' on the air transport lane, much like the original low-cost carrier model. This could then be complemented by dynamic pricing for all optional service-related attributes. Another later on top could optimize the blending of the total fare at individual customer level based on context, personal profile, and loyalty value. This is discussed further in this chapter.

8.5 Ancillary Products and Fees

Airlines have sought to make money by selling each part of their product separately. Choosing a seat in advance, enjoying extra legroom at an emergency exit or bulkhead, and relaxing with a beer or wine inflight now come at a hefty price tag. British Airways charges GBP 65 per checked bag (Euro 75). United Airlines will charge USD 35 for the first checked bag, USD 45 for the second, and USD 150 per bag for the third or any additional bag. Carry-on bags are free, but Spirit charges USD 41 per carry-on bag when travelers check-in online, but USD 55 when they do at the airport. Similarly, seat selection fees are popular as well. On KLM, the seat selection fee varies by section within the economy cabin, from 34.00 euros to 78.00 euros (depending on the flight). But this will also vary depending on how much forward the seats are inside the plane. There is variation between window and aisle seats, which was initially mainly determined through trail-and-error to test willingness to pay. Today, machine learning can help suggest optimal seat selection fees based on observed demand.

Over the years, airlines have added meals for purchase, priority-boarding as a chargeable product, lounge access for a fee, and more recently Wi-Fi on board at a cost. Insurance has been another product that sold well during the Covid-19 pandemic. Over the last 20 years, airlines have become extremely good at increasing revenues with ancillaries but the ceiling of flight-related ancillary revenues is nearing. It is for this reason that airlines must seek other cross-selling opportunities while ensuring they can service them after the sales.

8.6 Branded Fares and Changes

Pioneering airlines like Air Canada launched branded fares in 2004 to overcome the challenges of fare transparency enabled by the Internet. While hugely successful, branded fares still reflect the old ways of forcing customers into segments, one trip at a time. A request is made through a booking engine or travel agent's GDS, and RM systems then recommend how to respond based on the inventory that it has allocated in the reservation's buckets. This approach is arguably up for a big change. For instance, customer segments behind branded fares are used to control the distribution of seats. The perks (like seat selection and FFP points) or penalties (like no points and luggage fees) are not personalized or priced based on individual customer willingness to pay. Where there has been some automated steering in waving the seat selection fees or offering a discount based on loyalty tier status. This is an application of a rules-based system that could be further optimized dynamically using AI. But there are other important opportunities to modernize this area.

Most innovations in commercial airline management and technology at some point become obstacles to the next required transition, and with the continued use of GDS as the travel agencies' backbone, the industry is limited in adopting novel technologies. However, there are changes that can be made right away, such as potentially replacing the branded fare products. This may also be necessary to become more sophisticated and adopt true retailing and customer-based RM. In fact, more and more, the industry is encouraged to become a true service industry and enhance passenger experiences across the whole journey from shopping to purchasing and enjoying experiences at destination. Today, pricing methods and RM systems do not enhance any experience, and a rethink is required to bring benefits to people.

8.7 Modernizing RM with a Wider Scope

The application of AI in RM is necessary because of the amount of (new) data from emerging sources as well as the fact that analysis in real time is more important than historical data. Further, due to the slow but gradual convergence between capacity management and sales-oriented processes (online shopping and the use of MarTech and SalesTech), the scope of RM and decision intelligence technology must change.

There are two main streams of practices in airline RM. The first will be working on patches to update deficiencies exposed during Covid-19, the other creating modern customer retailing optimization through AI. Legacy RM systems will be used until older reservation system interdependencies can be retired and ticket auto-pricing has evolved.

The second new stream will be optimizing revenue including new content sourced from experience aggregators through application programming interfaces (API) and IATA's New Distribution Capability (NDC), a communications standard. It will support customer-centric retail bundling and better pricing and customers will see higher-value service bundles in their baskets.

Both these streams use AI, but in very different ways. Updating current RM systems involves patches to system components (such as demand forecasting) using intent-to-purchase analysis through online search. But this only applies to the selling of seats and not to other ancillary products, services, or features. This could therefore be called a 'local' application of AI.

The second stream of initiatives is what could holistically be called 'enterprise' RM. This is where RM philosophies can contribute to all commercial aspects. RM was (arguably) always about controlling distribution of seats. It was also about responding to booking requests. But the modern Internet of Things context is not necessarily about customer-triggered requests, but about data-driven offer management even when there is no request, or when the seat is the last item sought. The future is, in what I call, blended technology as 'SMartech' powered by AI and underpinned by RM philosophies and pricing psychology (Figure 8.1).

There are opportunities to redesign RM from the customer's perspective, not from the flight or seat distribution perspective. The starting point is the customer and their identity, past experiences, interests, and future desires.

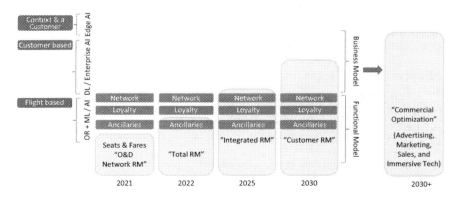

Figure 8.1 Evolution of customer-based revenue management.

The discovery of what they want is as much the task of the travel provider as it is of the customer. Both sides will analyze whatever content they can find.

This drive to modern offer and order management using 'SMartTech' will bring the benefits highlighted in Chapter 11. It can turn pricing and RM into contributors to passenger experience. Giving customers more control over what they value contextually is key. That means pushing the à-la-cart notion to its extreme, where the customer picks and chooses service items, attributes, amenities, and activities, with the value and willingness to pay going up as they choose more because they keep getting a more attractive deal. This increases share of wallet.

That is linking dynamic offering to in-process order management, linking order management to real-time procurement (aggregators and operators, i.e. the companies delivering the service), and re-pricing the bundle during the digital conversation with the customer. A win-win that also creates stickiness.

It also means treating the seat not just as a commodity within the passenger journey but as a value proposition for in-flight experience. How digital selling is executed depends on the stage of discovery, order cycle, and the visualization of the experience. This requires a complete overhaul of modern offer management systems.

It is not inconceivable that we will even start unbundling business class based on passenger needs, rather than the 'all-inclusive' model. The partitioning of the cabin can practically only go that far, but services can be sold based more on attributes even at seat level (e.g. massage function). This requires new thinking of how we bring RM philosophies onboard and apply them inflight using AI-powered 'SMartTech', which is use case I have worked on for a digital cabin but is beyond the scope of this book.

8.8 Conclusions

This chapter described the commercial function of RM, pricing, and ancillary revenues and how AI is helping the modernization in this area driven by changing markets and online behaviors. It argued that the move to personalized retailing is also making airlines reconsider commercial organization design and execution. It further demonstrates that novel technologies in marketing technology (MarTech) and sales technology (SalesTech) powered by Enterprise AI represent an effective bridge to building these new organizations that will deliver better customer experiences. It will also turn RM into a service department that has a connection to customers.

Notes

1 WestJet (2019) 'WestJet's Dreamliner takes first transatlantic flight'. Calgary: WestJet News releases. https://westjet.mediaroom.com/2019-04-29-WestJets-Dreamliner-takes-first-transatlantic-flight.

80 *Uses of AI and Emerging Opportunities in Commercial Management*

2 Vinod, B., 'Airline revenue planning and the COVID-19 pandemic', *Journal of Tourism Future*, 2021. https://www.emerald.com/insight/content/doi/10.1108/JTF-02-2021-0055/full/pdf?title=airline-revenue-planning-and-the-covid-19-pandemic.
3 Airline Weekly, 2022, via Skift Webinar. https://live.skift.com/how-ai-and-machine-learning-will-transform-airline-revenue-management/watch-again.
4 Hopper Research (2022) https://www.hopper.com.
5 Conversation with Lutz Vorneweg, Global VP Online, Amadeus, on 9 March 2022.

Bibliography

Achtari, G. (2018) 'Applications of machine learning in revenue management and routing'. Ph.D. thesis. Kingston: Queen's University.

Amadeus (2019) 'How AI is transforming revenue management'. https://amadeus.com/en/insights/blog/airline-ai-ml-revenue-management

HSMAI (2022) 'Prescriptive analytics and machine learning for revenue management leaders'. https://global.hsmai.org/insight/prescriptive-analytics-and-machine-learning-for-revenue-management-leaders/

Lee, M. (2021) *Is machine learning a magic wand?* Boston, MA: Boston University. https://www.bu.edu/bhr/2021/06/29/is-machine-learning-a-magic-wand/

9 Loyalty Management

9.1 Loyalty, or Frequent Flier Program (FFP) Management Described

Customer loyalty programs are the backbone of the customer loyalty strategy airlines have deployed since the mid-1980s. Originally launched to reward repeat business (based on miles-based and money-spent points) with perks they could redeem in a Frequent Flier Program (FFP), customer loyalty has matured and grown into full businesses. Eighty-nine percent of travelers now belong to at least one travel loyalty program (airline, hotel, OTA, cruise, or car rental), according to PhocusWright. Membership in these programs has also changed the way travelers shop for and book their trips, and it has helped airlines, hotels, and car rental companies to defend or grow their market share.

Customer loyalty management within the airline business consists of the FFP, campaign management, customer engagement, customer analytics and BI, partner integration and management, and the mobile application. Within the loyalty management system, the core, all loyalty propositions around the airline and its hotel, rail, cruise, and retail partners are hosted. The campaign manager allows managers to run campaigns based on narrow segments with targeted communications to generate high response rates. This function also tracks how customers respond and engage with the content and the program overall. Customer engagement acts as a glue to create and manage all communications to (and feedback from) the customers. But one of the most technically advanced components in loyalty marketing is the analytics and business intelligence function. In fact, the competency within loyalty management has become a strong enabling capability in transforming airlines to become more data-driven, at least in marketing, segmentation, and targeting of campaigns and promotions. It has, to date, not been integrated with the overall commercial function including pricing and revenue management, which does not function at the same segmentation level. While loyalty is about customers, revenue management is not. The latter is about segmenting the market based on observed willingness to pay price points in a competitive context. Aligning the two is complex but within the scope of some studies

DOI: 10.4324/9781003018810-12

82 *Uses of AI and Emerging Opportunities in Commercial Management*

and planned roadmaps for companies like FLYR Labs, based in San Francisco, USA.

The loyalty program is one of the most powerful mechanisms to collect information and generate insights about customers. The programs have comprehensive and centralized data repositories that gather all kinds of member information. Loyalty managers can get to know their members' hobbies, lifestyles, family ties, special requirements, member card, and activity history. This is important as loyalty tiers and qualifications are typically managed and thus awarded annually. And flying activity in general, or with a preferred airline, varies depending on the underlying derived nature of the need for air transport. While airlines would love to understand shifts in flying patterns better beyond the data they can collect, that is currently outside the consideration set. Artificial intelligence (AI) can contribute to a shift there, as discussed later in this chapter.

Often, customers freely enrich their profiles with interests and preferences, and combined with travel data, loyalty managers can use analytics to gain a deep understanding of their customer base. This helps with segmentation and the creation of targeted campaigns that can be better personalized than using the more generic data that general airline marketing has in its database. What is novel, as well, is that airlines do not need customers to be logged into their FFP. Using inference techniques (e.g. IP address, search characteristics), one can decipher whom the customer is by mapping it against the dimensions and attributes we already know of each customer. This also helps airlines to generate a consistent response to the customer and to avoid friction when customers that are not logged in obtain a different response (or offer) than those that are logged in. That is, once a customer is identified, the airline wants to ensure it is engaging consistently and meets its customer experience criteria. An obvious example is ensuring that a good offer is never shown to a new customer without having exposed it to a loyal customer first, likely at an even more attractive level (price-wise or by bundling additional privileges).

While airlines are predominantly concerned with their own customers that travel on their mainline flights, airline alliances and other marketing agreements have made it necessary for frequent flyers of partner airline programs to be recognized throughout their journeys. This means that Lufthansa Airlines' top-tier status travelers can also access Singapore Airlines' lounges, as part of STAR Alliance, for instance. There are clear benefits for the customer to share information, but airlines are generally still protective about granting tier status miles on their own flights, and grant miles-only accumulation on their partners' flights. What is not as evident for the traveler flying on multiple partner airlines is that each airline still has its own commercial interests within the partnership. And how this is managed through commercial agreements is sometimes reflected in how the flights are sold and inventory controlled. It is an area for revenue integrity and revenue assurance, and specific teams within airlines audit these aspects to ensure their own airline interests are served.

Airline loyalty programs over the years have gradually grown into merchandising programs by adding retail partners to the program, such as clothing stores, fuel stations, electronics stores, and the like. The tactic is to grow the engagement level with the program where stickiness is driven by the customer's eagerness to accumulate as frequent flier points as possible toward travel or other rewards.

But the strongest pillar of the FFP in the last 15 years has been represented by the banks and credit card companies. This group uses credit card products for frequent fliers that accumulate airline miles based on both credit card spend as well as flights. Often, there are multipliers when the co-branded credit card is used to purchase travel with the airline partner. Airlines would charge their B2B customer (banks, credit cards) often between $1ct and $3ct per mile. Besides, blocks of these miles were often purchased by banks in advance based on forecasts, providing the airlines with a sizeable cashflow.

Overall, FFPs like Aeroplan (Air Canada), Miles and More (Lufthansa), Flying Blue (Air France KLM), Skywards (Emirates), Etihad Guest (Etihad Airways), BIG (Air Asia), and KrisFlyer (Singapore Airlines) are all well-known and successful programs. At a high level, they appear similar, but there are many small variations with regard to how customers accrue points, how they can be redeemed, and what the particular perks and privileges are. Where those programs with density have been successful, is in building a stronger brand for the program itself, and indirectly for the airline. The rewarding nature of these programs has created umbrella brands that are powerful and allow airlines to monetize the membership data for other purposes, particularly as the industry moves to adopt further retailing beyond unbundling the air transportation component. Aeroplan (Air Canada) was, at some point, such a strong program and platform that Air Canada saw it beneficial to carve it out of the holding where it had previously structured it. It was sold for CAD 2.25 billion to Aimia in 2008 under a new partnership with the carrier.[1] It generated significant cash and spurred other airlines to evaluate this approach. However, in 2019 Air Canada re-purchased Aeroplan and launched a new loyalty program on a new platform.[2] As a case in point, an industry publication reported that in a June 2021 filing, United Airlines valued their MileagePlus loyalty program at $21.9 billion, which was around double the total market capitalization of the company itself (MarketWatch, 2021).

9.2 Loyalty Management Systems

Before discussing the smart processes, analytics–driven decision-making, and novel layer of automation, it is important to understand the systems that underpin loyalty management. Modern loyalty management platforms have a cloud-based infrastructure. While the current solutions are not cloud-native (code written in the cloud), the next generation will be. The systems have built-in modules based on a service-oriented architecture. This means that

84 *Uses of AI and Emerging Opportunities in Commercial Management*

services are provided from one module (component) to another, allowing flexible rewrites and updates. While the modules provide functionality as per the capabilities described earlier, an important element of loyalty management systems is that they exchange information. This exchange of data is required to integrate with partners to share programs and databases and recognize frequent flier members from partner airlines. It is also necessary to empower contact center agents with real-time frequent flier data and information about ongoing travel journeys and issues.

The campaign modules allow loyalty managers to boost ancillary revenues, track and manage engagement, and plan and launch targeted promotions that are based on multiple rules. This ability to personalize customer offerings accelerates time-to-market and relevance with a high level of automation. The engagement itself is tracked using website logins or App activity, including search.

Loyalty management solutions also require comprehensive customer communications capabilities along the same objectives as those described in Chapter 3. What is different from a loyalty perspective is that contact touch points and traffic have to be segmented in accordance with the expected recognition frequent fliers have. Those with the highest tier levels also expect to receive exceptional service. This has to be managed throughout all passenger communication systems.

Nonetheless, from a loyalty perspective, a complete record of communications sent via email, text messages, or customer service exchanges needs to be available with recommended actions to resolve issues, solve problems, and alleviate concerns or conflict. It also needs to be done in multiple languages, and templates are necessary to maintain a library of all use cases.

Part of the complexity of loyalty management systems is the automation required to handle all accrual, retroactivity, redemption, and billing activities. It necessitates exchanges of data in real-time among partner systems (via web services) and automation of the processes with non-airline partners. Often, this is handled through dedicated partner portals but it requires partner systems to interface with these applications. This always requires integration effort, while maintaining a service bus that allows processes (and operating models) to change.

Another layer of complexity lies in the calculation methods that are used for air/non-air and types of partnerships (alliances, non-alliance, retail) as well as the management of redemption, exchanges, expirations, upgrades, and vouchers for flights and points. These business aspects in loyalty management are mainly driven by human decisions using experience and trial and error. Data-driven automation here is not common as the business goals are not defined clearly or refined enough to allow machine learning and AI to automate more. That may change, as discussed below.

9.3 Impact of COVID-19 on Loyalty

The loyalty programs of airlines proved to be a foundational pillar for airlines during the pandemic. Not only did the programs turn out to be a good vehicle to maintain engagement and remain visible in the customers' mindset, but there were also monetizable aspects that supported the airlines commercially.[3]

First, even at much lower levels of air transportation and demand, the loyalty programs still hold their value because consumer spending had not collapsed. And customers in the loyalty programs vastly use their co-branded credit card, almost guaranteeing a predictable cashflow in the airlines' accounts. The additional benefit is that financial institutions purchase these 'miles' in bulk in advance, which came in handy during the crisis. However, there was one drawback as airlines were carrying higher liability levels as the travel restrictions led to a considerable reduction in redemption activity.

Second, most airlines simply adopted tactics to encourage their loyal travelers to get back into aircraft by demonstrating how new sanitary measures and protocols such as how aircraft cleaning had improved. Airlines were also distributing disinfectant kits and enabled new touchless travel options through the use of PDAs and self-check-in kiosks. Airlines such as American Airlines, United, JetBlue, Air Canada, KLM, Emirates, and Singapore Airlines all found creative ways to communicate safe health-related measures, including the use of animated clips on social media such as TikTok (Singapore Airlines) or YouTube (KLM, Wizz). Airlines were also relying on their loyal customer base to promote the notion of safe travel during the pandemic by showing people that were traveling.

A third set of tactics concerned flexibility to change dates at no cost and the option to cancel reservations with a full refund. Full refunds were offered as of 2021 simply for changing your mind up to 30 days before travel (Air Canada). It was at the emerging waves of COVID-19 that stimulating travel was the principal goal of airlines to maintain cashflow.

Fourth, airlines automatically issued elite status extensions, waiving points expiration dates and lowering award thresholds. All the major airlines, such as Air Canada, American Airlines, Avianca, British Airways, Delta, JetBlue, LATAM, Qantas, Qatar Airways, Southwest Airlines, Turkish Airlines, United Airlines, and Virgin Atlantic took this initiative.[4] Air Canada went so far that, for members that had already achieved their tier status, they extended the offer to gift an additional tier status to another family member or friend.

But the loyalty programs offered opportunities to leverage loyalty membership databases in other ways. The data and currency (points) in loyalty management systems can be monetized through other mechanisms, such as program partners. Airlines could sell data and loyalty currency to partners that also wanted to market to affluent customers that potentially had more disposable income if they were not traveling for a year. Economies the world over witnessed the inflationary pressure online retail shopping caused, in part fuelled by governments' wage subsidy programs to keep the economies going while businesses and stores were closed.

In addition, due to the business value of loyalty programs as monetizable assets, airlines started to use asset-based financing to generate additional

86 *Uses of AI and Emerging Opportunities in Commercial Management*

liquidity using loyalty management programs as asset.[5] Delta Airlines raised as much as USD 6.5 billion backed by its SkyMiles program. United Airlines evaluated similar options to obtain government loans. A lot of this is possible because airlines sell loyalty currency ('miles' or points) to banks and credit card companies who in turn offer these points as part of their own reward programs to customers. The crux is in the spread. Airlines sell these miles at a much higher price (in cents per mile) than it would ever cost them in incremental cost terms when travelers redeem points for travel. This is also because an airline can influence when reward travel is accommodated, even when airlines indicate they will dedicate a portion of their capacity for redemption travel (sometimes up to 8% of the seats on board). But this depends on seasons, blackout periods, and may not be the case in flights for which there is too much pent-up demand.

There is a clear evolution to loyalty programs as multi-partner programs that reach deeper into people's household wallets by adding retail breadth. And as a result, loyalty programs have become a big asset.

9.4 Artificial Intelligence Loyalty Management

According to Gunjan Kumar, airline loyalty expert,

> Airlines started to look out for new technologies and saw that consumer packaged goods (CPG) retail was using AI and machine learning to solve complex data issues and modeling engagement strategies that were developed based on customer segmentation, buying behaviour and most important their tastes and preferences.

All this led to airlines thinking about how AI and machine learning could help in member hyper-personalization.

Hyper-personalization was a two-step process. First, through enhancing the CRM platform to create segments and micro-segments of members. Second, by using AI and machine learning to crunch and mine massive datasets to produce personalized attributes of members that could be used for direct campaigns and promotions using marketing technology (MarTech).

The use of AI and machine learning resulted in the creation of advanced campaign management platforms that were rules-based. These rules could trigger personalized content for members and customers to ensure greater open-then-click rates thereby significantly improving the campaign KPIs. Another key use of AI and machine learning is how airline loyalty departments interact with members on social media. Social media can be seen as a double-edged sword where members can both vent their frustrations and comment on great customer satisfaction. Obviously, the airline loyalty department prefers to see only positive posts, but that is not realistic. AI and machine learning is used to create a single holistic view of the member using deep analysis of their past sentiments and experiences. The idea is to address their grievances better and create greater stickiness to the airline loyalty program. Airline loyalty departments are employing neural network specialists to develop correlations between member posts and their behavior to better segment members so they understand why a member has posted what they have. This has turned into a science of its own and is also used in contact centers, as described in Chapter 3.

> Airlines are re-inventing their entire redemption portfolio with the new knowledge gathered from enhanced analytics.
>
> (Gunjan Kumar, airline loyalty expert)

The airline loyalty department is in business only because it has members earning and burning points and they see the loyalty point currency as desirable and valuable. AI is helping in creating new products that help airlines understand the source of point accrual and the point of redemption using behavioral member mapping. This ensures that airlines can build a segmented approach pushing offers that relate to members better and build the loyalty program brand.

Another key area that has been impacted by AI and machine learning is churn modelling and analysis. In the new competitive world, it is 80% more costly to acquire a new member than to retain one. Churn rate is the health indicator for any loyalty program, and it is of paramount importance to ensure that churn is kept as low as possible. Some airlines have even set up teams to look at member churn. KPIs are monitored to ensure that churn for the program remains in the single digits.

Another interesting development is use of AI and machine learning to create greater cooperation between various partners (airlines and merchants). Airline loyalty programs make a lot of money selling points/miles to their partners and an extensive partner eco-system can create significant wealth to the loyalty program. Partner management is one of the first use cases that have seen the use of blockchain that will significantly reduce the biggest problem of miles or points being credited into the member account. Transactions done by members on partner brands can take anywhere between one day to several days to show up on the member's account and this really diminishes the member excitement. According to Gunjan Kumar, "several airlines are looking at employing blockchain powered by neural networks to create an eco-system that will facilitate greater interaction between partners and for real time upload of miles or points".

9.5 Fraud Prevention and AI

AI in loyalty management has existed since the mid-2010s. First applications were in recommender systems for campaign targeting, but most efforts have recently been directed toward fraud. Loyalty fraud is an area costing the airline industry an estimated $1.1 billion per year.[6] The Bond Brand

88 *Uses of AI and Emerging Opportunities in Commercial Management*

Report also reports that almost half of the reward membership is inactive in redemption, representing over $100 billion in reward points that are idling in accounts that become targets for theft. Airlines increasingly adopt AI to auto-detect fraud and flag it to take action to fight the estimated 1.2% in revenues they lose each year.[7] Cases of fraud have been widely reported by airlines such as Cathay Pacific. British Airways, Air Canada, and Delta Airlines.[8]

In most cases, the use of AI is about future prevention. For instance, Scandinavian Airlines (SAS) reduces loyalty program fraud in its EuroBonus loyalty program using Microsoft Azure Machine Learning.[9] It uses machine learning capabilities that also allow data scientists to interpret the model and explain its application and success in predicting the right result (fraud) to help users trust the solution. This is referred to as Explainable AI, as it is not shown in code but in conversation styles people understand. Chapter 19 explores explainable AI in detail.

> We use Azure Machine Learning to solve real business problems without worrying about building and managing infrastructure or creating new tools; we can focus directly on gaining value from the technology.
> (Daniel Engberg, Head of Data Analytics and Artificial Intelligence, EuroBonus/Loyalty, Scandinavian Airlines (Microsoft, 2020))

Loyalty fraud prevention helps SAS identify and mitigate fraud. Fraud can be related to attempts to accumulate miles that were not flown, or even theft. Also, purchases made on credit cards, and for which customers would normally accrue points, can be cancelled or returned. In these instances, processes have to be in place to detect and validate points accrual and removal.

SAS uses automated machine learning (AutoML) for automatic retraining and the InterpretML toolkit built into Azure Machine Learning for model interpretability. This allows data scientists to remove bugs and check the predictions of the model. SAS is able to catch scammers earlier, claiming they used to be a few steps behind the scammers.

The adoption of the technology also allows SAS to fight increases in fraud without having to add new staff. The technology identifies outliers and patterns based on the goal it is given, which is to find anomalies based on regular patterns. The regular patterns can be picked up from existing traveler data in historical databases. Advanced analytics can also detect 'normal' patterns of increasing activity, for instance, if a business traveler's points accrual suddenly goes up but is in line with other patterns about this passenger. A member could have started a new business or gained clients in a new region, for instance. But loyalty management also looks at how and where people log in, which email addresses they use, or whether the usual credit cards on file are used. Whether members are part of a points-sharing pool is often an area for potential fraud as well because accounts can be hacked, and points stolen.

9.6 How AI in Loyalty Fraud Prevention Works

Typically, airline developers or data scientists work with the AI platform provider. During a joint research phase, they bring data into an automated machine learning classification environment to prepare data before it can be trained. At the same time, the data pipeline can be prepared for release into the DevOps environment, where the end model will be built and trained. Because of the automation in continuous model retraining, as soon as there is a change in code (or the data that is infused from the pipeline), the model will retrain automatically. This enables it to become more and more intelligent.

Generally, the better the predictions are with fewer features or dimensions, the better. This is because it removes clutter, especially when it is not required to generate better results (predictions). In the case of SAS, the company was able to reduce the number of features factored in the model from 54 to 31 without losing accuracy, indicated Peter Gustavsson, Senior Systems Specialist at SAS' EuroBonus/Loyalty in a release by Microsoft. Additional features they built in account for data drift, which refers to a situation when the prediction accuracy degrades over time as member behavior patterns change. This functionality is very novel in machine learning and AI. Automatic retraining not only improves efficiency but also allows teams to monitor and control different rollouts as part of a continuous improvement process. This machine learning life cycle is called the continuous integration and continuous deployment (CI/CD) development model. Ranging from large to small fraud (one or few transactions), SAS has been able to catch even the smaller ones 300% more than they used to with larger, easily detected, ones.

9.7 Conclusions

This chapter explained how airline FFPs became important mechanisms to loyalty and what the role of analytics has been to improve their effectiveness. It also demonstrated that machine learning and AI are instrumental in enhancing future value by automating decision intelligence with richer, ingested insights. Illustrations included how improved and micro-segmentation can reveal customer tastes and preferences, which can be used for improved marketing and targeting. It also showed how AI is contributing to an evolution in loyalty fraud prevention.

Notes

1 BNN Bloomberg (2008) 'How Aimia and Air Canada got here: A timeline'. https://www.bnnbloomberg.ca/aeroplan-timeline-1.1116041.
2 BNN Bloomberg (2018) 'What Air Canada's new Aeroplane deal with CIBC, TD and Visa means for your points'. https://www.bnnbloomberg.ca/what-air-canadas-new-aeroplan-deal-with-cibc-td-and-visa-means-for-your-points-1.1176422.
3 PhocusWright (2021) 'Loyalty Programs Revisited'. https://www.phocuswright.com/Travel-Research/Consumer-Trends/Loyalty-Programs-Revisited-Key-Metrics-and-the-Impact-of-COVID19.

90 *Uses of AI and Emerging Opportunities in Commercial Management*

4 Adams, D. (2020) 'How Airline And Hotel Loyalty Programs Are Responding To Coronavirus'. Forbes. https://www.forbes.com/sites/advisor/2020/12/22/how-airline-and-hotel-loyalty-programs-are-responding-to-coronavirus/?sh=325a71174c0c.

5 MarketWatch (2020) 'Airlines are using frequent flyer programs to sell debt'. https://www.marketwatch.com/story/airlines-are-using-frequent-flyer-programs-to-sell-debt-heres-how-it-works-11600285585.

6 Benjuya, D. *et al.* (2019) 'Why fraudsters are flying high on airline loyalty programs'. *Security Intelligence.* https://securityintelligence.com/why-fraudsters-are-flying-high-on-airline-loyalty-programs.

7 IATA (2020) 'Fraud in the airline industry'. https://www.iata.org/contentassets/8a1d401955164c868258e7875edd5d5a/iata_whitepaper_fraud_july2020_digital_en.pdf.

8 Meyer, S. (2018) 'Airline data breaches worrying'. *CPO Magazine.* https://www.cpomagazine.com/cyber-security/airline-data-breaches-worrying.

9 Microsoft (2020) 'Scandinavian Airlines reduces loyalty program fraud with Microsoft Azure Machine Learning'. https://customers.microsoft.com/EN-GB/story/781802-sas-travel-transportation-azure-machine-learning.

Bibliography

Airlines for America (2021) 'Tracking the impacts of COVID-19'. https://www.airlines.org/dataset/impact-of-covid19-data-updates/#

Bailey, J. (2020) 'How loyalty programs are saving US airlines'. https://simpleflying.com/how-loyalty-programs-are-saving-us-airlines

Foussianes, C. (2020) 'How are airlines reacting to the coronavirus outbreak? https://www.townandcountrymag.com/leisure/travel-guide/a31295546/airline-coronavirus-covid-19-reaction

Gazdik, T. (2020) 'Companies extend loyalty programs in wake of COVID-19'. https://www.mediapost.com/publications/article/349446/companies-extend-loyalty-programs-in-wake-of-covid.html

Kumar, G. (2022) Interview with Gunjan Kumar, former executive at Hitit and global airline loyalty management expert, 15 March 2022.

10 Sales and Distribution

10.1 Sales and Distribution Function

The sales function within an airline is to build relationships with governments, companies, NGOs, and other entities that require their staff to travel as part of their business. Large multinational companies often have both executives and other staff travel for work, especially those organizations that sell products, services, or professional services such as advisory and consulting. Furthermore, travel purchasers examine the volume for meetings and in-house travel for training, rather than for client trips. Large companies like Philips, Johnson & Johnson, or Walmart usually have departments that handle travel purchasing and often go through corporate travel agencies or travel management companies (TMCs). These are B2B companies that often do not sell to individual travelers.

Senior sales positions within airlines deal with the biggest corporate accounts, like the banks, or firms in industry such as Samsung, Siemens, or General Motors. The negotiations are based on past and predicted travel and the budgets these companies assign to travel each year. Special packages and negotiated rates are part of the negotiations. They can include percentage discounts for higher fare classes which typically have available seats closer to the date of departure. But there can be (lower) discounts in lower fare classes as well. All these aspects are negotiated, including other perks such as access to business class or even granting senior staff a higher tier in the loyalty program automatically. Since most business travelers employed by firms must abide by corporate travel policies, this is typically maintained in the travel reservation application the travel department uses to communicate with the global distribution systems (GDS) used by travel distributors (Sabre, Travelport, TravelSky, and Amadeus) to communicate with airline reservation systems. In recent years, there has been strong pressure to move out of these GDS by establishing direct connections to avoid the steep segment fees and to overcome the limited capabilities of distributing richer content, like images or other retail products and services. The contracts with GDS themselves are often an obstacle and limit the airlines' ability to innovate in the distribution landscape, other than their website. Many airlines, such as Scandinavian

DOI: 10.4324/9781003018810-13

Airlines (SAS), in October 2022 negotiated an overall package that would see it distribute improved content (full access including lower fares through New Distribution Capability-NDC Direct Connect technology) in parallel to its existing Amadeus GDS contract.

Lufthansa and Amadeus have announced similar 'NDC-based GDS agreements', following those that had already been announced with Sabre and Travelport. The arrangement was called the "NDC Smart Offer" and is available only on a bilateral basis to agencies. Cory Garner, CEO of T2RL, in a LinkedIn post explained that it offers the best content and does not involve the distribution cost charge that Lufthansa maintains for GDS bookings made through other agencies for other fares.[1] These changes are causing shifts in the distribution industry (the intermediaries) but there appears to be a looming integration between the GDS and NDC content aggregators.

What the changing landscape brings to bear is the multitude of arrangements and the complexity involved in understanding all the (transaction) costs involved as well as the impact that distribution cost charges (i.e. fees laid on top of fares sold through certain agencies) may have on demand complicates the steering of demand. This is especially the case if there is any focus on margin and optimization beyond the initial cost recovery of channel costs today. This complexity can of course not be handled by a human or a set of business rules in these channels without data analytics in real time to provide smart automation.

Further, due to the increasing airline industry consolidation (despite a flurry of new startups), negotiating corporate travel agreements has become even more difficult. For example, airline mergers can lead to a shift in the negotiating power when the travel buyer appears relatively smaller on the new combined list. Or airline mergers that cause a rationalization in networks can make the combined carrier less of a fit for the travel needs, in terms of destinations, connections, and frequencies.

Airlines are mainly concerned with the biggest corporate travel buyers that may provide more solid predictability in travel. This is also why airlines track whether the amount of travel that took place each year compares well with what was forecast. In fact, it is monitored closely month-over-month and year-to-date, but moreover in the wider context of the economy and related factors. Route managers look at this booking velocity on a weekly and flight-by-flight basis (as discussed in Chapter 8). But none of those teams is concerned with the cost of the booking channel used to generate a confirmed reservation.

Most airlines have a small business program for smaller companies, offering moderate discounts, loyalty accumulation, and other perks. These programs are intended for companies that have no negotiated contract in place. In some cases, these small business reward programs are like frequent flier programs for individuals. KLM's small business program is called BlueBiz. Travelers can earn blue credits on every used ticket and spend them on free tickets, upgrades, and flight-related services. Within the program, one blue credit equals 1 dollar, but the traveler can still earn Flying Blue miles to use privately as well. In addition, companies that enroll in BlueBiz get their staff to have priority boarding or permitted flight changes. Finally, KLM will guarantee a seat on a flight even though it is fully booked, granting the most flexibility to program members. Other examples of these programs are American Airlines' program called Business Extra, Delta's scheme called SkyBonus, and Southwest's SWABIZ. In the case of Delta's program, a company needs to spend at least USD 5,000 for five individual travelers per year in order to qualify. It also recognizes spending within the SkyTeam alliances (with Virgin Atlantic, Air France-KLM, and Aeromexico).

10.2 Artificial Intelligence in Corporate Sales

Today, most business planning in corporate sales is based on information obtained from more traditional reporting tools, including business intelligence solutions such as PowerBI or Tableau embedded into CRMs, or analytics tools used outside CRMs but with information ingested from passenger service systems (PSSs) and loyalty databases. Other popular BI systems are Microstrategy, IBM, SAP, Birst, SAS, Information Builders, SiSense, Oracle, and Microsoft.

As discussed in the introductory chapter on data analytics and the evolution to artificial intelligence (AI), a modern analytics and BI platform supports analytic content development. It often enables nontechnical users to autonomously run analytic workflows from data access, ingestion, and preparation to interactive analysis. This means that within sales, provided all the dimensions are captured in the commercial systems, staff using BI can pull up the reports they need to (1) assess the performance of the contracts they granted, (2) do their planning for future seasons, and/or (3) design new programs aimed at achieving their sales targets.

Today, a great deal of how this is managed is supported by insights and technology but still relies on judgment and manual work. There is an opportunity to move from descriptive to advanced analytics, including predictive analytics, and ultimately automated corporate sales optimization using AI. Below, the case for this evolution is presented.

As is always the case in machine learning and AI, you must define a goal and describe problems you need to solve toward achieving that goal. The problems you describe will unveil which types, which kinds, and how much (quality) data you require to find solutions to solve those problems. It is only at this point that the logic for using data to achieve the goal can be created by writing the set of rules (algorithms) that machine learning will apply and learn from to automate any decision-making you want to achieve in airline corporate sales. These are several goals we can use machine learning and AI for:

- Optimize contract rates for an enterprise (or TMC representing a corporation with staff frequently traveling), by:
  - Maximizing revenues (or profits) for the account (built up by segment).
  - Predicting optimal customer retention and reach based on trade-offs for each of the categories of travelers for that firm.

94 *Uses of AI and Emerging Opportunities in Commercial Management*

- Taking into consideration past travel volumes, revenues generated by this customer, as well as insights into the likelihood this customer is lost based on competitive schedule and fare analysis.

In order to solve this problem, the data strategy would dictate us to ingest the following inputs based on historical as well as predictive and prescriptive insights:

- Past rates.
- Uptake (usage of rates and all related deep insights).
- Performance analysis against negotiated targets.
- Estimates of past displacement (revenues compared to estimated lost business).
- Estimates of incremental revenue of the deal per company as a whole, or by category, even broken down by corporate passenger, per pax mile.
- Benchmark of average profitability score of this customer against other companies (by size), by region and origin–destination.
- Estimated growth for each account and market segment based on both macro- as well as micro-economic factors obtained from third parties.
- List of variables and estimated elasticities (obtained from other algorithms), including not only projected market capacity (by OD, cabin, and service products) but also projected Forex and interest rate changes.
- Estimated loyalty program stickiness and expected market changes (new algorithms to be developed to support decision intelligence) coupled with changes in tax regulation on frequent flier points and its impact on demand.

Figure 10.1 below captures the potential scope of enterprise AI applications around corporate sales applications powered by AI. It would entail the alignment of many business rules around core goals, but it is technically feasible to harmonize business model practices that enhance overall value for the airline.

To solve the end model, deep learning is required to link all dimensions and aspects to each other so that meaningful insights can be created about cause and effect (causation), but also which aspects appear related (correlation) in specific contexts. A corporate customer will never be profitable on all routes. For simplicity's sake, discounts are often negotiated off published/ public rates using a blanket approach, for example, 35% off the market rate, plus automatic status, bonus miles, and access to lounges. While this works well and is simple to understand, using machine learning may propose a much more sophisticated structure that would generate higher margins for the airline. Nonetheless, the key issue to solve is to come up with the optimal level of discount that not only secures the business but also maximizes the revenues for the airline across the network.

For the time being, the opportunities are there to use machine learning to generate deeper insights into the actual behavior and performance of

Sales and Distribution 95

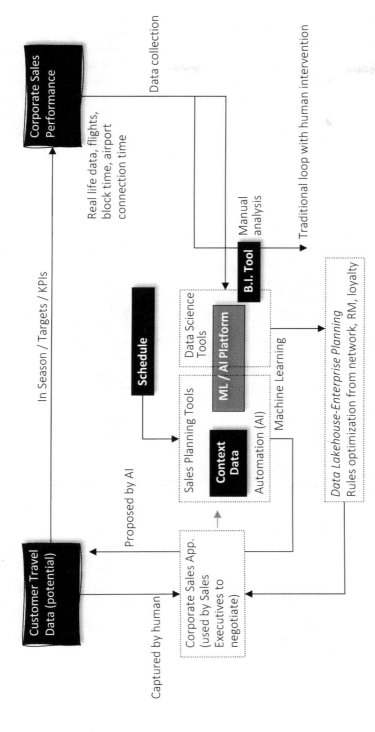

Figure 10.1 Scope of enterprise AI for corporate sales optimization and sales App.

96   *Uses of AI and Emerging Opportunities in Commercial Management*

negotiated corporate sales programs. This will help generate ideas to develop creative plans that can be executed with more automation because they can be tracked and steered in real time. But that does require a cultural shift in the mindset of both the airline as well as the corporate customer, which largely depends on how competing airlines work. It is therefore not that simple to radically change this approach. Most in the business agree that what works best are incremental steps in improved analytics and prescriptive techniques in defining optimal discount levels. This then essentially serves to gain deeper insights and provide more timely inputs into decision-making for proposal development and contract negotiations. It could help quantify passenger displacement as well.

10.3 Potential AI-Powered Use Cases in Distribution

There is a great potential to apply AI in use cases around the optimization of distribution based on the need or expected importance of content penetration in each of the channels. Airlines will always be encouraged to drive bookings to direct, lower-cost, channels that also enable better engagement with end customers. But doing so can undermine their negotiating power with traditional intermediary channels like the GDS or traditional agencies using the GDS. Further, airlines have contracts in place with GDS that dictate what restrictions airlines have on offering content (e.g., the lowest fares) exclusively outside the GDS. Figure 10.2 provides a high-level illustration of some of the complexity around wholesale distribution and related costs. The purpose is not to provide a detailed analysis but to highlight future decision intelligence automation opportunities.

With SAS announcing a modified wholesale model and return to paying commissions to agencies on 3 October 2022, the playing field shifted. SAS proposes that the agencies can use commission revenues to pay for content facilitated by new NDS players that provide full content including the lowest fares.[2] Travel agencies, depending on their size and target markets will have to look at trade-offs on absorbing the cost of full content (NDC) versus commission payments on higher-yield traffic.

Since the airlines still pay segment fees on GDS bookings, there is an interesting use case for machine learning to understand the impact of demand by category, segment, and possibly at individual customer level of

- The airline passing on channel costs to the agencies including IATA BSP or other payment costs.
- The travel agent passing on the GDS cost recovery fee charged by the airline to the end customer (like Lufthansa).
- The travel agency taking on the cost of NDC content and propensity and quality of incremental bookings for the airline.

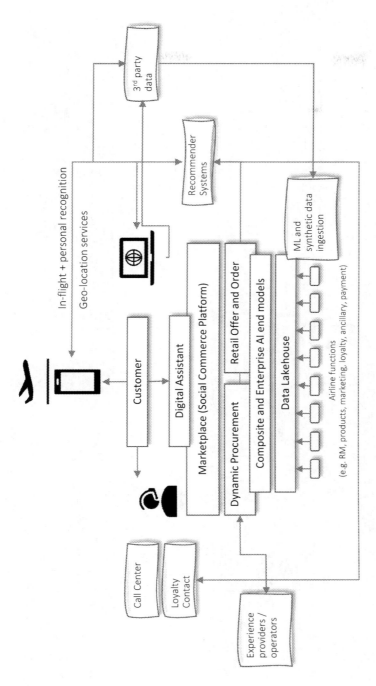

Figure 10.2 Scope of potential distribution and contract steering using AI.

98 Uses of AI and Emerging Opportunities in Commercial Management

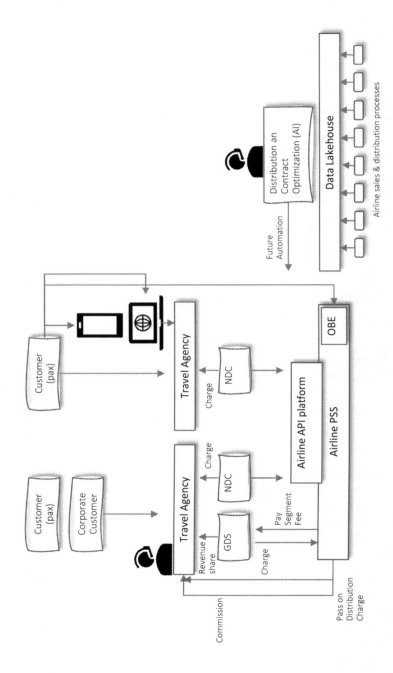

Figure 10.2 Continued.

The distribution analytics could generate invaluable insights that AI-powered end models could use to steer commercial decisions and optimize:

- What distribution costs (segment fees) to recover and how much.
- Which content to promote through GDS or NDC only.
- Which channels generate the best quality density and optimal yields.
- Which markets to treat differently using distribution tactics to obtain the best results.
- How to distinguish between corporate TMCs or leisure-focused agencies and Online Travel Agents (OTAs).

Building in the rules and basing potential channel shifts on cost/benefit cases will involve calculations that AI can assist in. It will be able to generate recommendation that also reflects the risk of losing customer segments, even at the individual corporate customer level. Given the trend to offer full and enhanced content through NDC-enabled distribution and the aggregators' intention to gain traction in the agency community, there will be many opportunities for more decision intelligence in (1) impact analysis, (2) contract negotiations, (3) operationalized channel shift mechanisms, supported by MarTech solutions and loyalty products.

Therefore, the following is a list of use cases for ML and AI in optimizing distribution management based on market penetration and margin goals:

- Channel optimization/shift based on cost, retailing optimization, propensity to spend, and new revenue-generating products.
- Impact analysis of GDS channel cost recovery on bookings per product/ market combination such as corporate agencies and big banner chains tied to GDS.
- Point of sale pricing based on observed willingness to pay with ingested insights.
- Embedding payment services and optimizing attributes in fare products.
- Improving agency sales contracts and commission levels, notably with large OTAs like Expedia, Kayak, and Booking.
- Distributed AI and distribution penetration using NFTs in blockchain.
- Text-to-image generation using AI for NFTs to create unique artifacts.
- Enabling agencies to extend the benefits they enjoy to their customer base through B2B2C metaverse where they hold a space.

It is evident that the above examples of use cases represent an illustration of the possibilities. For instance, by coupling loyalty to distribution channels and sales programs, a more complex mix of optimizations could be run using deep learning. This is a very promising idea of a roadmap that would elevate the skills of the teams concerned with this with the help of smart technology. Chapter 20 on Hybrid Intelligence describes how this combination could work in practice.

10.4 Conclusions

This chapter delved into the sales and distribution functions of airlines to highlight a few key use cases where AI could enable positive changes. It is shown that the sales function could benefit from prescriptive analytics in corporate sales steering, negotiations, and demand stimulation. Applying AI in use cases related to distribution management can provide decision-making support and intelligent distribution channel optimization management in real time, taking into consideration the (transaction) cost of each booking by channel while mitigating any potential negative passenger displacement. The conclusions are that these are only the tip of the iceberg on what AI can be used for in this discipline.

Notes

1 Garner, C. (2022) 'NDC offers–offer'. Cory Garner on LinkedIn: NDC OFFERS–OFFER https://ca.linkedin.com/posts/cory-garner-19a21_ndc-offers-offers-in-detail-activity-6975382196484284416-ND9pSINDETAIL.
2 T2RL (2022) 'SAS's distribution commission program: a new distribution model is born'. http://t2rl.net/insight/display.asp?ID=713.

Bibliography

Harteveldt, H. (2016) 'The future of airline distribution'. The Atmosphere Group – Research conducted for IATA. https://www.iata.org/contentassets/6de4dce5f38b45ce82b0db42acd23d1c/ndc-future-airline-distribution-report.pdf

11 Retailing and Digital Assistants

11.1 Introduction

In this chapter, we are starting to move a bit into a hipper and more modern space of commercial aviation transformation. While there is a great deal of talk about 'retailing', the retailing the industry is referring to is better defined by adding products and services to the list of things to sell as ancillaries, i.e. adding items during the booking path as people work their way to check out and complete their purchases, for instance a fun bumpy jumping experience off the Sky tower in Auckland, New Zealand.

In the last six months of 2021, IATA worked with onboard distribution stakeholders to remodel NDC and One Order certification. The current NDC and One Order certifications move into a new Airline Retailing Maturity (ARM) index with a broader scope covering airline retailing using offers and orders. The ARM index would also serve to help transition airlines and offer a certification model. The use of the word retailing is arguable because it is not necessarily referring to end customers that shop and browse freely off digital shelves. It is still based on distributing (push approach) products through intermediaries, i.e. travel agents-based GDS and direct-connect technology for agents in parallel to GDS content. Agents also do not have freedom or choice in their shopping path; it is sequenced by the distribution systems or NDC as explained in the previous chapter. In essence, there are still many opportunities to innovate around customer intimacy differently. This chapter aims to shed more light on this retailing.

11.2 Startups in Commercial

While aviation is full of exciting startups, commercial is an area where three challenges put the brakes on innovation. When you think of startups you might imagine whizzy tech companies led by inspirational entrepreneurs. Brands like Tesla, Airbnb, Uber, Spotify, and Airportr and their founders are synonymous with the space. But close to where you might happen to live, these days there are many trendy new entrants that want to create their position in the travel industry.

DOI: 10.4324/9781003018810-14

102 *Uses of AI and Emerging Opportunities in Commercial Management*

Aviation is no stranger to startups. Caeli Nova has an innovative solution to opening shorter flight routes by allowing aircraft to fly higher and further in the event of a cabin depressurization.[1] Statusmatch.com makes it easier than ever before for airlines to attract new high value fliers.[2] The Butterfly seat converts between long-haul business class beds and regional business class seats to grow revenue. And Plusgrade monetizes unsold business class seats, although the extent to which this revenue is all growth or potentially displacement can be disputed.[3]

However, airline retailing is proving a tough nut for startups to crack. Alaska Airlines recently introduced subscription pricing for flight passes by Caravelo, although it has some limitations.[4] Even so, incumbent and new entrant vendors seem to have difficulty in innovating and in accelerating go-to-market for solutions. There are three challenges that startups need to overcome.

The first one is that ancillary revenues are likely saturating by 2025 as airlines run out of new things to add to the current booking path set up around flights. There is very little room to add more steps and not make a booking or order process too lengthy and painful. This will turn people off. It is becoming too cumbersome.

The second challenge is around misaligned goals. Airline organizations are not designed to use a data-driven approach to achieve common goals centered on specific customers. The industry has tried to offer rich content that inspires shoppers to buy using NDC, a communications standard, and application programming interfaces (APIs) with intermediary vendors. But most airlines are still not able to identify the specific most-desirable customer. Or build a relationship around one that is consistent across each transaction, every time they travel. The biggest hurdle is a silo mentality within airlines where teams work apart towards different objectives rather than together towards the same goal. Enterprise artificial intelligence (AI), discussed in Chapter 18, shows promise in terms of delivering better results around customer goals, but because organization is an internal matter for airlines it is hard to see startups gaining traction in this space. Meanwhile, it is hard for startups to gain traction when groups of stakeholders and their airline prospects are pulling their business in opposite directions.

The third challenge involves asset gaps. In the famous words of Facebook founder Mark Zuckerberg, "startups like to move fast and break things".[5] In a highly regulated and safety-conscious industry it can be hard for airline staff to have the necessary mindset to work effectively with small and agile organizations. Airline technology is not set up to use in this way either. It would need to be high-tech, high-touch, customer focused, operating across both electronic and real-world spaces. But many of today's airlines are still powered by legacy distribution platforms which had their origins in 1960s mainframe computers.

Even modern apps follow customers using the same 'from > to' structure. You can check any booking engine. Moving to personalized ticketing will require skills, attitudes, and commercial logic that airlines lack today. Put all these together and no wonder we are seeing little disruption from startups. So, what would building an airline startup in commercial aviation look like today? It would be a true retailing platform with inspiring window displays that help travel shoppers see the airline as a lifestyle company, not a purveyor of seats in a tube. How would it work?

11.2 Digital Assistant for (Airline) Experiences

There is an opportunity for a digital marketplace offering a digital assistant built around each individual customer. A new digital airline retailing experience can inspire shoppers and grow airline profits but is designed by and with the client. There are several reasons why this is commercially necessary.

According to Google, web browsers are looking at more sites than they used to.[6] The average person surfed through 35 sites for travel experience planning in 2022, compared with eight sites in 2011. The look-to-book ratio in travel agents' Global Distribution Systems, like Amadeus, has increased from 200–300 to 1,600 per confirmed booking.[7] Clearly, the selling part of travel is not working well. To win a shopper's business, web retailing platforms need to be more compelling than ever to inspire the shopper to stick around and buy. Unfortunately for airlines their current internet booking engines are mainly lackluster, based on legacy 'from > to' technology that does not represent the way people shop for travel in the real world.

True retailing requires an experiential and experience marketplace with attractive window displays as well as well-stocked shelves. An inspirational shop is full of exciting and interesting things to touch, experience, and buy, with more on offer than the owner's own products and more than just one shelf. Airlines who want to be real retailers need to become lifestyle businesses and avoid being seen as merely selling seats and let customers figure out what is included or important not to miss. The way they offer products should be based more on how people shop in the real world rather than 'stackable' sequences dictated by how we have structured airline distribution since the 1960s.

Building social proof into the retailing experience will be important too, as consumers gain confidence to buy when they see believable insights from third-party influencers they trust. Hotel chains like Accor now include Trip Advisor ratings in their booking engines and airlines should show similar things – passenger photos, tweets, videos, and trip reports, the list is limited only by their imagination. We can stream it live, as well.

Flexibility is also needed. Accommodation is a higher priority than food for some, for others, a good swimming pool might beat any hotel room's features. Golfers often stay at an inexpensive three-star motel because they insist on the expensive tee time at a high-profile course. The same applies to air transport.

104 *Uses of AI and Emerging Opportunities in Commercial Management*

Airlines creating such an experience marketplace will need to figure out how to play around with the options, trading off flight price against other travel spend and any commission earned from partners, a shopper's previous brand loyalty, and many other attributes. This concept is depicted for illustrative purposes in Figure 11.1 below. It highlights the need for a digital assistant that uses AI to help individuals navigate their shopping paths and sift through increasing amounts of content. Below the dynamic procurement level, providers can optimize the offerings and set commercial optimization rules, as discussed throughout the remainder of this chapter.

11.2.1 Content and Control

Shoppers want more content than airlines offer today, and the shopping experience is not well aligned with how flights and the current ancillaries are sold. Airlines start with a schedule, constructing an origin-destination pair, departure time, and price from there. Travel or experience shoppers on the other hand start with their budget, why and where they want to be, and what they want to do. Some may have a specific experience in mind, but others choose either a beach, a mountain, or a city with the exact location as a secondary decision level. Other important things shoppers bear in mind are weather, distance, budget, and maximizing their time at the destination, which may be based more on arrival time rather than departure.

Shoppers also want more control over how content is delivered to them and to choose which third-party sources they trust. They need a digital assistant that automates the heavy lifting of search, profiling, and many recommendations into a simplified, customisable user interface.

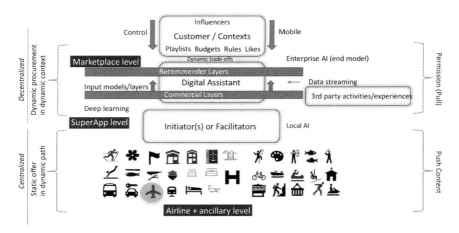

Figure 11.1 Democratization of airline retailing with digital assistants.

Retailing and Digital Assistants 105

Who will offer this experience platform? Airlines have a simple choice. Either they do it themselves (costing time and money) or they pay someone else to do it (costing more money but less time). If they do not, they will lose money to a nimbler competitor. Even if airlines decide to do some of the building work themselves, such a project is likely to be a collaborative effort. There are four possibilities for how it might pan out:

- Big-tech company (e.g. a FAAAM[8]) plus an enterprise scale AI platform, and a startup.
- Airline company (e.g. an existing IT vendor, an airline, an alliance) plus an AI platform and a software service company, plus a startup.
- Travel service company (e.g. online travel agent like Expedia, Booking, Kayak) plus an airline plus software integrators plus a startup.
- A remarkable startup bringing in the above stakeholders.

The big question is to what extent a startup can be a major player. For the right team and the right execution plan the rewards could be huge.

11.2.2 Content Creation is King

Pushing airline-approved content to shoppers is not the sole function of the marketplace. A good marketplace will make it worthwhile for shoppers and travellers to create their own content and stick around, and for retailers to join the marketplace without the airline telling them what to do. This does not only give the social validation referred to before to other shoppers, but it also increases the power of the marketplace at low cost by offering a more complete range of services without any high-cost centralized organization. Such content has a third benefit too, it generates deep data that modern machine and deep learning algorithms can use to find trends and patterns that airlines would not see otherwise. To address privacy and GDPR concerns, content creation can be an opt-in process.

11.2.3 Airline Experience Marketplaces Need AI

Experience marketplaces of the future will be like an improved Amazon of travel with immersive experiences (pre-experience). On top of a well-designed selling platform, non-airline travel service providers will be able to make their own listings without any coordination with the airline. Virtual reality interfaces will be a given, too. AirAsia's super-app is a good example of where to start but is still at an early stage and is more centralized.

For full impact, the platform will need to work on modern aircraft, too. The A320neo, A330neo, and A350 families are ready to go with each having high-capacity technical backbones and communications capabilities able to handle the necessary data processing. But the experiential experience marketplace will likely need yet a more advanced platform-based aircraft, perhaps an imaginary 'Boeing 797' or 'Airbus A370'.

At the back end, the platforms will need five AI-powered components to work:

- Input layers with airline-own, third-party and live-streaming content.
- Output layers of recommendations relevant to a single shopper.
- Customer segmentation rules and filter engines.
- Optimization layers incorporating loyalty, pricing, revenue management and other commercial (sub)rules, all cost factors, linked to a measurable and meaningful end metric like share of wallet.
- Integration with order and offer management systems for fulfillment plus revenue accounting.

If the experience marketplaces of the future are open-source, open-standard, and peer-to-peer they are likely to deliver better long-term results to airlines than high cost and highly centralized alternatives. This requires designing the analytics, experimental layer and DevOps layer where commercial strategies designed by humans can be executed by AI. When the concept was developed and the architecture designed, it looked something like the illustration below:

11.2.4 Three Startup Opportunities

Building websites, sourcing content through APIs and selling plane tickets now have turn-key solutions. The potential for startups in these spaces is low. But there are three high potentials, high reward opportunity for truly transformational startups helping to build experience marketplaces:

- Finding a way to calculate what a flight should cost based on a shopper's journey an overall propensity to spend through the retail experience.
- Estimating the transactional as well as longer term wallet size value of identified customers, including their potential to bring new business through referrals, which can be tracked.
- Building an enterprise scale system for making multiple recommendations for shoppers, including all price components in real time.
- Offering a dynamic platform through which all experience providers can generate and even develop new product offerings in real time.
- Developing a comprehensive airline commercial system that does not just price itineraries, hold reservations, check tickets, and accept passengers for travel but incorporates all shopper data, live-streamed traveler insights, third-party insights and experience content into recommendations for shoppers. These systems will create offers and manage orders independently of traditional airline fare classes and be powered by enterprise AI platforms with live-streamed data and content.

11.3 Case Study of Experience Marketplace

Consider the following case study to illustrate the airline experience marketplace underpinned by AI. Mélanie was following top Moroccan chef

Mourad Lahlou in San Francisco through Instagram, a social media network focused on photo and video sharing. She decided to log into the Airline Experience Marketplace (AEM), where she maintains several travel and experience playlists. As she logged in, AEM had created a recommended playlist for a trip to Morocco based not only on what she had liked and preferred within AEM itself but also through her Instagram and other social media engagement.

Last year Mélanie added a budget for 2022 and ticked options for 'no travel restrictions', 'solo', 'family', and 'retail', creating a few playlists to bundle recommended content on things to do that make fun combos in the process. AEM showed Mélanie a separate bundle with tables comparing trade-offs given her budget. Some choices were more related to different accommodation and luxury categories, others more to culinary and beverage experiences. It also helped Mélanie understand the cost of upgrading the flight experience in the context of shopping in Morocco, i.e., her opportunity cost. As a teaser AEM had also recommended a Moroccan cookbook, shipped today, if she made a purchase.

Mélanie saw that the recommendations ranked high on a combined metric of travel platform reports from GetYourGuide and Tripadvisor, as well as her own influencers across social media. The child-friendly score of the pottery classes by Karima in Moroccan city Marrakesh particularly got her attention. The layout of potential experiences from seeing the Atlas Mountains and three valleys (without the camel ride for her two-year-old), the Ouzoud falls, and the proposed cooking class with local chef Khmisa all fit well to balance the experience.

The recommended Mandarin Oriental hotel seemed perfect but was flagged as pricey compared to the Hilton. Becoming a Mandarin fan would mean flying Premium Economy on Air Canada with an economy connection on Air France rather than a business class all the way featuring Air Canada's Signature Class flat beds over the water. AEM showed helpful videos and photos of the hotel and air travel alternatives seats to help Mélanie make her decision. The price was displayed with up-front and buy-now-pay-later options, each with a loyalty points bonus to help sweeten the deal.

Every time Mélanie clicked on an activity she saw other recommended experiences and their impact on her budget and spending. She chose

- Palmaraie buggy trip.
- Traditional Berber night with free babysitting at the hotel.

Critically, Mélanie was not overwhelmed by the choice so the decisions were easy to make, AEM showed her what they thought she would find both most to her liking and within her budget. And when products were combined Mélanie got better and better deals. Mélanie knew that confirming her basket and being able to control all changes through her PDA would be the most hassle-free way to enjoy her trip and make changes along the way.

108 *Uses of AI and Emerging Opportunities in Commercial Management*

Of course, the AEM does not exist today. But in this marketplace case study, I described shows the potential of using commercial logic and AI to build and deliver powerful and engaging platforms with dynamic offerings created by real-time sourcing as matches are suggested between supply and likely demand. It goes beyond the products that are pre-built (static) on digital shelves. It uses convolution algorithms, deep learning, and stacks models using Composite AI on Enterprise AI platforms, discussed in Chapter 12.

What makes this concept unique is that it democratizes retailing by allowing the customer to drive the shopping experience and path. It supports this through a digital assistant and gives customers control using their rules and allows the presentation of offers to be optimized to meet their goals. Below is a simplified rendering of the 'pull' and permission-based marketplace with decentralized offers.

11.3 Use Case of Use Cases: AI-Enabled Retailing and Embedded RM

Fundamentally, the previous section described an ultimate use case that represented a set of use cases and can only be designed and built around a data fabric architecture (refer Chapters 18 and 22). This type of architecture enables the use of enterprise data by providing the data, at the right time, regardless of where it resides. Using Enterprise AI, a data fabric can allow these types of use cases to be executed by automating the discovery of (required) data and how it is governed and consumed to recommend the solutions that will solve the problem. In the illustrations above, it is about sourcing products and services that an airline is just discovering it needs to offer but does not have in its ecosystem. It is that dynamic procurement component that could be (literally) at the 'edge' of customer behavior's footprint where it will be priced and commercially optimized. Building smart rules and automated customer-based revenue management in that retail scope presents a big set of challenges by itself.

In order to embark on AI-enabled journeys that resemble the experiential Airline Marketplace of Experiences platform above, an airline could start off by sketching the superdome as a child would imagine it with 'lantern' consciousness. Lantern consciousness is the opposite of spotlight focus, where people only see details and micro-processes. So, this refers to the lack of blinders or constraints to paint the overall objective, which is goal-centric at an individual customer level. A 'green lake' approach is necessary to identify what all the necessary building blocks are so that the recommendations are delivered at the right time and follow the customer's erratic, irrational, and inter-mitted thoughts and actions. The complexity can only be built over time, or it would never be finished. And herein lie all the difficult discussions in which layers and what level of complexity and how accurate it should be at least at the start. Despite all the literature on whether traditional project planning or scrum methodologies are best, the reality is that a combination of both at different stages of such undertakings is most likely going to push retailing in this direction. It would be more powerful than Amazon.

11.4 Conclusions

Airlines can only become truly data-centric if they become goal-centric. This chapter demonstrated that AI could help build transformational retail roadmaps to deliver more convenient customer propositions that are powered by sophisticated commercial processes using AI. The chapter provided a practical use case for an experiential Airline Marketplace of Experiences to demonstrate a vision. Machine learning and AI have the capability to enable these unique platforms. They would transcend online to onboard digital platforms inflight that will inspire a new breed of retail revenue management solutions to optimize revenues generated from identified individuals using physical and digital assets onboard, including advertising on in-cabin billboards.

Notes

1 Caeli Nova (2022) 'A breath of fresh air'. https://caelinova.com/news-and-blog/a-breath-of-fresh-air.
2 StatusMatch (2022) 'How it works'. https://www.statusmatch.com/#how-it-works.
3 Plusgrade (2022) 'Premium upgrade'. https://www.plusgrade.com/solution/premium-upgrade/.
4 Alaska Airlines (2022) 'Flight pass terms and conditions'. https://alaska.caravelo.com/alaska-flightpass-terms.pdf.
5 Taneja, H., 'The Era of "move fast and break things" is over', Harvard Business Review, 22 January 2019. https://hbr.org/2019/01/the-era-of-move-fast-and-break-things-is-over.
6 Travel-related searches for "tonight" and "today" have grown over 150% on mobile, over the past two years. https://www.thinkwithgoogle.com/consumer-insights/consumer-trends/travel-related-search-statistics/.
7 Conversation with Lutz Vorneweg, Global VP Online, Amadeus, on 9 March 2022.
8 Facebook, Alphabet, Amazon, Apple, Microsoft – the famous five of American tech companies.

Bibliography

Butterfly Seating (2022) https://www.butterflyseating.com/
Inflight-VR (2022) https://inflight-vr.com/
Migacore (2022) https://www.cirium.com/data-innovation/contextual-demand-insight/

12 Total Revenue Optimization (All Commercial Functions)

12.1 Introduction

Even in the early days of automated revenue management using the Expected Marginal Seat Revenue (EMSR) methodology, there was talk about adding functionality to find novel ways of problem solving around pricing, capacity, interlining, and group sales. In the 1980s and 1990s but even into the early 2010s, it was not possible to use revenue management systems for real-time management or dynamic what-if planning. As described earlier in the book in Chapter 8, the need to modernize both the approach and the technology used in revenue management became more urgent during the COVID-19 pandemic. Not only was it important to ingest emerging data in real time to measure intent in shorter booking cycles, for lack of reliable (historical) data, but it also became more important to include ancillary revenues in the calculations. This was because of the rising popularity of revenue from ancillary products related to seat sales. These products were branded as differentiated products with different price points and contribution margins, such as checked luggage fees, seat assignment fees, a refundability premium, or bundles including a meal, like the Value Pack fare on Air Asia. Given that it is important to know what the likelihood is that a customer will purchase additional ancillary products, machine learning and artificial intelligence (AI) are now applied to account for this and recommend which products should be for sale, and how much capacity should be allocated to this. In addition, and within bands or branded fare products, AI can enable dynamic pricing, which is the calculation of the optimal price in the market for the product at that time without the need to file fares or open capacity first. Technically, it is no longer necessary to use fare classes if we utilize the full potential of dynamic pricing. Also, this supersedes the need to have capacity controls at all, although airlines still use them for network, point-of-sale, and alliance or interline control purposes. This has led to increased complexity as multiple logics operate simultaneously, leading some to question what the overall performance of modern systems is in terms of net profitability, productivity, and efficiency. Nonetheless, they do offer a more dynamic approach to generating higher revenues, especially in unpredictable times.

DOI: 10.4324/9781003018810-15

12.2 Total Revenue Management

The approach of including ancillary revenues in pricing and capacity optimization is referred to as Total Revenue Management by some, including by vendor FLYR Labs, based in Santa Monica, CA, USA. But this approach is limited in its scope, and the term 'total' is misleading. Figure 11.1 illustrates this and the potential evolution toward customer-based revenue management which de-emphasizes the airline seat level for more sophisticated levels of optimization with ambitious goals. In the hotel industry as well, total revenue management can broadly be defined as the goal to manage each revenue source to the highest profitability. To illustrate, by incorporating several revenue points-of-sale, hotels can increase overall profitability by applying this to their restaurants (food and beverage), banquet/conference space, leisure, pool or spa, and other facilities based on selling features to individuals.[1]

For airlines at least, there are two improvements that should be made. First, I argue that it is preferred to change the basis of management from revenue to profit. Second, we should include all additional revenues that passengers can generate beyond seat and ancillary products at individual passenger level in our predictions and adopt a more holistic approach to profit optimization by identified guest.

Regarding the first part, even when passengers buy the same fare, their profitability will not be identical. One could be using a different payment option that carries higher merchant fees. And even if they use the same credit card to purchase the fare, the cost of servicing one passenger over the other may be different. One can be a frequent flier with status and expect to use the lounge or consume more, whereas the other can be known to shop in an airline-airport affiliate duty-free store. The latter could be a modern in-store continuation of modern retail platforms that airlines can launch in partnership with Boeing or Airbus. As described in the chapter on retailing, the digital platforms will likely have reach beyond inflight to online, at airports, and in the metaverse in Web3.0. All the monetizable products and services that passengers may purchase need to be included in a full profit maximization exercise, even those for which no capacity management is needed. The propensity for each passenger to generate value for the airline must be captured and optimized through retailing optimization using engaging tactics.

But the latter is not the only angle to total revenue optimization. It may be that the core product (e.g. air transport) is not in demand, and as such the ancillaries are not being sold either. This is where total revenue optimization approaches can be used differently, that is, by creating incentives to purchase the core product. One creative way of doing this is to waive additional fees for checked luggage, seat selection, or offer extra loyalty points to induce the customer to travel. While arguably not an environmentally friendly approach, there are ways of doing this using Sustainable Aviation Fuel (SAF)

112   *Uses of AI and Emerging Opportunities in Commercial Management*

or on electric propellor aircraft, too nowadays. The benefits of total revenue optimization include the fact that it will:

1   Bring silos closer together.
2   Increase overall productivity.
3   Lead to higher aircraft utilization.

Total revenue optimization can also pave the way for better engagement with customers. This brings us to the area of loyalty.

12.3 Loyalty Based Revenue Management

For most airlines, loyalty (frequent flier program, or FFP) is a separate business in which the most profitable customers are the banks. When airlines enter co-branded credit card programs to drive loyalty, they sell frequent flier points to banks. Based on projected credit card spend as well as frequent flier miles, banks and loyalty firms purchase these points at USD 0.01–USD 0.03 per point on average. From the airline side, when the loyalty program is in-house and not a stand-alone enterprise, the miles passengers accrue are a short-term liability. They can be redeemed for travel or merchandise in many affiliate marketing programs.

Loyalty itself is 'revenue managed' in that how the tiers are set, how the points are monetized, and what additional fees are charged for redemption (award) tickets can be optimized. Adjusting tier qualification levels can also induce more travel, and oftentimes analytics are used to assess which members have the highest likelihood of purchasing additional travel (or taking longer itineraries for more points accumulation) to make it to the next status level. Using advanced analytics, or better yet, with applied AI in marketing technology, these individuals could be targeted with a personalized offer for double or triple the miles on specific routes. These routes could be those identified by machine learning as the most likely routes that would be relevant for personalized campaigns to be on target and be effective.

There are other ways in which loyalty can contribute to a wider scope of revenue management. That is, by tapping into the credit card spend from the financial institution that is the co-brand partner, for instance, American Express or TD Toronto Dominion bank for Air Canada's Aeroplan. Airlines know which tickets are purchased with credit cards but getting access to the entire spend on a customer's credit card is very valuable. Credit card purchases are invaluable for gaining deep insights. Analytics can help create predictive links between the customer's interests, willingness to pay, and all life-style related aspects and attributes that appeal to the customer. Credit card spend can reveal that a customer may have a low willingness to pay for air transportation but spends disproportionally on luxury social clubs or lounges. Golf enthusiasts are a good example. They spend a great deal on tee times and special dining experiences. As deep insights are obtained, airlines

Total Revenue Optimization 113

can predict travel patterns and ensure that an improved mix of passengers is attracted to flights for which the revenue and profit potential has been identified to be higher, using AI. Campaigns and retail offers can be bundled this way, increasing the optimal mix of customers on flights.

But the most promising opportunity for aligning loyalty and revenue management better is to define the goal of revenue management in loyalty terms. For this to work, revenue management must adopt different metrics and KPIs to monitor its performance against, that is, in profitable loyalty terms. Customers would be expressed and ranked in loyalty terms against a dynamic indicator of both current and future profitability. By using deep learning and AI in MarTech-driven revenue optimization, any request that comes in for a booking can be assessed against criteria and the value of the expected remaining customers groups to come in based on their long-term impact on the airline's contribution margin. The airline would be prioritizing a customer based on overall expected spend (lifetime), not the single transaction at hand, provided that a customer also has the highest propensity to purchase other products and services. A win–win on a transactional as well as lifetime basis. These approaches are novel and experimental compared to today's practices, but they become use cases to look at thanks to the capability of AI.

12.4 Customer Revenue Management

Customer-focused RM can move the goalposts for regular customers that are not of particular importance to loyalty as well. It can use a creative combination of algorithms in a process called 'convolution' to amalgamate different data sources, business rules, and objectives defined at the level of the buyer. The convolution algorithms combine lower-level objectives and the results of multiple processes and outcomes into a single input for a further (higher) layer of 'total customer value' revenue optimization with richer insights, a layer which simply does not exist in today's airline workflow or systems.

This approach is not only analytically more advanced than current processes but also cheaper as multiple data sets stored in a single place are used to evaluate different stages of the passenger journey and integrated into one single flow.

I have argued before that I recommend loyalty to drive customer-focused RM and retailing. Best practice in modern organization design is driven by data and structured to achieve specific goals. Moving beyond organigrams with boxes and straight lines, today's most agile teams are enabled to work across traditional functions to solve tricky problems that would otherwise be left alone. This is the enterprise-level capability of AI and the topic of Chapter 18.

It will be a collaborative effort. Humans will establish the objectives and figure out how to monetize travel shopping and buyer behavior, but they will be assisted by enterprise-level AI that spots the trends and act on opportunities to source and sell related products and services from third parties in

114   Uses of AI and Emerging Opportunities in Commercial Management

real time. This will be explored further in Chapter 20 (Hybrid Intelligence). Organizationally, loyalty teams have the best profile to co-ordinate this process for four reasons:

1   Strategic skillsets: Loyalty people were the first to adopt customer-level analytics and use this data to drive new propositions. Since they alone in the airline follow individual customers across all their activities beyond just travel, they already understand their customers better than other departments.
2   Creativity: Airline commercial infrastructure was developed from punch-card computers in the 1960s and everything else has been built on top with little real innovation in the way things are done. Loyalty on the other hand is comparatively young, only really getting going in the last 20 years so today's loyalty people have much more experience handling change.
3   Fit for purpose: Since loyalty managers work with individual travellers, they are used to developing products and services consistent with the way people shop for, buy, and value travel rather than the stack of traditional airline seat sales.
4   Retailing: Airlines have been talking about retailing for years, but the practices are more focused on incremental ancillary and not dynamic offer creation. Loyalty people already work with real retailers and although they might need a bit of help along the way, they already have access to the contacts, knowledge, and mindset necessary to make airline retailing a reality.

12.5 Business Level Profit Optimization

From a revenue model perspective, the typical airline business model has many sources of revenue. Each division has its own revenue-generating capability as well, such as maintenance and engineering, loyalty, and even finance (leasing out aircraft or through investments). Most attention is typically paid to the core business and adding layers of products (premium space, lounge access), services (refundability, flexibility), amenities (on board), perks (100% points accumulation and status), and ancillary products (insurance) or cross-selling services (car rental, hotel, experiences).

The question thus arises whether there are opportunities to optimize profit at business, not divisional level, through improved enterprise-level analytics and steering. Figure 7.1 in Chapter 7 demonstrated this scope, which would include all day-to-day revenue operations. To illustrate the point, the leasing market for aircraft (e.g. dry lease, or ACMI) fluctuates heavily depending on the backlog of aircraft manufacturers. Airlines typically manage their fleet over different time frames, and there have been opportunities to adjust planned capacity and schedules and temporarily remove aircraft. Norse Atlantic Airways even decided to lease out four Boeing 787s (two 787–8s

Total Revenue Optimization 115

and two 787–9s) for 12 months to Air Europe when it became clear that it needed to downsize the airline's fleet size even before they launched.[2] But it is not uncommon for airlines to review market values of their aircraft, the state of the leasing market, and assess whether incremental revenues can be made from leasing out aircraft against the contribution margin those aircraft otherwise deliver to the bottom line of the airline. These opportunities must be thought of, and business cases prepared, but they are complicated undertakings. Not only is the data and knowledge spread out across the company, but there is also no common denominator that would make it easy to do comparative analysis should all the required data be in place.

Using an enterprise data lakehouse and designing potential workflows that would allow an approximation of these types of business-level analysis would be ambitious. It is also ambitious from a people and personality aspect, as discussed in Chapter 25.

Other examples are about digitally positioning the catering or maintenance and engineering (or even oil refinery business in the case of Delta Airlines) so that a higher level of planning efficacy and efficiency can be achieved. Already, meal planning and food waste are use cases for AI as we have seen in Chapters 2 and 5. And capacity levels and meal discrepancies can be monitored in real time to re-allocate or promote meals dynamically to people hours before they check in and offered at a discount, so that the loading of aircraft can be updated. In all these applications, the potential benefits are perhaps small but recommended from an environmental, societal, and governance (ESG) standpoint.

Business-level optimization requires several important elements to be in place:

- A clearly defined goal that can be expressed in the least number of KPIs.
- An enterprise-wide scorecard that translates well to divisional characteristics.
- An enormous amount of data.
- A thorough understanding of workstreams at the divisional level.
- A level of automation within departments that are already advanced.

This is how some of the work using AI would look like:

- From the standpoint of data, the airline is a collection of production outputs that are affected by a variety of factors (operations, events, external influences).
- The addition of variables has specific effects in both the short and long term (i.e. other operating units producing outputs).
- Each variable has its own set of statistics regarding its impact on the operation.
- Data is combined to form an assumption about the best course of action based on the available information.

116 *Uses of AI and Emerging Opportunities in Commercial Management*

- The various outcomes and changes in the airline's performance are then considered.
- This is then how assumptions are validated and it is at this stage that recurrent neural networks handle the analysis of data point sequences.

Chapter 18 explores how AI at enterprise level will deliver the first phase of total revenue optimization at business level, given that a divisional level of problem solving, and automation already presents a considerable challenge for the adoption of data. The main obstacles in these efforts are not around the technology or the required quality of the data, but the human and interpersonal aspects of work, communication, emotional systems, and the realities of what change is and triggers in people.

12.6 Profit Load Factor

Within revenue management, all analytics and decisions are based on probability. The projections of demand and likelihood of demand to arrive at specific times and willingness to pay price points, considering the restrictions (differential pricing) and rules in place are part and parcel of the art and science of revenue management. Revenue management also applies its own KPIs, particularly with regard to booking and final load factors, average yield (by cabin), and other more granular indicators such as point of sale (location) and channel.

The potential revenue that a customer or flight and a combination of flights on a particular day could generate is not within the scope of today's RM practices. This is mainly because RM is tasked with optimizing the demand (request for seats) as it comes in, against assumptions of what is expected to come in. It is essentially allowing the sale of open seats in predetermined buckets (that can be more dynamic as well) as long as it and other itineraries that are mapped to the same inventory meet the minimum yield the system predicts it can generate (bid price). Even with the inclusion of the potential spend on ancillary revenues (for each request) added on top to improve the basis of decision intelligence (refer Chapter 8), there is no assessment of what the real potential revenue by customer and for a flight or combination of flights is. In order to get to that level, commercial optimization needs to include retail and loyalty optimization as discussed before.

Therefore, when customer revenue management becomes a model that can be constructed and executed, it would produce new KPIs. It would become possible to map these KPIs to the current revenue management systems and identify the gap. I would call this KPI the profit load factor. It highlights to what extent revenue management performs against the maximum estimated profitability by customer, flight, and O&D. It is therefore an assessment of its performance and should inspire a collaborative effort to integrate commercial functions into a more sophisticated logic, at both customer and flight level that meets joint but fundamentally aligned KPIs for an improved business score card.

12.7 Convolutional Neural Networks

In order to achieve some of the things set out earlier, we will need to employ advanced computational methods. As described in the introductory chapter defining AI, the field of machine learning has taken a dramatic turn in recent times with the rise of the Artificial Neural Network (ANN). These networks were inspired by biology and helped develop computational models that far supersede the performance of AI in common machine learning. One field within ANN is that of Convolutional Neural Networks (CNN). It was initially invented to solve pattern recognition in images (such as identifying roads in satellite images, or recognizing letters in handwriting), but it has since been applied to deep learning, too. Amazon, for example, utilizes CNN image recognition to make suggestions in the 'you might also like' area. The hypothesis is based on the user's expressed behavior. The products are matched based on visual criteria, such as red shoes and red hat with red belt for a red outfit. Pinterest also uses CNN image recognition in a novel way. The organization focuses on visual credentials matching, which results in simple visual matching enhanced by tagging.

ANN and CNN allow us to create deep linkages and data relationships that a human would not easily find and would only imagine, without any statistical support and with a lot of creative thinking. The simple architecture of CNN offers an easier way of getting started with ANN and uncovering these hidden layers of relationships in data and real life so we can use them in new business use cases.

Essentially, just like the human brain with interconnected nodes (neurons), ANNs work in a distributed way to collectively learn from the input to optimize the final output, which could be a recommendation or optimized retail bundle, or whether to operate or lease aircraft. Applying it at that level requires multiple sets of ingested data from across the enterprise in a data lakehouse. The convolutional neural network can then be created with deep learning and multiple layers of computation along a set of goals, trying to solve an overriding problem or achieve a goal. For instance: operate or lease out this Airbus A350–1000, within the context of a consideration set of market dynamics, routes, financial gearing, and AI-powered recommendations on commercial viability vs. predicted outcomes of leasing out aircraft.

12.8 Conclusions

This chapter proposed the new concept of total revenue management based on aligning, then integrating commercial optimization logic across departments. It discussed the limitations of revenue management and proposed other dimensions, each representing an incremental step. Loyalty-based,

118 *Uses of AI and Emerging Opportunities in Commercial Management*

customer-based, corporate, and business-level-based approaches are explored to highlight areas for improvement using convolutional neural networks in AI. This could result in a new set of KPIs culminating in a 'profit load factor', as suggested. This indicator highlights to what extent revenue management and related commercial functions achieve their potential. The chapter concludes that this approach becomes a potent driver of advanced prescriptive analytics for strategic business management underpinned by AI.

Notes

1 RevFine (2022) https://www.revfine.com/total-revenue-management/.
2 World Airline News, 14 April 2022. https://worldairlinenews.com/2022/04/14/norse-atlantic-to-start-flying-in-june-leases-out-its-idle-boeing-787s/#:~:text=The%20new%20airline%20made%20this,a%20period%20of%2018%20months.

Bibliography

Banciu, M. *et al.* (2021) 'Distribution-free bounds for the expected marginal seat revenue heuristic with dependent demands', *Journal of Revenue and Pricing Management,* 18, pp. 155–163.

Ciresan, D. *et al.* (2012) 'Multi-column deep neural networks for image classification', *Computer Vision and Pattern Recognition (CVPR),* 32, pp. 3642–3649.

Genter, J. (2020) 'How Airlines make billions from monetizing frequent flyer programs'. *Forbes.* https://www.forbes.com/sites/advisor/2020/07/15/how-airlines-make-billions-from-monetizing-frequent-flyer-programs/?sh=45512e3314e9

O'Shea, K. *et al.* (2015) *An introduction to convolutional neural networks.* Lancaster, PA: Lancaster University. https://arxiv.org/pdf/1511.08458.pdf

Thomas, C. (2019) 'An introduction of convolutional neural networks'. *Towards Data Science.* https://towardsdatascience.com/an-introduction-to-convolutional-neural-networks-eb0b60b58fd7

Zeiler, M.D. *et al.* (2014) 'Visualizing and understanding convolutional networks, *Computer Vision–ECCV'.* In M. Franke (Ed.), *Managing airline networks,* pp. 818–833. New York: Springer.

13 Brand Management, Reputation, and Social Media

13.1 Introduction to Brand Management

An airline brand is not its product or the services it offers. It is a position it holds in a current or potential customer's mind, which is subject to many influences. A brand is not a tangible item that can be seen or touched, but it can bring people together; employees, customers, and other stakeholders, for instance. This is because a brand, which often centers around a name, an image, logo, or theme, with or without a slogan, represents the values a company stands for and positions itself as a distinct entity people can relate to and build a relationship with. For airlines, since the early days of commercial aviation, a particular glamorous, adventurous, and pioneering allure has always existed. The luxury and personal attention that First and Business Class offers has also frequently been used as a key tactic to create a halo effect of excellence and distinction, and it can indirectly attract higher margins across the entire range of products and services an airline offers. This explains why global and full-service carriers have traditionally advertised heavily in global media, not only in traditional media such as new channels, CNN, BBC, and Al Jazeera but also in magazines such as National Geographic, World Traveller, and now in social media like Facebook, Spotify, and through Google Ads.

Effective brand management can help to achieve a number of important objectives. It can:

- Increase the likelihood of retaining customers and increasing their lifetime value.
- Attract new customers.
- Increase revenues and margins.
- Improve the adoption of new products and services.
- Improve employee engagement.
- Create competitive advantage.
- Build better relationships with people.
- Stand out from a crowd where perceptions matter.

It has been proven that brand management builds loyal customers through positive brand association and that this has a positive effect on an airline's

DOI: 10.4324/9781003018810-16

120   *Uses of AI and Emerging Opportunities in Commercial Management*

bottom line. But the reason brand management has become so important is that the world has fundamentally changed with the introduction of the internet. This has also required new technological solutions to support modern brand management. For instance,

- There are more opportunities for customers to be influenced (positively and negatively) by the abundance of online information.
- There are more direct relationships between suppliers (airlines) and their customers.
- Customers can openly share opinions, frustrations, or complaints and directly influence what others perceive.
- Everything that is shared can instantly escalate.

Airlines traditionally worked with marketing agencies to design and execute campaigns around the company's vision, commercial strategies, or tactical promotional campaigns. While this is still important today, the acceleration of information sharing and activity in social media channels has called for a different set of techniques that can be deployed swiftly.

Famous professor and scholar Philip Kotler argues that brands need to differentiate more and that 'brand activism' is a means to show customers that the companies not only care about customers and meet their needs but also support social, political, economic, and environmental reform.[1]

> Customers are the voters. They can make a brand or destroy it by a shift in their purchases.
>
> (Philip Kotler)

13.2 Artificial Intelligence in Brand Management

Most of the application or artificial intelligence (AI) within brand management is mainly around analytics and digital advertising and tightly related to marketing and sales campaigns. AI-backed predictive technologies can deliver contextualized recommendations onsite and even optimize Return on Ad Spend (ROAS) by predicting which users are most likely to convert and for which products. Delivering these experiences in real time helps personalization and loyalty because the overall 'AARR' (acquisition, activation, retention, and revenue) funnel is consistent and seamless. Consistency in (digital) experience will help branding as well.

Now, consider the following story as published by Relay42[2]:

> Your return customer, Hailey, visits your airline's website to look for a flight. Upon her visit, she is recognized as a Silver Status customer. Unfortunately, she doesn't convert on her first visit, so she's automatically entered into a retargeting customer journey for loyalty members. Then, because AI uses her history to understand her, it predicts that Hailey is

most likely to interact with visual content and based on that prediction it shows Hailey a personalized display banner. When she doesn't click on the banner but visits a metasearch website to compare flights instead, that data is collected and stored in her profile. AI then uses that data to retarget Hailey with a dynamic travel video, including personalized pricing and the number of loyalty points she can earn by booking her flight with your airline. When she clicks, she lands on a personalized landing page. When she books her flight there, she's automatically excluded from receiving irrelevant retargeting offers and retargeted to receive relevant ancillary offers for her upcoming flight.

In the above example, digital marketing and targeting can keep track of and re-engage with Hailey because it is underpinned by AI. It keeps solving problems until a solution has been accepted by Hailey that also meets the airline's objectives. And since the path and choices Hailey makes are not linear, it would be difficult for a human to observe and act on the actions.

While this is about sales conversion and advertising, there is a relationship to brand management. Brand managers in the past had to rely on little information from a few sources, such as surveys. Therefore, experienced brand managers had to rely more on instinct, past experience, and traditional sources of information. In an information age, past information is almost less important because there are so many new information sources generating an overload of instant information through many channels. With information in abundance, it is almost impossible to focus or narrow it down manually. The data itself cannot be followed or interpreted by humans anymore because of the sheer volumes and complexities, coupled with new and micro-generations of people that behave and express themselves differently, and through an ever-increasing number of platforms.

Therefore, AI applications in brand management originated around the primary objective of proper interpretation of data. This hinges on the appropriate and clean sources of data and since AI functions best with large data sets, it became important to prioritize the simplification and structure of multiple data streams around clearly defined goals. An additional benefit of AI is also that it can ingest new data as it emerges from existing or even new sources. As such, when we use machine learning to detect patterns and evaluate complex datasets of peoples' opinions expressed on various platforms or through different channels, we can use AI to structure and make sense of them. This also helps airlines to be reassured that when actions are taken, they are based on proper statistical analysis and less on gut feel.

The future of brand management will be faster and more creative. With the use of AI, it can also help define categories better and liberate those professionals in brand management from repetitive tasks or mundane work collecting dated information. The quality of the data will improve which will indirectly provide airlines with the confidence to release more creative and personalized content. Measuring and refining the success of branding exercises will also

122 Uses of AI and Emerging Opportunities in Commercial Management

allow real-time optimization. In order to capitalize on the promises of AI the most in brand management, the two critical success factors are speed and scale. Customer intimacy can only be optimized if it is as close as possible to real time, and the airline must be able to scale the level of intimacy to each and every customer at the same time, without compromising speed. This remained one of the principal challenges during the Covid-19 pandemic.

13.3 How AI in Brand Management Works

In Chapter 3, it was discussed how airlines use modern technology underpinned by AI in contact management, conflict resolution, and social media. But airlines also use modern solutions as digital growth management platforms, such as Singapore Airlines using Insider.[3] These platforms are used for digital marketing and brand nurturing purposes. For Singapore Airlines, other than delivering great experiences in real-time, the airline also wanted to "improve its key metrics such as conversion rates, ancillary revenue, and customer satisfaction scores", as indicated in the press release. Another example is KLM Royal Dutch Airlines using Relay42 for personalized marketing and branding. These airlines use technology to tie together service, profitability, and branding.

In 2017, American Airlines launched an interactive map with geo-markers to spot and keep track of where in the world AA was mentioned on social media.[4] It also uses automated filters and prompts staff to look at situations that demand attention or intervention. Geo-targeting has become much more convenient with real-time data and available tools to reach people directly. This has a direct impact on how customers experience the service and how they feel about the brand.

AI in practice always starts with defining a clear goal. In the airline's case, it is to secure the brand value and position it wants in key customer groups, while building brand awareness in other markets or customer groups. Second, airlines want to increase user frequency that can lead to more consistent interactions and ultimately sales at the right margins. In addition, and because airlines still deal with large groups of intermediaries, they want to entice online and brick-and-mortar travel agencies plus increasingly prominent influencers into favorable behaviors for the airline.

How this works in practice, is by defining, describing, and listing the terms by which a particular airline wants to be perceived as articulated by (potential) customers. These are words that have positive associations that transfer well across markets, digital media, and can inspire people to explore the airline, its services, values, and social and environmental standards and decide to engage. Airlines also want customers to become individual ambassadors of their brand and re-share their opinions.

What is described above is supported by graphical design and content generated from marketing agencies but built into digital marketing campaigns. These campaigns are executed using modern MarTech platforms that can personalize the message to individuals and bring in relevant past, current, and

Brand Management, Reputation, and Social Media   123

potentially other information. Meanwhile, how airlines' score is measured through quick 'I appreciate this: Yes/No' surveys as well as more elaborate surveys after they experience a meal, a flight, or an interaction with the call center. In practice, AI brand management platforms automate the execution of campaigns for different categories (but same individuals) to see what works best for the customer to their satisfaction and learn from this reinforcement. The goal is to keep delivering on and solving problems so that customers are satisfied along their shopping paths and across behavioral tracks.

However, through digital media, opinions can spread quickly, negative news can travel fast, and even go viral. So, airlines also use AI-based technology for reputation management as part of brand management. Perceptions matter and posts on social media can do a lot of damage to the reputation of an airline. Also, customer review websites such as TripAdvisor can play a big role in raising awareness among travelers and airlines as to what is not working well, or what is hurting the business. It is for this reason that airlines watch these social media closely. AI has been used to develop systems that allow companies to guard their online reputation. An example of such a firm is Mentionlytics in London, United Kingdom. Their similar solutions are allowing companies to achieve advanced brand management by enabling brand managers and product managers to conduct large-scale research and analysis on social media platforms or any public forum.

13.4 Potential Use Cases for AI

The list of use cases and potential enhancements in brand management underpinned by AI is extensive. These are some of them:

- Identify at-risk customers that are disconnecting from the airline brand or start to hold an unfavorable opinion.
- Deploy emotional analytics, such as eye tracking and emotions reading applications, to read consumers' attitudes and feelings and detect when people appear to be offended by messages.
- Perfect the delivery timing of messages based on learned effectiveness and response behavior.
- Test which brands appear to do well in collaboration for joint campaigns.
- Learn which colors, type of music, or other image-related contexts are received well.
- Prescribe how to engage customers in collaborative behaviors that will help the airline improve its brand and communication (entice to share positive news).

13.5 Conclusions

This chapter has demonstrated some ways through which AI helps companies in brand management. By doing the latter better and in real time through any emerging channel, airlines can improve customer service, pre-empt conflict, solve more problems faster, and protect their reputation. This further leads to more loyal customers and improved revenues. Those airlines that perform best are those that embrace the technology the best, such as Singapore Airlines, Emirates Airline, KLM, Southwest, Air New Zealand, and Air Canada. The chapter concludes with a number of new or potential use cases for AI applications in airline brand management, such as emotional analytics using AI cameras.

Notes

1 Tesseras, L. (2018) 'Father of modern marketing' Philip Kotler on avoiding brand decay and preparing for disruption', *Marketing Week*. https://www.marketingweek.com/philip-kotler-modern-marketing.
2 Relay42 (2021) 'How airline marketers are using AI to improve the customer journey'. https://relay42.com/resources/blog/airline-marketers-using-ai-improve-the-customer-journey.
3 Singapore Airlines (2019) 'One of the World's best airlines chooses insider'. *Cision PR Newswire*. https://www.prnewswire.com/news-releases/singapore-airlines-one-of-the-worlds-best-airlines-chooses-insider-to-deliver-ai-powered-experiences-to-its-20-million-fliers-300906164.html.
4 AltexSoft (2022) 'Airline marketing and advertising use cases from American Airlines, Ryanair, AirFrance, and Others, Altexsoft'. https://www.altexsoft.com/blog/airline-marketing-advertising/.

Bibliography

Alexsoft (2022) https://www.altexsoft.com
BCG (2022) 'Artificial intelligence and AI at scale'. https://www.bcg.com
Karaağaoğlu, N. *et al.* (2019) 'An evaluation of digital marketing applications in airline sector', *Journal of Human Sciences*, 16, pp. 606–619. https://www.researchgate.net/publication/333057977_An_evaluation_of_digital_marketing_applications_in_airline_sector
Mentionlytics (2022) https://www.mentionlytics.com
Relay42 (2022) https://www.relay42.com

14 Cargo Warehouse and Handling

14.1 Introduction to Cargo Handling

According to industry association IATA, airlines transport over 52 million metric tons of goods a year, representing more than 35% of global trade by value but less than 1% of world trade by volume. That is equivalent to $6.8 trillion worth of goods annually, or $18.6 billion worth of goods every day.[1] Unlike passengers, cargo is not homogenous. The goods that are transported by air can consist of air mail carried in bags and containers, parcels, any dry consumer goods or machinery as well as perishable products such as fruit, flowers, seafood, and other foods. While most cargo is carried on combination aircraft (passenger aircraft with belly holds used for cargo as well), oversize cargo is often carried on main decks of full freighters.

Due to the volume and diversity in dimensions of individual boxes that need to be combined (stacked) on pallets or flat beds, cargo handling is a complex task handled by experienced staff. There are also many regulations and safety measures to follow, particularly around prohibited items and dangerous goods. It has traditionally also been very hands-on work.

Most cargo is arranged for by freight forwarders. They act as service providers for shippers (such as manufacturers) and handle the logistics of the transportation of goods from the manufacturer's premises, the export process, all transportation modes (sea, rail, air, and truck), and import. Freight forwarders have contracts in place with various third-party logistics companies to deliver a turnkey solution. They bundle all service and transportation-related fees and charge an overall 'handling fee'.

For individual shippers or smaller firms that want to make their own arrangements, these are the typical steps:

1 Check (inter)national restrictions
  Not all cargo is equal. Some restrictions and prohibitions may apply for safety and other reasons. Shippers need to make certain the goods will be allowed into a country.
2 Choose a service product
  Shippers need to choose the product and service that is best going to suit them based on the features which are important.

DOI: 10.4324/9781003018810-17

126 *Uses of AI and Emerging Opportunities in Commercial Management*

3 Make a booking

It is customary that the space for the cargo must be booked in advance. This naturally aids demand and capacity planning and thus revenue optimization, as discussed in Chapter 15. Typically, this occurs one to seven days prior to a preferred departure day. Sometimes cargo is simply delivered to an airline's cargo warehouse, in which case it needs to be booked into the cargo system upon acceptance. Depending on the service level, the cargo will depart or will be transported by the air carrier on another day, it is occasionally up to their discretion. Most cargo is booked for specific dates, though.

4 Prepare the cargo and paperwork

The company arranging for the transportation is responsible for the preparation of the cargo. It means the required documents need to be provided as well. A label with a consignee address (recipient), the number of pieces, and an Air Waybill (AWB) number with a bar code. All declarations and certificates (such as Dangerous Goods) need to be provided when the cargo is delivered to the cargo terminal.

5 Complete Air Waybill

The AWB is a document required to ship cargo internationally and is completed on behalf of the shipper usually by a Freight Forwarder, an airline office, or an agent appointed by the airline to create documentary evidence, a proof of receipt of the goods for shipment, the freight bill, and the guide for handling, dispatching, and delivering the consignment.

6 Cargo drop

Once the physical cargo and paperwork has been prepared, the cargo can be taken to an acceptance location, which is typically the air cargo terminal where all air cargo is handled. Trucks typically check in at (un)loading docks to tender the cargo.

7 Track cargo

Radio Frequency Identification Device (RFID) tags are increasingly used today to monitor and track cargo location as well as temperature for climate-controlled ULDs. Customers can see at which stage the cargo is at all times.

8 Collect cargo (at arrival airport cargo terminal).

This is the last step in the airport-to-airport process, where freight forwarders pick up the freight for last mile delivery.

14.2 Automation in Air Cargo Handling

During the last two decades, a great deal of investment has gone into developing a modern generation of core cargo management solutions, such as by companies like Accelya, IBS Software, and SmartKargo. The core cargo management solutions typically contained booking/commercial modules as well as functionality to perform cargo acceptance and terminal handling, cargo revenue accounting, ULD planning, and in some cases weight and balance support.

While there has been a steady increase in the level of automation in air cargo booking and handling, the majority of functionality centered on rule-based management, such as respecting cargo embargoes and whether certain types of cargo were allowed to be packed together for safety, hygiene, or other reasons. The types of goods that cannot be shipped by air usually include aerosol sprays and cans and weapons, firearms, ammunition, and explosive devices. The list of items also includes gearboxes, generators, engines, life jackets, and fire extinguishers.

Rule-based management is about the function of controlling the security of communications and IT events through rule- or filter-driven systems. These rules and filters are pre-built and create hard stops in a workflow or require an air cargo terminal employee to take other steps to process and complete a task, such as checking in cargo ('acceptance'). Also, assigning cargo to another flight ('rebooking') is a manual process. When cargo is physically accepted it must be measured and weighed. The dimensions of the cargo as well as the weight are necessary so that a calculation can be made in the core cargo management system about any chargeable weight differences based on what was booked or committed, but also with regard to the contract or market rate (spot) that was quoted to the freight forwarder. There are machines that weigh cargo automatically, but traditionally, the dimensions were taken manually and input in the booking system. Once accepted, the cargo must be placed temporarily in the cargo warehouse where there are racks and locations. The cargo is scanned with a handheld device and assigned to a location. Most cargo, especially perishable cargo and pharmaceutical products is kept in a cold store, a separate area with careful temperature control. The cargo handling software is updated in real time and this information is stored.

On 17 October 2022, Siemens Logistics and Qatar Airways Cargo announced a partnership and MOU to study use cases, build proof of concepts and prototypes to introduce robotics and AI-powered solutions to improve cargo operations planning and handling in the warehouse. This is an illustration of the increased focus on smart digitization of workflows and processes, some use cases of which are explored in this chapter.[2]

14.3 AI Use Cases for Air Cargo Handling

With the proliferation of eCommerce and digital marketplaces, there is an increasing need by shippers, freight forwarders and logistics providers for control, convenience, simplicity, traceability, transparency, and speed. The required visibility in supply chain is driven to a large extent by the acceleration of booking to delivery cycles people have grown accustomed to in consumer markets. And with the ever-growing share of small parcels compared to larger, bulky air cargo, the overall volumes to be handled by air cargo staff at cargo terminals have gone up dramatically, particularly during and following the COVID-19 pandemic. There are many opportunities to automate tasks and processes in air cargo terminals using artificial intelligence

128   *Uses of AI and Emerging Opportunities in Commercial Management*

(AI). Like in car assembly lines or factories, robotics can take on tasks that are repetitive and do not require specific reasoning other than what can be automated and repeated with 100% accuracy. New technologies in cargo facilities can improve productivity, operational efficiencies, and even improve safety. The enhancements in productivity can help improve responsiveness to customers and help mitigate service interruptions faster. This is because with improved insights and optimized planning, AI-driven automation can think and act faster and thereby solve multiple problems at the same time.

During and following the COVID-19 pandemic, cargo organizations were focusing more on strengthening their supply chain and logistics capacity. The attention shifted to AI more and more as an effective way to accelerate this. McKinsey estimated that the implementation of AI had already helped improve logistics costs by 15%, inventory levels by 35%, and service levels by 65%.[3]

Another research by McKinsey estimates that logistics companies will generate $1.3–$2 trillion per year for the next 20 years in economic value by adopting AI into their processes.[4]

The crux in adopting machine learning and AI in cargo facilities is in capturing all activities and movements as digital information (data), even visual aspects (such as scanning items in 3D at acceptance). Then, by connecting all tasks and machines on a digital network, smart allocation of resources and all physical handling movements can be coordinated in real time, with predictive insights into solving issues before they become one.

14.3.1 Warehouse Storage and Cargo Movement

According to an MHI study in 2020, only 12% of businesses are using AI technology in their warehouses and this is not significantly different in air cargo warehouses.[5] There is a high level of manual work involved today that could be automated to remove physical strain from people.

Within a cargo warehouse, cargo must be stored and is often moved around once or more before it is moved to the area where pallets are built up. In some cases, freight forwarder-built pallets are accepted as ready for transportation, weighed, and temporarily stored in a warehouse location. In the past, forklifts were used to move cargo and place it in a lane or high rack depending on destination. Recent innovation allows warehouses to be mapped digitally, with free-roaming autonomous vehicles, or 'automated guided vehicles', also called 'pallet moving robots'. These self-guided vehicles are also an ideal solution to labour shortages or boost consistency and constant productivity levels throughout all shifts and peak times, which are very prevalent in cargo (in terms of time of day and day of week). And these vehicles are also reliable, safe, and require little maintenance. Self-guided industrial vehicles are on the job 24/7 and do not get tired. There is also no room for mistakes, which is helpful in areas where both perishable and dangerous goods are handled. The automated storage and retrieval systems (AS/RS) described here also have

Cargo Warehouse and Handling   129

another additional benefit. They allow racks to be closer together in a high-density facility. This saves personnel and equipment time.

Process flows, workflows, and organization charts are used by warehouse engineers to input into robots. Robots are also trained on locations and distances, at different speeds through trial and machine learning. With computer vision and intelligent computations, they perform situational awareness and consider the speed of other moving objects (and thus prevent collisions). They can spot obstacles, people, as well as known and unexpected objects in their way. All operational rules are uploaded such that the robots know, upon scanning, where to move the cargo to and on which rack to load it. In some of the most advanced types, the routes can be altered in real time as operations dictate them. Some are designed to move large, heavy loads, and offer flexible transport thanks to a rotating table. This is a magnetic belt guidance system that is ideal for assembly lines but can also be used in logistics warehouse when the pallet must be pivoted in orientation (especially ULDs that are asymmetrical). This allows terminal operators to optimize the capacity, speed, and safety of their processes.

Even without self-guided vehicles, AI can aid in improving warehouse operations through augmented reality (AR) technology. AI helps to fight traffic jams that often affect the streamlined operation of many operational processes and the flow of pallets. It improves punctuality and can help optimize routes with real-time traffic data through dynamic traffic support. AR driver assistance and apps already exist. This technology uses glasses or windshield displays and can be used to present information in real time in the driver's field of vision. This type of modern assistance also helps employees focus once they have grown accustomed to wearing or using the technology.

The software behind this technology recognizes serial and barcode numbers, identifies objects, and helps employees navigate the warehouse floor to expedite the picking process.

14.3.2 Cargo Acceptance, Truck Docks and (Un)Loading

AR in wearables (like glasses) can also streamline the process of truck loading. It can effectively replace printed cargo lists and load instructions. For instance, it can show loaders which pallet to take next, where to find it, and where it is needed to be placed in the vehicle. But from an air cargo terminal perspective, the arrival process is also critical.

Before truckers deliver their cargo at the terminal facilities a lot can be improved. Traditionally, even though cargo was booked by freight forwarders, truckers can show up early or late due to a variety of reasons. Often, there are traffic jams around cargo terminals where drivers must wait their turn, walk into the building, and request permission to park their truck/trailer at an unloading (or loading) dock to have their cargo handled. In the past, and depending on some countries or airport locations, drivers spent hours waiting. Sometimes up to 50% of time is spent by drivers looking for the cargo

130 *Uses of AI and Emerging Opportunities in Commercial Management*

and paperwork or permission to dock.[6] Further, it is important for drivers to identify themselves and traditionally this was done using ID cards and signatures. With face-recognition technology, this can be improved and expedited tremendously.

Truck congestion at airports, particularly in the United States (Chicago, Los Angeles, and Anchorage) has been a rampant issue in recent years. The problem stemmed from the rush of ad hoc all-cargo aircraft being substituted for grounded passenger jets during the COVID-19 pandemic combined with the rapid rise in e-commerce orders. Backlogs in ocean shipping have further been complicating matters. All this was colliding with staffing shortages at airport warehouses.

One of the ways to address truck congestion is through an Air Cargo Community System (ACCS) that connects all the supply chain and logistics parties digitally. This does not merely aim to establish a connection link to send or disseminate information between all parties. The aim of an ACCS is for this platform to enable functions and features that benefits all stakeholders through enhanced coordination throughout the supply chain. This means that forwarders, ground handlers/air cargo terminals, customs brokers, shippers, and consignees and also GSAs, security agencies, airlines, and trucking companies can action information that is disseminated in advance.

As mentioned, congestion often represents a serious impediment, this is also due to a lack of timely coordination leading to bottlenecks. With an ACCS, air cargo terminals would be able to better manage the flow of incoming traffic on trucks. For instance, if we were to equip trucking companies with mobile applications in each truck, the drivers could book their arrival and offloading slots at airport terminals in advance. But as they leave the shipper or forwarder's warehouse, the applications can communicate about real arrival times with more accuracy. This can trigger an optimization process between all truckers across the chain in case there are unexpected delays, accidents, or incidents, automatically alerting each driver with an improved slot time. Conversely, the terminal will be able to optimize the incoming flow in terms of expected commodities, required equipment, and necessary staff levels and skills.

The richer the data and the more tasks are digitized across the overall process, the more can be planned, and optimized. It can also help to optimize routes and track entry/exit times at the airport. The ACCS will further be able to trigger the release of electronic and required documents at the right times, without any interventions. This will alleviate workload for drivers. Equipment will be more secure as well, being monitored with QR codes or vehicle tokens in real time.

It is important to highlight that the described connectivity requires a number of technologies. This combination of communication and identification technologies makes up a connected community system with geo-fencing. Is uses video cameras, RFIDs (or 'RFID tags'), radar, Global Positioning Systems (GPS), 5G, and IoT connectors.

There are a number of airports that have adopted an ACCS. Today, they include Brussels, Mumbai, Bengaluru, and Atlanta. The latter is reportedly saving over 7 million copies of paper through the adoption of the digitized process.[7] The reduction in paper is not only an environmental benefit. Combined with the acceleration of information dissemination it leads to insights that enable many efficiency improvements.

Overall, there are tremendous benefits to an ACCS underpinned by machine learning and AI. Here are some specific gains by stakeholders:

- For airlines: the automated integration of data from forwarders and handlers will improve the accuracy of delivery information to the parties on the import side (IATA eAWB e-freight program).
- For freight forwarders: advance notification to handlers and airlines on shipment information, and customs clearance.
- For trucking companies: reduced waiting time and optimized loading time through automated dock-slot booking, drop-off, and pick-up planning.
- For ground handlers: improved facility planning and staffing due to early notification of accurate shipment details, arrival information, and special handling requirements. Automated dock-in, warehouse acceptance, and dock-out events through ground handling (GHA) mobile applications.
- For the airport: improved visibility and reduced congestion around access roads.

14.3.3 Cargo Screening

By law, cargo is required to be scanned and screened. Screening equipment at acceptance can be designed to be integrated into the workflow so that no additional touch points are necessary to update the cargo handling system. As the cargo gets secured upstream, the security status can also be communicated to the freight forwarder. They can be notified about any issues, based on the controls and flags that occur in the process.

What is interesting in the automation that AI can bring is the combination of technology and data around activities that can occur simultaneously while removing any manual intervention. As a case in point, three-dimensional (3D) scanners can be used in a smart way. Companies like SPEEDCARGO in Singapore have pioneered with products like CARGO MIND that go beyond just scanning.[8] For scanning purposes, these solutions measure the dimensions and weight, scan the Waybills with all the commodity, handling, and destination details, while the screening function runs its protocol against rules. The AI script then automatically creates and sends instructions digitally to other connected systems. For instance, available self-guided forklifts are called to take the cargo and move it to a specific location. This could be a location on a rack or a holding location for manual follow up rectifying irregularities with the cargo, booking, or known shipper. All of these can be automated and

132 *Uses of AI and Emerging Opportunities in Commercial Management*

aligned through integrated AI functions, essentially connecting all (a) data, (b) rules, (c) procedures, and (d) workflows toward a common goal.

As a case in point, AI is particularly powerful in advanced molecular screening. There are many applications in the medical world that will transfer into other domains. IATA has also hinted at these opportunities, by suggesting using molecular scanning to analyze commodities such as pharmaceuticals, live animals, or lithium batteries and perform regulatory and safety checks. It will be useful to identify prohibited products or illegal trade articles such as drugs and ivory artifacts.

14.3.4 Pallet Build-Up

Cargo pallets or ULDs are often built up by warehouse employees with the help of forklifts, whereas boxes are stacked by hand. While self-guided vehicles can roam around autonomously to pick up cargo from racks, the final build-up and installation of nets is done by hand. With modern machinery equipped with computer vision (3D vision) combined with the holding data on the content of boxes at piece level (stored by scanned code), AI can provide smart assistance in automated pallet build-up. Given that the weight, content, and dimensions are known, operational rules that are configured in the cargo management system can provide all the guardrails the AI pallet build-up bot has to follow but optimize how boxes are stacked on top of each other. This optimizes the number of boxes and the dimensions that will maximize the use of available space within the aircraft belly-hold or main deck.

AI-assisted software generates optimal configuration for cargo and essentially embeds some of the experience of warehouse employees by learning from overrides. Together, they optimize the total cargo that will be carried, minimizing the spoilage of space and maximizing the economic benefit relative to the environmental externalities. The process also works in reverse. Reverse planning is when the pallet must be partially dismantled due to any commercial or operational reason.

14.3.5 Service Recovery

The capabilities of modern cargo management systems underpinned by smart processes using AI not only aid the acceleration of commercial and operational planning but also help remove inefficiencies. But with the digitization of information and machine learning, it becomes increasingly feasible to predict outcomes. This helps in predicting service interruptions such as misconnections and potential offloads very early on. If connected to ACCSs, airlines know well ahead of time that cargo will not show up for the booked flight, or that there will not be sufficient time to complete all the handling tasks. Therefore, when things go wrong or deviate from the plan, AI can create service recovery scenarios and recommend corrective action. Cargo can be reassigned to other flights and the stakeholders in question can be

Cargo Warehouse and Handling 133

notified ahead of time about the situation as well as the corrective action that has already been taken. This level of automated support (of autonomous automation) is valuable in maintaining service levels and business relationships.

There is another application for this functionality. It allows commercial and operations managers to create what-if scenarios. By being able to play around with different events, managers can often identify new opportunities for improvement. Similarly, it has happened that new routing or other service opportunities create commercial opportunities, particularly when partnering with other airlines in cargo (interlining). At the warehouse level, the artificial assistance has reduced manual and time-consuming calculations, manual shuffling of cargo, and increased staff morale in situations involving irregular operations (IRROPS), such as aircraft on ground (AOG), equipment swaps, downgauges, and other unexpected events.

14.3.6 Staff Planning

With the digitization of information, particularly the fine-tuning that an ACCS enables, the accuracy of cargo shipment and volume information aids the planning of required staff in the cargo warehouse. It becomes possible to assign staff members not only at loading docks, cargo acceptance, or document handling but also at pallet break-down or build-up locations. Staff levels can be planned ahead of time and people can be assigned to work flights. The dispatching using alerts can be done automatically. If employees use handheld and are logged in, they can receive instructions on where they are expected to be on their handheld.

14.3.7 ULD Planning

ULDs are managed in ULD management modules within cargo software. They are either standalone solutions or integrated into cargo management systems. ULD management systems track the serviceable units by identification number and have planning support based on historical and actual cargo movement data. They also provide support in predicting at which airport locations the ULDs will be required. AI can take ULD management to another level in terms of improving the accuracy and level of automation in ULD planning, predictive maintenance, and minimizing the carriage of empty ULDs (ferrying) to other locations. With the integration of images obtained by cameras, computer vision can not only determine the seriousness of the damage and predict out-of-service likelihood but also alert staff to prevent more permanent damage.

14.3.8 Last Mile Delivery

In the cargo transportation industry, last-mile delivery is considered a costly activity and a step in the logistics value chain. While not the responsibility of air cargo terminals, it is important for air cargo carriers to make sure that when cargo is accepted for carriage by air, there is trucking capacity available to bring the freight to its final destination. While this is often the responsibility of the freight carrier, airlines often accept to carry air cargo to destinations that are remote from their destination for commercial and market share reasons. That means they have to contract trucked air freight.

The steady rise of eCommerce and small parcels has created more challenges. There is a need for faster and low-cost delivery, and online retailers such as Amazon even create subscription models to recover some of the last-mile delivery costs. But airlines are also looking into drone delivery. An example of this is Air Canada, which in partnership with Drone Delivery Canada created a new service offering.[9]

Other than drones, self-driving cars and even small flying warehouses are being looked at to address the growing problem and availability of surface modes for last-mile delivery. Automated pickup stations, such as those offered by Amazon and UPS are also a growing trend. Customers need their bar code and digital identification for the package to be released, while the records are updated to complete the tracking cycle.

14.4 Other AI Applications

There are a few other applications of AI that can be added to a cargo warehouse management system. These include

- Automated damage detection of damage to equipment, ULDs, or cargo.
- Predictive maintenance of autonomous vehicles or other handling equipment.
- Predictive and automated self-charging of robots.
- Automated lighting management and lighting level based on predictive movement to reduce energy consumption.

14.5 Conclusions

This chapter described air cargo handling as an excellent candidate for smart automation using AI. There is a high amount of manual and repetitive work that takes place in a cargo terminal. Simultaneously, there are numerous (regulatory) information exchanges. The opportunity to digitize the information under industry eFreight initiatives also enables many smart functions both upstream and upstream. The benefits of advanced planning, improved productivity, and efficiency are evident in the areas of cargo storage, acceptance, screening, and pallet build-up, while there are new applications in service recovery, staff planning, ULD management as well as last-mile delivery. The percentage of airlines and freight forwarders that will adopt AI in air cargo handling, warehouse management, and logistics will exceed 60% by 2030 according to industry observers.

Notes

1 IATA (2022) https://www.iata.org/en/programs/cargo/.
2 Siemens Logistics (2022) 'Siemens Logistics, Qatar Airways Cargo and Qatar Aviation Services (QAS) Cargo agree on cooperation to digitalize cargo processes'. https://www.siemens-logistics.com/en/news/press-releases/siemens-logistics-qatar-airways-cargo-and-qatar-aviation-services-qas-cargo-agree-on-cooperation-to-digitalize-cargo-processes.
3 McKinsey & Company (2021) 'Succeeding in the AI supply-chain revolution'. https://www.mckinsey.com/industries/metals-and-mining/our-insights/succeeding-in-the-ai-supply-chain-revolution.
4 McKinsey & Company (2021) 'State of AI in 2021'. https://www.mckinsey.com/capabilities/quantumblack/our-insights/global-survey-the-state-of-ai-in-2021.
5 MHI (2020) https://www.mhi.org/publications/report.
6 Journal of Commerce (2014) 'It's Time to Face the Real Problems with Port Trucking'. https://www.joc.com/trucking-logistics/drayage/it%E2%80%99s-time-face-real-problems-port-trucking_20140124.html.
7 Kale Logistics (2021) 'New Kale Logistics solutions study at Atlanta Airport […]'. https://kalelogistics.com/new-kale-logistics-solutions-study-at-atlanta-airport-demonstrates-environmental-benefits-of-digitization/.
8 NVIDIA Developer (2018) 'Singapore based research institution uses AI to improve the air cargo process'. https://developer.nvidia.com/blog/singapore-based-research-institution-uses-ai-to-improve-the-air-cargo-process/.
9 Newswire (2021) 'Drone Delivery Canada announces multiple agreements for project at Edmonton International Airport'. https://www.newswire.ca/news-releases/drone-delivery-canada-announces-multiple-agreements-for-project-at-edmonton-international-airport-809641864.html.

Bibliography

AI Multiple (2020) https://research.aimultiple.com/logistics-ai/
Chopra, A. (2021) 'Is AI and digitization new avatar for air freighters and forwarders', pp. 1–7. https://doi.org/10.1109/ICAECT49130.2021.9392594.
IATA (2021) 'Cargo facility of the future'. https://www.iata.org/contentassets/ea37 0e43f1e84cf6835650c2bec61885/stb-cargo-white-paper-cargo-facility-future.pdf

15 Cargo Commercial Management

15.1 Introduction to Cargo Commercial Management

Cargo has always been an important part of air transport. On the very first commercial flight in 1910, there were 200 pounds of silk but no passengers.[1] Fast-forward to the present and once again cargo is at the heart of aviation, carrying COVID vaccines and wrangling great supply chains both when the container ship Ever Given blocked the Suez Canal in 2021 and more recently when logistics in the port of Shenzhen were disrupted by a lockdown.

Air cargo can be divided into two categories – freight and airmail. Within air cargo, there are differentiated service products with value-added premiums like cold chain, high security, and live animals. But since mangoes and postcards do not need flat beds and are not concerned where on the plane they sit or with comfort or not, cargo is not as colorful as the passenger side of aviation.

Nonetheless, the technology of cargo and passengers has both advanced together. One record is the cargo compliment to One Order and One ID, products introduced by industry trade association IATA to make it easier for airlines to serve their customers by integrating everything about people and their air travel needs into one place. One Record is the digital integration of all documents that are required throughout the supply chain for the processing of freight as they leave the factory until they arrive at the final recipient's premises. It centers on the eFreight initiative of IATA.

Core operating systems and mobile apps for cargo have been developed like iCargo from IBS, an Indian software company. Digital distribution platforms like CargoAI, cargo.one and webcargo are finding novel ways to bring cargo into the modern commerce age. But despite progress the processes behind air cargo are still rather heavy. Personal relationships between airlines, freight-forwarders, and the end-users they serve matter. There is no well-established loyalty program, and the cargo professionals find that their tools are not smart enough in forward planning. Overall, there is an awareness that in terms of decision intelligence, air cargo relies too much on human judgment. In fact, IAG Cargo, the freight arm of a British-Spanish airline group with many brands has moaned that youngsters are not attracted to careers in cargo.

DOI: 10.4324/9781003018810-18

15.2 Cargo Commercial Capability Gaps

Early attempts by software vendors to offer cargo revenue management software relied on philosophies borrowed from the passenger side of the business, even though that is a transactional B2C business. Also, in the cargo vertical, including in commercial cargo management, the adoption of science and automated decision support had traditionally been slow and lagging other industries. What is worse, the 'black box' approach of first- and second-generation cargo revenue management systems since the early 1990s that would generate minimum entry rates ('bid prices') for spot capacity were not popular with managers. Metrics such as load factors were often looked at because they were more tangible and credible than whether the system generated the highest transactional margins on local or connecting lanes (point-to-point vs origin-destination pairs with connections, often at constrained hubs). Furthermore, most systems in cargo revenue management operate at revenue level. As such, they are not able to assess what the net profitability of a booking with a spot rate request is. Airlines such as Air France KLM Martinair Cargo have addressed this, using home-grown analytics systems with ingested data from finance.

First-generation systems struggled with modularizing and aligning the business into medium-term and short-term. This is the different planning cycle for network and schedule compared to the commercial operations of selling and optimizing capacity closer to and up to departure, typically the last seven days. Within the booking cycle of these last days, a bid price or minimum entry rate would be calculated by the cargo RMS based on the pace of current bookings relative to historical bookings for that flight/lane profile. There were no good performance metrics and confidence levels, and often, the workflow was not automated. It would allow revenue analysts to override recommendation (and distort future historical data).

As older generation companies and technology often put on weight in terms of their heavy, slow, and antiquated processes and technology, so does their capability to adapt swiftly and capitalize on new opportunities. The systems were based on overnight batch calculations thus not in real time. And many executives did not believe in software packages that were relatively static and created rigid or archaic decision-making that did not reflect relationships in business (B2B). These systems are perceived to be inadequate to solve problems in crises and come with hefty subscription fees when the underlying business has fluctuating and unpredictable levels of activity (transactions).

What needs to be addressed? Air Cargo is a B2B industry and built around relationships. This requires any modern cargo revenue optimization to incorporate this in a smart logic. It requires a solution that looks past individual transactional data. But vendors have not built-in loyalty-based logic into more holistic business systems. They have also not been able to align the business models between the spot market and contract space because the operators

138 *Uses of AI and Emerging Opportunities in Commercial Management*

have not created a revenue model that bridges the two. There is no reasoning that harmonizes it today, but it is not inconceivable to design it.

Indeed, one can automate relationship-related business processes leading up to the point just short of transacting. CRM systems are the most used tools to handle that part of the sales function. And many can now support the transaction (digital commerce). But they do not handle the problem-solving part holistically. They take a snapshot in time with a limited business scope.

And while airlines sell spot capacity under one-off transactions, these same customers are the most important customers (forwarders) representing most of the annual contract business. They are thereby responsible for a large part of the revenues on the same flights, and moreover, on trade lanes as routings can be flexible. And these customers are global, with regional headquarters, supporting a myriad of local and global business from the airline's network perspective. In some markets, the carrier will help the forwarder in their business (shipping community), in others, the forwarder needs to help the airline to solidify commercial operations in those markets to get approval from network executives. And all this is even more complicated with capacity fluctuations and passenger aircraft. It became very hands-on with the managing of passenger freighters 'preighters' during the COVID-19 pandemic.

The reality is that in cargo revenue management you must be discriminatory, opportunistic, and sensitive to the overall relationships. And only small parts of this can be fully automated. Therefore, real-time pricing cannot optimize it all, as capacity commitments are important, too. This is because the identity and relationship with the freight forwarder matters as well. For instance, if you allow Willingness to Pay (WTP) to run the show, capacity may be decremented by a hot source market without allowing your key global strategic partner to cover their (network) needs. This always escalates above and beyond software.

15.3 Cargo's Changing Role

The cycles and complexity of removing and adding passenger freighters had never been more obvious than during the Covid-19 pandemic. The landscape shifted. But so did the profile of cargo as a key contributor to free cash flow and an important driver of the industry enabling eCommerce. It also closed a chapter on the generation of cargo revenue management and cargo RM packages. But this is not only related to the composition of capacity, but more so due to a new generation of players, distribution channels, people, and technologies and how relationships evolve.

This has overlapped with a flurry of newcomers and activity the venture capital (VC) market[2] has demonstrated in investment in startups in modern science. No less than 4,785 companies ventured into artificial intelligence (AI) and Machine Learning (ML) services in 2020, and 79% of companies surveyed in transportation have high expectations of 'more aggressive AI adoption' from modern providers.[3] In June 2022, former Seabury and

Accenture executives also launched a cargo commercial optimization startup in Amsterdam called Rotate.[4]

There is therefore an opportunity for a new generation of problem solvers in cargo using modern science on AI-enabled platforms, at a more holistic level. It would look beyond individual transactions and use logic that has multiple dimensions and KPIs, including loyalty and business objectives by trade lane or source market. That way, Singapore Airlines could – for instance – be more aggressive ex-Vietnam but drive higher margins in Jakarta-Singapore-Amsterdam where it faces less competition out of Indonesia. While dealing with the same freight forwarders with regional offices, it would balance the relational risk at headquarter level. It can demonstrate, with actual data, how much value it is driving for both the forwarder group and itself, but balance the interests.

15.4 Artificial Intelligence in Cargo Revenue Optimization

Depending on how you count there is a handful of traditional cargo RM vendors. Each relied on models and algorithms using fundamentally similar techniques. But this market is rapidly changing, and it is coming from the outside with more modern technology. It is around the application of AI, combining multiple decision-making layers and considerations, using richer data than had been available historically. This can also include loyalty and relationships and drive new pricing schemes thanks to computing power.

By 2021, science started to get cool. Also, the science used in digital commerce surpassed what had ever been used in air cargo revenue management, and even the passenger business. More modern, younger organizations and startups started hiring scientists that demonstrate the relative ease of using science once they define their business problem, scope, and business process.

15.4.1 Artificial Intelligence in Cargo Revenue Optimization

The science that was of interest to airlines like Cathay, IAG Cargo, Lufthansa Cargo, Cargolux, Qatar, and others was around dynamic pricing. Instead of relying on historical data, airlines started asking for solutions that could estimate willingness to pay per kilogram based on the observed market in real time. This was considered important and is now integrated into the automation of request-for-quote processes that can accelerate the booking process. Freight forwarders can enter a portal and enter the shipment, origin, destination, dimensions, and special handling details in an online request and obtain a quote in real time. The forwarder can then select a preferred option, click on it, and obtain a confirmation that is generated automatically.

The application of AI in dynamic pricing relies on ML. In order to solve the problem of recommending optimal spot rates to individual customers,

140 *Uses of AI and Emerging Opportunities in Commercial Management*

rich data and loop algorithms are required. The various dimensions and attributes of data required to feed the algorithms include:

- Business user-defined goals of profitability and market share.
- Aircraft capacity on selected (and alternative) routes in weight and volume.
- Estimated market capacity on like-for-like origin-destination or alternative routes.
- Required volume and weight.
- Estimated current market rate.
- Customer identity.
- Shipper identity.
- Commodity.
- Handling fees.
- Rate elasticity of demand (given supply/demand in the past and current market).
- Cost and margin data.

This list is simply for illustration as any granular dimension that is found to be statistically relevant through deep analytics will be used or can be trained to be used by the algorithms. Nonetheless, the results of dynamic pricing are promising and are preferred over the conventional bid price approach.

15.4.2 Allotment Management

Depending on the region, trade lane or freight forwarder in question, allotments (or 'allocations') are negotiated between the airline and the customer. These Block Sale Agreements (BSA) are essentially contracts under preferred rates. They guarantee that cargo space will be sold while providing the freight forwarder some certainty that their customers have supply chain and business continuity. The use of allotments fluctuates a great deal but has generally been in a bit of a decline as a business practice. The difficulty in allotments is that history is no longer a good predictor of future business, even for the entire supply chain. The shifts and micro-seasons are more pronounced. The forwarders often see ad-hoc variations in volumes and number of pieces, making them less reliable partners for the airline when they tender more or less cargo than initially booked. The question is therefore at what point in time it becomes certain what the final shipment details will look like. Herein lie the opportunities for AI.

As described in the previous question, the digitization of the supply chain and the potential of Air Cargo Community Systems is in accelerating and improving the quality of information exchanges. This drives efficiencies at each step but moreover throughout the supply chain. The AI models can assist in generating alerts about expected deviations to shipment volumes and weights or even number or pieces. Automatically having this analysis performed by machines to drive recommendations is important. For instance, as freight forwarders book shipments into their allocations, AI can assist to predict whether the allocations will be fully used or not. It can dynamically recommend the release of the remaining space or automatically trigger it. Other logic can be built in as well as part of smart commercial processes. For instance, forwarders can be sent an incentive to commit to the space or lose it, and forwarders may wish to pay a fee for the privilege. Alternatively, cargo carriers can allow AI to optimize the recommended contract rates as well as the best amount of allotment space by forwarder and lane. The benefit of using AI is that (1) more (what-if) scenarios can be run and faster, (2) the predictions will have high confidence level and not rely on human judgment, and (3) the adjustments can be made in real time, allowing for very dynamic and commercially optimal business operations. The fourth benefit is that the experience that is gained will improve results incrementally using ML.

15.4.3 Network Optimization

Network optimization in air cargo is similar to the passenger business except when it concerns freighters, which typically fly circular routes (multiple pick up and offloading points in a rotation). But in essence, the goal is to maximize the revenues and profits from the carriage of cargo across all combination of flights. This means that where cargo competes for space from outstations on flights to central or regional hubs and onwards to destination airports, the cargo that is accepted and flown each day on all flights combined should yield the highest profit. In practice, this goal is not achievable. It is the focus on the commercial side and that of cargo revenue management analysts, but often not the end reality. There are many reasons why little trade-offs are made each day to accommodate individual clients, provide preferential treatment to maintain relationships, or overcome operational constraints and cushion the unforeseen circumstances in passenger operations.

There are other reasons why sub-optimal commercial performance is acceptable. Even though profit is the end goal, the cargo business is characterized by B2B relationships, and airlines and freight forwarders cannot base all daily decisions on the profits of single flights. Also, it is generally preferred to utilize the weight and volume capacity that is available with the cargo at hand, even though they may not be the most profitable mix of shipments to fly that day. There are trade-offs that are made, and sometimes cargo is flown earlier because it had already been tendered and the cargo warehouse wants to clear backlog. The cargo terminal is also more focused on ensuring the optimal dimensional fit of cargo on pallets than the profitable mix. After all, they are operations people and may not have the information at hand with regard to the profit by shipment and how to load an aircraft as such. That is simply not realistic, also for weight and balance reasons.

Nonetheless, early generation cargo RM systems did offer some decision support for network optimization by discriminating access to capacity based

142 *Uses of AI and Emerging Opportunities in Commercial Management*

on the estimated value of cargo. It used the bid price approach described earlier. Modern computing and AI offer a completely new capability that is more powerful and allows cargo managers to achieve more, faster, leading to better results and improved planning for next seasons. One of the key benefits is that AI can work in real time, whereas older techniques require overnight calculations and uploads based on the data collection points in a booking cycle. Using AI, accurate and detailed data is available to work with in real time. What-if scenarios can be used to compare outcomes for shifts in network or capacity, providing instant views into expected profitability. Ultimately, KPIs and targets can be set (market share, load factor) for the AI to pursue and solve. The underlying logic can also be used to support decisions on upgauging, downgauging, rerouting, or which flights the cargo to assign to in case of irregular operations (IRROPS).

15.4.4 Business Level Optimization: Pax vs. Cargo

All airlines that operate as combination airlines struggle with tensions between the passenger and cargo business. They each have an interest to utilize the most payload and range capabilities of aircraft. On short haul flights operated by narrow-body aircraft, the constraints for cargo are usually based on volume. On long haul flights, even for wide-body aircraft, the constraint for the cargo business is the weight restrictions because of sector length. However, there are instances where the aircraft has the range and no weight but pure volume restrictions. For example, Air Canada operates five high-density Boeing 777-300ER aircraft with 458 seats to Paris. This leaves practically no space for cargo because of all the extra passenger bags.

Traditionally, and the fastest decision to make, is to restrict cargo tonnage to maximize the sales of seats on the passenger sides such that the range of the aircraft is safeguarded with maximum take-off weight (MTOW). These calculations are easy because the expected weight and volume of passengers and bags are more predictable than that for cargo, even when based on historical data. This is because cargo is not homogenous and trade in identical lanes can change in composition. For instance, on flights out of Seoul, South Korea, you can expect consumer electronics and chips for manufacturing, but this can shift when tuna from Japan is rerouted due to regional supply chain interruptions or when trade restrictions currently in place make that impossible. There are many shifts possible, mostly for economic but also market force reasons.

To protect or obtain more capacity for sale for the cargo division, the cargo people sit down with their passenger colleagues. Using historical data and forecasts produced by predictive analytics, they can present or construct internal business cases together. The debates are often over the reliability and confidence levels of the forecast and must be based on projected revenue as well as net profit (margin). Regarding the latter, assumptions must be made about the cross-charging of costs, such as incremental fuel, incremental

Cargo Commercial Management   143

handling costs, and potentially incremental costs related to longer turnaround costs. The finance department plays an important role, almost as a referee, both in providing and validating cost data and accounting assumptions.

The opportunities for AI at the business level are enormous. First, ML in advance analytics will decipher all the links, relationships, and trends that are potentially missed today at granular level. Imagine the missing information about cargo that did not get captured or carried because there was no space available in the past. Or the fact that because the departure times are 4 hours too early for cargo to be tendered and processed, the airline is not capturing cargo from one market on that lane but is not aware. Deep learning can map all the interdependencies and relationships between rates, cargo, schedule, forwarder, and other dimensions to estimate the value of the lost opportunities.

Second, AI can provide the smart automation required to solve the joint optimization problem. Once the goal is well defined, which can have multiple facets and be specific to each origin–destination market, deep learning and AI scripts can optimize the number of seats and ULD positions that should be reserved for passengers and which positions should be reserved for cargo. This would include the optimized weight and volume dedicated for cargo at net profitability to the airline level.

While this is a new application of AI at business level, some progress has been made, albeit on a more manual level using analytics. It is also only done where the low-hanging fruit is, which is typically on a handful of long-haul routes. For instance, Air Canada and Air Canada Cargo look at this for flights from Toronto to Seoul with the Boeing 777s. Air France KLM Cargo also concentrates this joint planning on routes over 6,000 nm. Airlines such as Air New Zealand and Qantas have relatively more of these cases, particularly on flights to London, UK and New York. The pacific flights have fewer constraints, depending on the season (summer posing more challenges). There are clear benefits in infusing real-time insights and predictions with high confidence levels to optimize decisions based on restricting or promoting the sale of seats to passengers or space for cargo carriage based on their respective revenue and margin contributions.

15.4.5 Focal Shift to Smart Sales Steering

Cargo sales is about optimizing both relationships and cargo revenues or profitability, depending on the context. And with new technology, cargo sales professionals can have all the insights they need to make informed decisions in front of the customer. Not only for a space request but to respond to the forwarder's business and their customers' (shippers) business needs. Other than the descriptive analytics they have today, they will eventually have more consumer-friendly and intelligent digital cargo assistants that will help make recommendations. For instance, India-based IBS Software has developed a sales App mobility module that supports sales and marketing teams at Korean

Air Cargo. According to IBS and Korean, the tool allows "maximum conversion of opportunities by providing real time access to customer profiles, customer analytics and capacity predictions to support Korean Air cargo operations" (AIthority, 2019).

Cargo loyalty is also already emerging from the company LoyaltyPlus (2022), based in Cape Town, South Africa. It will also include AI-based models to recommend better accrual and redemption propositions that drive business results and generate new customers. Figure 15.1 provides an overview of the scope of commercial optimization use cases that will contribute to a modernization of workflow, processes, and practices using AI.

These new AI programs in air cargo strategic sales will have two components:

First, they will be underpinned by a digital assistant for cargo sales professionals that does more than simply issuing price quotes and booking space. It will be a real assistant allowing them to build and develop business based on a deeper understanding of the market. Showing how demand conditions are evolving will help sales specialists target their business and automate aircraft deployment decisions based on real-time demand forecasts. This is how smart freighter planning or route development will be possible by using deep insights and business recommendations based on predictions with confidence.

The second component of cargo platforms will be crafty AI algorithms that look at the supply chain and air cargo holistically, ingesting real-time data and 'listening' to the market. The associated deep learning models will integrate with the digital assistant to 'push' recommendations to sales teams. The underlining analytics will incorporate at least:
- Manufacturing & sourcing shifts.
- Current market rates, capacity, and trends.
- Economic growth and commodity markets.

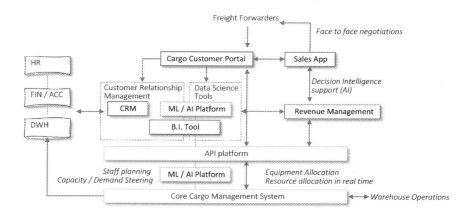

Figure 15.1 Modernization of cargo commercial practices using AI.

Cargo Commercial Management 145

- Ocean, rail and road feeder services capacity.
- Interest rates and foreign exchange prices.
- BSA vs. spot capacity commercial logic.
- Trade & border restrictions.
- New entrant freighter capacity.
- Freight forwarders launching in-sourced & leased freighters.
- Changes in alliance partner strategies (incl. JVs).
- Value-added service potential (e.g. temperature control, security, and live animal carriage).
- Space and revenue optimization across both freighter & passenger fleets.
- Circular flight vs. origin-destination network controls.

A tool like this would help cargo airlines sift through all the noise, solve problems, and produce compelling recommendations based on robust analytics. It will show the low-hanging fruit as well as harder-to-spot opportunities. All strategic and commercial logic starts with a unified goal. Salespeople like to know how to achieve it and how they can get support in finding opportunities through trends they cannot pick up manually.

Creating this workflow, identifying all possible data sources, and writing the set of rules to be executed using enterprise-level AI will power digital carriers and enable strategic sales efforts that will ultimately make airlines more commercially successful. Imagine having this available on a tablet. This is the foreseeable future.

15.5 Conclusions

Air cargo is a fundamental component in commercial aviation. It has traditionally been an industry that has lagged in the adoption of technology, particularly in automating commercial optimization. This chapter described some of the commercial capability gaps and highlights how the shift to eCommerce has necessitated new management techniques in real time. The second part of the chapter elaborated on new practices and opportunities by using advanced analytics, ML and AI to improve automated decision intelligence. Use cases such as dynamic pricing, dynamic allotment management, network optimization, and smart sales steering based on uncovering all macro-economic and micro-economic trends were described as the most promising areas for revenue, margin, market share, and customer service improvement. More integrated approaches at business level are recommended and likely become a common practice.

Notes

1 Freightwaves (2019) 'Flashback Friday: the history of air freight'. https://www.freightwaves.com/news/flashback-friday-the-history-of-air-freight.

146 *Uses of AI and Emerging Opportunities in Commercial Management*

2 VentureBeat (2021) 'Venture capitalists invested over 75 billion in AI startups'. https://venturebeat.com/2021/09/30/vcs-invested-over-75b-in-ai-startups-in-2020/.
3 CB Insights (2021) 'Top 100 AI startup, where are they now?'. https://www.cbinsights.com/research/2021-top-100-ai-startups-where-are-they-now/.
4 Stattimes (2022) 'CargoTech grows and welcomes its fourth member: rotate'. https://www.stattimes.com/air-cargo/cargotech-grows-and-welcomes-its-fourth-member-rotate-1346422.

Bibliography

AIthority (2019) 'IBS software has launched an integrated revenue management system at Korean air to boost cargo profitability'. https://aithority.com/machine-learning/ibs-software-has-launched-an-integrated-revenue-management-system-at-korean-air-to-boost-cargo-profitability/

Chitragar, V. *et al.* (2022) 'Artificial intelligence in air cargo system'. *SAE Technical Papers.* https://www.sae.org/publications/technical-papers/content/2022-26-0022/

Hoffmann, R. (2013) *Dynamic capacity control in air cargo revenue management.* Karlsruhe: KIT Scientific Publishing.

Rizzo, S.G. *et al.* (2019) *AI-CARGO: A data-driven air-cargo revenue management system.* Doha: Qatar Computing Research Institute (QCRI). https://arxiv.org/pdf/1905.09130.pdf

16 Human Resources Management

16.1 Human Resources Management Defined

Human resource management is the function in a company that is responsible for staff, well-being, and compensation. The basic functions of human resource management include planning, controlling, directing, and organizing company activities, utilization of workforce, recruitment, and staffing. In the airline business, safety is of the utmost important, and regulatory agencies also ensure that employees are trained and certified in the proper areas, such as handling dangerous goods, aircraft loading, and the piloting of aircraft. Similarly, ground staff and cabin crew need to pass training for certification.

Regarding organization structure, chief HR officers typically follow the directives of the executive management team. Airlines, however, have typically been structured around conventional functional pillars of operations, network and commercial planning, sales, finance, and HR. The advent of low-cost carriers following deregulation in the 1970s and even the introduction of the internet has not fundamentally altered airline organization design. New functions and roles have been added and embedded in the existing foundational framework. In fact, HR has not really had a big role in redesigning profoundly different airline organizations. In few cases, however, the separation of talent and build-up of a more diverse talent pool was necessary when tour operators launched in-house airlines (such as Thomas Cook in the UK), or when they were spun-off (such as Condor). Air Canada has also gone through a series of low-cost start-ups at arm's length (Zip, Tango, or leisure division Rouge). These shuffles created heavy workloads to manage staffing requirements, iron out union contracts, remove duplication and ensure the proper operating procedures and certifications were in place.

16.2 Airline HR and Recruitment Challenges

A 2018 survey of HR leaders conducted by Oracle uncovered that 58% indicated they were using AI in their hiring processes.[1] Later in that same year Deloitte, in their Global Human Capital Survey with 10,000 business leaders, observed that 71% believed AI was an important trend.[2] Only 31% said they

DOI: 10.4324/9781003018810-19

were ready to accept it. That changed when the COVID-19 pandemic hit in 2020.

Following the pandemic, there were several challenges in human resource management at airlines, airports, and even among suppliers. Not only had airlines laid off over 400,000 staff in 2021,[3] about 20–30% of the overall workforce decided to leave the industry according to Bloomberg.[4] And when travel started to return, many airports and airlines had to cancel thousands of flights due to workers that called in sick and had contracted COVID-19.[5] Some airlines were forced to increase the average pay to attract new hires.

The Great Resignation that commenced during the pandemic resulted in employers paying much more attention to employee well-being, in five categories: financial, mental health, social, physical, and career well-being. According to Forbes,[6] 62% of employees identified well-being benefits as key a key factor in deciding whether to apply for a new job. The shift to remote, and later hybrid work mode also disrupted many people, jobs, departments, and company cultures. It even changed the demands from Generation Z and other groups in the workforce. According to BrightPlan's 2021 Wellness Barometer, a survey concluded that over 80% of employees want support and guidance on mental health as well as personal finances.[7] Financial planning assistance and mental well-being had traditionally not featured on employee needs. It was evident that the workforce and dynamics had changed.

16.3 Toward AI in HR, Analytics and Automation

A 2018 analysis by McKinsey estimated that 56% of all hire-to-retire tasks could be automated with current technologies.[8] As AI technology advances, it will become capable of taking over even more HR functions that currently depend on employees. There have been several trends toward the adoption of analytics and analytics-driven automation in HR. Conventional use cases centered on staff planning, rosters, and absenteeism. It has been used in the passenger as well as the cargo business. For instance, providers like Data-iku even developed an application that generates graphical representations of conversational flows and can map activity within discussion groups to iden-tify (opinion) leaders. In cargo, workforce analytics and AI is used for cargo terminal planning and staff rosters, as described in Chapter 14. Table 16.1 provides an overview of the main use case categories and AI technologies used in AI that will be explored in this chapter.

Workforce analytics is the use of data-informed methods to improve work-force planning and management. As opposed to people analytics (discussed in the next chapter), workforce analytics takes a broader perspective on work in general instead of focusing solely on the people. The practice measures the impact of workforce behavior and related factors on overall business perfor-mance. During the pandemic, for the airlines that were even using work-force analytics, the approach, and metrics changed. Whereas previously it was about productivity and performance measured in commercial metrics (calls

Human Resources Management 149

Table 16.1 Overview of technologies and use cases of AI in HR

Function	Use Case	Technique Used	Tools Used
Staff planning	Ensure availability and productivity	Workforce analytics to measure absenteeism, productivity, patterns	Machine learning
Retention	Retain target level and quality of human resources	Workforce and conversational analytics; remuneration analytics with ingested salary data sets	Natural Language Processing (NLP) bot on-the-loop of chat platforms; ML to main benchmarks on compensation levels
Recruitment	Attract and assess suitable candidates	Automated document scanning and video interview collection and pre-assessment	Computer vision in video and NLP for analyzing interviewee response and non-verbal cues
Motivation	Increase staff motivation	Conversational analytics for sentiment analysis in combination with workforce analytics for attitude mapping	NLP bot on-the-loop of chat platforms; email content monitoring using ML to filter out key attitudes

handled, sales, and revenue per seat mile), analyses shifted toward attendance vs absenteeism, completion factors, process time (delays due to exponential growth in volumes), and turnover.

Workforce analytics data can be applied to three major categories: recruitment, retention, and talent management. Recruitment is discussed in the next section. In terms of retention, analytics in workforce can automatically run comparative analyses of market as well as internal compensation, do productivity checks over time and observe important patterns, or flag behaviors or early signs of employees that are looking for other opportunities or otherwise leaving the company.

Employees who are engaged tend to work harder. They frequently also stay with the same company for a long time. In addition, research by Gallup[9] highlights that companies with highly engaged employees make 21% higher profits and 17% more productive, when compared to others. So, employee engagement measurement is important and increasingly companies turn to software solutions for support in assessing and managing this. Some of these tools require employee engagement (surveys, frequent one-on-ones, exit interviews, run focus groups), whereas others are more subtle, and work based on derived insights from observing how people work. Retention rate and productivity metrics are often used but they are frequently after the fact and do not provide sufficient steering capability. Using organizational analytics

150 *Uses of AI and Emerging Opportunities in Commercial Management*

tools, supported by AI as discussed in Chapter 17, airlines can analyze how employees engage with their work and their colleagues to draw inferences on other matters like employee engagement, well-being, and attitude.

Regarding talent management, the third component, the tools available in workforce analytics help in establishing important milestones for performance checks, evaluations, or assess potential within a role or for other roles. Depending on the metrics used, these analytics can expose training requirements or potential areas in which there will be a lack of skills. This is aimed at identifying learning opportunities and shaping training programs. For instance, the time it takes a route analyst to assess demand forecasts on their routes and build a case for promotional fares can be an indicator of the overall understanding of the work and context. Measuring the time spent and functions used in a group of applications can be benchmarked against best practices maintained in the knowledge center.

All the use cases across all airline functions depend on what data is captured and how. If it involves multiple processes on a multitude of applications, this must be built in. For instance, in airline fleet planning, many teams and departments work together with finance to build scenarios and business cases. Measuring how these cases are solved and how capable the teams are in working together requires a subset of goals and metrics. Therefore, regarding performance or skills, what is captured depends on the objective of measurement and the benchmark used to evaluate the performance. This can be an overall case, or a subtask as part of the process. Therefore, this is somewhat of a gray area because there is potential bias in how performance is assessed or how the same work is completed differently by individuals in the same team. The person evaluating the performance does not necessarily have hard KPIs or metrics and is using personal judgment if they have not been pre-established. There is now validation of this and when this data is entered digitally, any model that is constructed to map or analyze it will assume the quality of the data is a given. As more people are added, new benchmarks can be established.

In the case of hybrid intelligence, as discussed in Chapter 20, assessing skills becomes easier because of the interaction between machine and AI. That is, human skills are required to complete tasks (data scientists writing script) and the time required from DevOps to results can be measured and benchmarked. The quality of the predictions can be measured, as well. So, the higher the interaction with technology, the better these analytics will be and the more useful they will become. This is a bit of a self-fulfilling prophecy, which nonetheless aids in the generation of ideas toward talent and training analytics.

Companies like Workday deploy more sophisticated technology to power their engagement measurement solutions, even underpinning the surveys. For instance, with their proprietary 'Workday Peakon Employee Voice', the intelligent listening technology is automated in that it can trigger it to ask the right questions at the right time to create more meaningful insights and

Human Resources Management 151

change. They can also allow people to compare their situation with other peers in the same or other industries through benchmarks. These solutions are typically integrated with human capital management (HCM) systems. They also provide integrations with Microsoft® Teams and Slack so that employees can receive alerts to answer questions right in the communication tools that their companies use.

The above approaches are effective mostly for items that are blatantly disruptive in a company and less for organization-related issues that people do not wish to speak up about. It also does not necessarily solve the fact that humans are often compelled to provide socially acceptable or desirable responses in order not to attract unwanted attention to themselves.

16.4 AI, Video, and Recruitment

In recruitment, automation can be used to scan and analyze CVs automatically or run scripts against social media profiles and content against criteria or red flags. In addition, comparing public profiles against obtained resumes can also generate shortlists for candidates, even against the existing current talent pool already employed. Some of the benefits include an accelerated recruitment cycle, reduced time requirements, and thus lower costs, but it may also help remedy race and gender bias.

According to Gartner,[10] only 21% of human resource leaders use data to "shape talent acquisition and recruiting strategies, improve employee engagement and inform other business decisions". But more data does not always mean more action and companies are not all reaping the benefits of investments in analytics. So, there are companies that have embarked on trying a different approach, using video for pre-screening candidates at larger scale.

The use of video calls and video in recruitment has become more commonplace since the Covid-19 pandemic. Now recruitment firms use videos submitted by candidates that contain the recordings of their responses to questions. Often, a time limit as well as deadline data is used. But AI is now used to capture, play, and interpret videos generated from candidates.

One such company that offers this solution is Myinterview, based in Israel. It was founded in 2016 based on the principle that traditional CVs were fast becoming obsolete.[11] The company developed machine learning and artificial intelligence models to enable faster and more effective hiring processes for HR teams. Myinterview customers include Marriott Hotels, Meta (Facebook), Billable, Agoda, and McDonald's.

The benefits that automated analysis of candidates' submissions brings include time savings of up to 70%. Recruiters can process and filter applications faster while benefitting from deeper insights that are necessary to match good candidates to open roles. The video component also allows recruiters to meet the people behind the resumes, while creating shorter and more efficient hiring funnels.

152   *Uses of AI and Emerging Opportunities in Commercial Management*

The information that is extracted from video is supported by models using AI. Natural Language Processing conducts text analysis to identify keywords and phrases to uncover personality learnings. It also looks for soft skills, certain vibes, and alignment with the company goals. But it can also ensure that bias is mitigated by filtering out gender or racial profiling.

It does this by training a machine learning model using a database of thousands of interviews. These interviews were rated by different behavioral psychologists using a set of specific criteria. By doing so, Myinterview, for instance, finds that these models reveal important data that is otherwise missed by focusing exclusively on the text in resumes. Conversation and expressions add many dimensions to a person.

Other than saving time, using AI in analyzing applicant videos also generates new value that is important in today's competitive labor market. There are benefits for the candidates, too. The company can process more applications and provide feedback to job applicants quicker.

Modern recruitment tools with video analysis using AI are used by firms such as Google and Facebook, but even recruitment outsourcing process firms for airlines such as Air Canada. The added advantage of this technology is that it can handle large volumes at scale, and it is thus a great candidate to serve large online job boards and marketplaces. The leaders in this space are Spark Hire, Jobvite, TestGorilla, CodeSignal, and Workable.

16.5 Other AI Use Cases in HR

Workforce analytics uses historical data collected either by HR in a company to improve operations and ultimately financial performance. There are different software solutions and statistical tools that allow measuring, characterizing, and organizing employee data, but the basic steps of the process are similar:

- Identifying a problem or pain point that must be solved.
- Deciding on what data is necessary to understand and solve the problem.
- Building the workforce analytics dashboard to visualize the operations.
- Identifying an appropriate benchmark to assess company results.
- Deciding on the right analysis method and report your results.
- Develop and deploy AI to automate the use of ingested insights into automated tasks.

There are many use cases for applied AI that are in its infancy or are being considered for testing. Not only do end models have to be tested, but the ingestion into best practices also requires careful consideration. Potential goals to which AI can contribute better performance include:

- Removal of favoritism in promotions or influence of informal powers by using objective metrics and analytics.

Human Resources Management 153

- Removing bias in performance appraisal by looking at fact-based results against agreed objectives and metrics, including reducing the optics of academic degrees and awards by reviewing performance over qualifications based on paper.
- Background verification with the help of AI (automated process).
- Predicting burnout by analyzing complex performance, sentiment, and attitude data.
- Knowledge creation and management, such as capturing intelligent conversations and intellectual property-related ideas.

16.4 Conclusions

This chapter discussed the opportunities of artificial intelligence in human resources in aviation in recruitment, retention, employee engagement, and well-being. It concluded that AI is slated to empower workers to dedicate more time to tasks that require a human touch, relative to processes that can be automated. It demonstrated that AI can assist in the early stages of recruitment or candidate screening by deploying algorithms that can help to diversify the candidate pool while ensuring the removal of bias. The chapter further highlighted additional use cases where AI can also. For instance in overcoming the negative effect personal relationships humans have by ignoring favoritism, which often impacts when and how people are considered for new positions or promotions. Overall, AI will accelerate many of the HR functions and tasks while solidifying an objective and diverse workplace.

Notes

1 Forbes (2019) https://www.forbes.com/sites/tomdavenport/2019/02/10/ai-and-hr-a-match-made-in-many-companies/#1faa8cf83cd3.
2 Deloitte (2018) 'Global human capital survey'. https://www2.deloitte.com/insights/us/en/focus/human-capital-trends/2018/ai-robotics-intelligent-machines.html..html#endnote-sup-3.
3 Kelly, J. (2021) 'Airlines lost over 400,00 workers'. *Forbes.* https://www.forbes.com/sites/jackkelly/2021/02/01/airlines-lost-over-40000-workers-united-airlines-announced-another-14000-jobs-may-be-lost/?sh=7c11029624b3.
4 Bloomberg (2020) 'Jobs are being wiped out at airlines, and there's worse to come'. https://www.bloomberg.com/news/articles/2020-07-23/400-000-jobs-lost-at-airlines-during-coronavirus-pandemic.
5 Koenig, D. (2022) 'After wave of cancellations, Delta sees recovery in 2022', *ABC News.* https://abcnews.go.com/Business/wireStory/delta-loses-408-million-8000-employees-hit-infection-82240726.
6 Meister, J. (2022) 'Top ten HR trends for the 2022 workplace, *Forbes.* https://www.forbes.com/sites/jeannemeister/2022/01/05/top-ten-hr-trends-for-the-2022-workplace/?sh=6c06474a3006.
7 Brightplan (2021) '2021 Wellness barometer survey'. https://www.brightplan.com/2021-wellness-barometer-survey.
8 McKinsey & Company (2018) 'Human resources in the age of automation'. https://www.mckinsey.com/capabilities/people-and-organizational-performance/our-insights/the-organization-blog/human-resources-in-the-age-of-automation.

154 *Uses of AI and Emerging Opportunities in Commercial Management*

9 Gallup (2017) 'State of the American workplace'. https://www.gallup.com/workplace/238085/state-american-workplace-report-2017.aspx.
10 Gartner(2022)'Makesmarterworkforceplanningandbusinessdecisionswithtalentan-alytics'. https://www.gartner.com/en/human-resources/insights/talent-analytics.
11 MyInterview (2022) https://www.myinterview.com/.

Bibliography

Dataiku (2019) 'Use cases for AI in human resources'. ebook. https://content.dataiku.com/ai-in-hr
Eubanks, B. (2022) *Artificial intelligence for HR*. New York: KoganPage.
Ferrar, J. *et al.* (2021) *Excellence in people analytics*. New York: KoganPage.
Workday (2022) 'Workday peakon employee voice'. https://www.workday.com/en-us/products/employee-voice/overview.html

Part 3

Artificial Intelligence and Organization

Part 3 of this book reveals a novel and promising application of AI beyond human resource management into organization design. It also elaborates on how AI technology can help overcome internal intra-organizational barriers and create new value at enterprise level. It delves into the use of integrated, composite, and Enterprise AI as tools and systems that will enable new organization forms and business execution models.

Part 3 is structured as follows:

Chapter 17 addresses AI as a tool in airline organization design.
Chapter 18 delves into composite AI, Enterprise AI use cases and benefits.

DOI: 10.4324/9781003018810-20

17 AI and Organization Design

17.1 Introduction

Organization design is concerned with how functions, departments, job roles, and human talent fit together to use resources and deliver the outcomes necessary to achieve company goals. In its most simplistic form, it is displayed graphically with organigrams (organization charts) that show how the company is divided into subsidiaries or divisions, departments, and to which individuals the people or departments report to. Organization design is a specialist field within business administration and there is abundant research on how company performance and organization relate, as well as which type of company structure is best suited depending on its geographical or demographical make-up or in which industry it is. For airlines, this has typically been quite straightforward, as they have been principally designed around their operating nature, and less as customer-facing service companies. As such, airlines have global headquarters for the main (corporate) functions while operations are geographically spread out from one main or two or more regional smaller bases.

The purpose of this chapter is to briefly discuss organization structure design as part of transformational business models in commercial aviation. The main point that is made is that the enabling capabilities of modern technologies drive new organization design, which in turn determine new talent strategies in aviation. This is because the technology can do at enterprise level what humans with traditional skill sets could not. It explains why we used to group people with training in specific disciplines in more traditional functions together, such as marketing, pricing, revenue management, sales, and network planning. I will show that there is a need to let go of specific specialists to enable them to become more strategic across the airline as an enterprise, by simplifying and automating some of the more conventional jobs, roles, and system functions. We can elevate the workforce and execute modern business models by taking advantage of enterprise-level artificial intelligence (AI) platforms. For instance, somebody who is specialized in placing digital advertising content and improving its ROI will be able to move up and manage an AI-driven customer experience booking platform

DOI: 10.4324/9781003018810-21

that is automating how inspired customers engage with and get exposed to personalized content in social commerce communities. In short, the MarTech part can be automated within a tactical platform that becomes more strategic, while lower-level tasks that are more repetitive can be automated and managed based on exceptions. At more strategic levels around network and product propositions, even more can be done to give airlines a different purpose to fulfil.

The starting point of organization is always up for debate. Does company strategy determine organization strategy? Does organization strategy determine organization structure? Does the existing talent pool determine organization structure? Either way, I am more of the opinion that future technology drives the execution of new business models and has a disproportional (but positive) influence or bearing on organization design, because the design is part of the strategic execution. It is the way the outcomes and benefits are brought to people and customers, and how customers service themselves (-self-service). I argue this because of how we engage with customers now, that is, digitally, and through the Internet of Everything (IoE), otherwise known as Internet of Things (IoT).

Now, the technology is not invented or created in isolation. The technology itself is based on overcoming today's obstacles and hurdles of things we cannot do, not make, or bring to customers in ways we envision. In short, it is invented to bring new benefits and solve more problems. Therefore, the critical element in this dynamic is ongoing research in computing, programing, and conversation between thought leaders. Without research, whether academic or commercial, we simply do not make progress.

Going back to organization design, we need to be aware of fundamental design principles, such as structuring an airline company around (1) specialization, (2) coordination, knowledge, and competence, (3) control and (4) commitment, and innovation and adaptation. Specialization is typically linked to decentralized organizations with local excellence centers. Organizations structured around control and commitment tend to depict those with big central headquarters. As this chapter will demonstrate, Enterprise AI can help airlines design organizations that combine all these into a holistic paradigm that serves customers better.

17.2 Airline Design Challenges

It is useful to take a case of one airline that has a strong functionally oriented architecture and shed light on it from a modern angle. KLM has done well during the pandemic. In 2020 their revenue fell 54% but they were able to cut costs by 46%, limiting EBITDA to (€75m). A fully executable turnaround plan was developed in only ten weeks.

It was KLM's ability to pivot its organization and work with its stakeholders that led to these good results. Their organizational structure allows department heads to rationalize costs and maintains a corps of experts to

158 *Artificial Intelligence and Organization*

accelerate change on the cost side. This is achieved by a strict hierarchy that keeps certain managers directly accountable for specific business issues.

The KLM organization is supported by three pillars. One is maintaining sensible financial policies like paying almost its bills in 85 local currencies to help to save millions. Strong network initiatives help too, such as using the airline's relationship with Philips, a medical equipment and consumer electronics company. During the pandemic, KLM used its relationships to create an air bridge with China and pivoted its business and operations toward emerging opportunities swiftly. The final pillar is cargo and engineering, since the airline's technical division service aircraft for third parties, this part of the organization generates revenue even if KLM does not even operate a single flight.

The three pillars together supported a skeleton network for KLM during the COVID-19 pandemic. They maintained service to 90% of European destinations, although with only 50% frequency. Sufficient density supported network reach, and almost no permanent staff were furloughed.

The Dutch flag carrier's organization comes with drawbacks though. Like Lufthansa, Cathay Pacific, Qantas, Air Canada, easyJet, Ryanair, and other similarly organized carriers, they have isolated 'factories' in the airline. And while these factories are great for cost control, they do not facilitate the commercial agility and innovation necessary for successful revenue generation. This matters because controlling costs can only impact profitability to the extent that the airlines, already lean organizations, currently spend money.

The upside of generating profitability through revenue growth however is effectively unlimited. And since almost all the factories touch or impact the end-customer they each have a role to play in this side of the profit and loss accounts.

17.3 Airline Progress

After the 2007–2009 global financial crisis the world's most successful airlines were those that addressed their governance. Ed Bastian at Delta, IAG's Willie Walsh (head of the airline trade association IATA at the time of writing this book), Alan Joyce of Qantas, and then Air Canada's CEO Călin Rovinescu made change happen by insisting on faster decision cycles and higher quality teams.

Madrid-based IAG, who own the Aer Lingus, British Airways, Iberia, and Vueling brands among others, are particularly well-known for tight governance. Australian Qantas is, too. But even within these airlines, the various departments don't work together when it comes to enhancing profitability or customer experience. On FlyerTalk, an Internet bulletin board, it is a meme that any British Airways 'enhancement' announcement will certainly cause pain for passengers.

AI offers a solution, but not within the current structures. AI and machine learning are often touted as definitive solutions to airline challenges.

Unfortunately, these technologies will fall short because in the current organizational environments even if decisions are data-driven the technology will be too laser-focused to spot the hidden patterns and insights that traditional computational methods miss because the goals are not holistically defined.

Current airline organizations will not meet future business needs or facilitate recovery post-COVID-19. At least, not if airlines are to reach their potential. This is because airlines need better organizational analytics.

17.4 Organizational Analytics

At KLM and most other airlines, the organization structure is not based on data about the design of the organization but on a functional structure that had been in place for decades. How the structure performs or impacts the business performance is not measured either. The accounts show profit or loss but are silent on how this was created by the company's organization itself, i.e., the processes are not measured.

So, what is the problem? An organigram is not an organization, and it is not how people work either. Real organizations are messy, and people tend to talk to each other independent of reporting lines. But org charts do show how goals are transferred for execution, that is how the box-like factories become a problem. The most important issue is that breaking down a complex process into existing departments leads inevitably to information loss. This leads to a further problem, when shielded from other units the frame of reference changes, meaning there is no logical sequential system and neither AI nor machine learning methods can find the links that humans miss if another silo's data is invisible to end models that are to bring benefits to customers.

Airlines will need to use organizational analytics to actively understand how their organization impacts their performance if they wish to implement AI at enterprise levels. Or simply to improve organizational and business performance today first. In practice, this means airlines need to understand how each job and task is related to another person's job to see how the two add costs and contribute value to the end customer and the bottom line. Essentially this is also about taking Six Sigma to another level using AI. However, Six Sigma was more related to identifying causal relationships to solve problems, for instance, why certain parts in factories came out defective.[1] AI and deep learning can do a great deal more, provided data is collected first.

There are two ways in which AI can help airline organization design. First, it can be used to collect data on people and how people work together and complete processes to achieve results. Secondly, machine learning can interpret the insights and generate prescriptive analytics on how to better design the airline's organizational structure. Companies like re:config in Norway have specialized in this but we have not witnessed the application of this or similar solutions in the airline industry.[2]

160　*Artificial Intelligence and Organization*

Using AI for data-driven organization design consists of three overall workstreams, that is

1   Mapping the current organization. This is concerned with visualizing the workings of the organization today by mapping which individuals work together and how. The insights are obtained from telephone, text messages, corporate chat (e.g., Slack), and email. In order to do this, language and sentiment is inferred using AI models in combination with Natural Language Processing (NLP). Morrison (2015) developed software that generates different types of visualizations of organizations using colors and easy-to-interpret diagrams that show the makeup of a company and how the value is generated throughout the types of hierarchies. It was not possible to obtain permission in time to procure illustrations for this book, unfortunately.
2   Identifying a more suitable organization. This involves the machine learning model that identifies patterns and maps them to the current organization design to highlight mismatches or overlaps. Another end model recommends a new structure based on how people work and the processes, and tools, they use.
3   Integrate planned Enterprise AI applications. This is about integrating planned changes to the value chain within the firm. An airline could launch new service products or a digital service for which the execution involves multiple departments. An example is the launch of a separate premium Economy cabin. An additional model can use synthetic (created) data to help optimize the integration of this in an improved organizational structure.
4   Implement the new organization. This is part of the change management and applied psychology techniques the airline chooses to use.

The capabilities that exist, such as re:config, can be enhanced by introducing sentiment-based optimization that measures which individuals and personalities match better in teams, while removing bias, favoritism, or other diversity-related risks, as discussed in Chapter 16.

17.5 Potential Use Cases

A data-driven approach to organization design using AI has many valuable use cases and can help satisfy people, organizational, and business requirements provided the company is goal-centric and the objectives are clearly defined. Below are a few potential use cases for the application of AI-base organizational design tools:

•   Uncovering new value by combining departmental processes and optimizing them around a common goal, to run faster and smarter based on observed work and collaboration analytics. In other words, the solution could identify use cases for Enterprise AI (refer Chapter 18).

AI and Organization Design 161

- Better group people and teams based on observed dynamics and personalities.
- Assign work colleagues to optimize healthy climates and avoid interpersonal conflict while stimulating creativity.
- Remove bias when assigning teams to managers by highlighting what works based on work practices around people.
- Design new organizations in preparation for mergers or acquisitions by performing organizational analytics around new or common goals.
- Perform comparative analyses of organization to learn from cultures and enable people to work using their practices and languages, also for M&A due diligence.
- Remove favoritism by superiors in team creation by allowing employees that work well together to create teams together.

The list of potential use cases is much longer, especially if we look at evolving organizations impacted by emerging technology and required skills. In that context, AI in organization design will be very powerful in combination with Enterprise AI, discussed in the next chapter. Enterprise AI stacks departmental AI 'problem solvers' (such as market analytics, trends, demand generation, ancillary, revenue management, fleet, finance, aircraft acquisition, and slot requests) on top of each other and compares this to a higher overall logic (the end model) that integrates all workflows along a common goal. It takes the customer's perspective of how airline products and services are received, perceived, and used, as well as where and when. Then there is room for further monetization of augmented data hubs that can be created around these digital footprints as each touch point could ingest valuable insights into consumer behavior. However, it will need to align well with how people work and whom they communicate with the most to achieve their results, which is where data-driven organization design comes in.

The types of organizations that AI can design will simply be better for the employees and the customers, for example by enabling flights scheduling, ticket, and other sales based on the day and time a passenger arrives rather than departs. I can foresee an airline organization which changes the day-to-day tasks for most people working at airlines and where there are multidisciplinary experts. That sounds more like the future to me. Especially with Generation Z gradually entering the workforce.

17.5 Conclusions

There is a lot of room for commercial evolution and differentiation by enabling new airline organizations designed with the help of AI. This chapter outlined how AI can support and improve organizations. It first elaborates on the field of organization design and then discusses airline design challenges. It then shows how the use of machine learning in workforce and workflow analytics leads to organizational analytics that can drive better organizations

162 *Artificial Intelligence and Organization*

using AI. The chapter then concludes by listing potential use cases of data-driven organization design coupled with applied Enterprise AI across workflows that help design modern airline organizations which combine people, processes, and modern technology in a high-touch–high-tech manner.

Notes

1 Six Sigma Daily (2022) 'What is six sigma'. https://www.sixsigmadaily.com/what-is-six-sigma/.
2 re:config (2022) 'Reconfig designs organizations from the ground up'. https://reconfig.no/.

Bibliography

Anderson, C. (2015) *Creating a data-driven organization*. Cambridge: O'Reilly Media.
Burton, R. (2020) 'New trends in organization design', *Journal of Organization Design*, 9, p. 10.
Morrison, R. (2015) *Data driven organization design*. London: KoganPage.
OrgVue (2022) https://www.orgvue.com/solutions/
re:config (2022) https://reconfig.no/
Slinger, G. (2014) 'Will organization design be affected by big data?', *Journal of Organization Design*, 3(3), pp. 31–39.
Stanford, N. (2007) *Guide to organization design*. London: Profile Books.

18 Enterprise, Composite AI and the Real-Time Organization

18.1 Introduction to Enterprise AI

Previous chapters have concentrated on functions within airlines and how they can use artificial intelligence to solve problems and automate processes in each of those areas in a smart way using data. Enterprise AI takes this to another level by integrating functions that support workflows that cut across the organization, especially in areas such as planning or the different parts of the company that have interactions with customers at different touch points in their journey.

Enterprise AI can help airlines design organizations that serve customers better by allowing an optimal fit between customer needs and wants and delivering on its promises in real time. This is because the underlying organization is flexible enough to detect and respond to customers and what they want. Not only when they are planning to travel or plan their experiences but also when they are in transit, in-flight, or anywhere during their journey. Recommendations-based offers and servicing requests in changing contexts in real time dictate a different execution from the organization. The servicing aspect is increasingly important as customers demand more control, convenience, and flexibility or room for spontaneity. Previous chapters of this book have highlighted how artificial intelligence is driving this agility. They contain use cases in individual functional areas where large volumes of data can be used not only for operational efficiencies but also to improve context-driven sales by offering products and services that are relevant. The chapter on retailing (Chapter 11) speaks to this and related opportunities.

Enterprise AI applications will be increasingly important because of three trends, that is (1) the evolution to real-time selling and servicing, (2) increasing desire for personalization, and (3) higher levels of instant flexibility. While the consumer demands or wishes are clear, there is tremendous work to be done and novel technologies required to make that happen at enterprise level. It is therefore important to explore what applications at enterprise AI level would generate the most value.

DOI: 10.4324/9781003018810-22

164 *Artificial Intelligence and Organization*

18.2 Enterprise AI Described

Enterprise AI refers to a category of enterprise software that uses advanced artificial intelligence techniques to drive digital transformation across all departments of a company. It is essentially a higher level of smart alignment and even integration of logic that allows business processes and workflow to work in tandem to deliver a common goal. These goals are higher-level goals than, for instance, customer retention within loyalty, or controlling revenue dilution on specific flights within RM. From a business standpoint, it is difficult to do that because defining and agreeing on these higher-level goals is a challenge. It is also not simple to do at a high level. For example, the goal could be 'maximized enterprise profitability', but that may dictate several trade-offs between divisions (e.g., maintenance and engineering, loyalty, corporate investments and asset management, and finance) that themselves have their targets, CSFs and KPIs by which they are measured). Enterprise AI can help balance these trade-offs, but only if humans are able to identify which goals can be adjusted by which set of business rules and work closely with models to understand how they get to their predictive results. This requires techniques within AI, which are grouped under Explainable AI and Hybrid AI, the topics of Chapters 19 and 20. Once these goal-centric business rules are known and agreed on by people, they can be written into code for AI (algorithms), trained with data and tested. But that is almost the end game. Working with big data is where all the complexity starts.

From a technical standpoint, Enterprise AI involves the development and deployment of a technology stack at scale. This can be done for one or more use cases. But to develop an effective airline enterprise AI application, it is necessary to aggregate data from across many enterprise information systems. That includes commercial systems, planning and operational systems, finance systems, and all databases that are housing transactional and other data. Today, almost all applications that are used on wider enterprise infrastructure generate data, and it is making data management more complex.

If we include inflight operations and sensory experiences, even sensor networks (seats, tray tables, cabin movement, and climate) must be connected to provide a (near) real-time view of the extended enterprise. This is how we would be able to recommend merchandise for sale depending on what customers are shopping for in their seat using either their phone through Bluetooth on the IFE screen, or the IFE screen itself when a customer is logged in with a loyalty account (or creates one). The connectivity is one thing, but the enterprise application of this level of personalized experience requires more than just data. And it may have to operate close to the source through Edge AI, as discussed in Chapter 22.

The velocity in data is already dramatic today. The data sets across an airline rapidly amount to hundreds of petabytes, even exabytes for an airline the size of British Airways. The required ability to ingest and aggregate so much data from so many sources (millions of endpoints) at a high frequency is complicated by the need to process the data at the rate it arrives and to use it in real time to run other processes and applications. It is increasingly argued that this type of scale requires 'elastic distributed' processing capability that only modern cloud platforms and supercomputers can deliver. It is for this reason that, as a first step, airlines such as Air Canada and Finnair prioritize the relocation of enterprise data in a data lakehouse to the cloud. Once the data is there, other layers towards enterprise AI application can be built. That is a long journey.

Today, there are many products that are useful. Many claim to be full 'AI platforms', such as Snowflake, AWS IoT, Databricks, Hadoop, Cassandra, Cloudera, or DataStax. But there is no product in the foreseeable future that offers the full scope or functionality required to operate a full airline enterprise AI application. Most of the obstacles in this space are represented by the multitude in data types, data interconnections, and processes that act on the data that is associated with multiple entities (for instance, the customer and the supplier). This creates many distractions in trying to structure data and should not be the focus of application developers. Therefore, companies like C3 have proposed the model–driven architecture,[1] which elevates the task to a model (such as customer) while automating the integration of data types and independent of data interconnections or other data structure dependencies with the help of other software products.

18.3 Composite AI Described

Many predictive and prescriptive analytics applications require different approaches or techniques to use machine learning and artificial intelligence effectively. They are often built on different technologies and development languages, such as Python, Jupyter Notebooks, R, Scala, and DIGITS. There are also extensible curations of machine learning libraries such as Amazon Machine Learning, AzureML, Caffe, TensorFlow, and Torch. These are pre-built algorithms a developer can use for common tasks (time–series analysis, forecasting to name but two). Using multiple AI tools for building applications to solve problems toward an end goal is what composite AI is about.

Composite AI combines different AI techniques to achieve more with better results. It offers two main benefits in the short term: (1) dealing with multiple sets of 'small data', and (2) helping to expand the scope and quality of AI applications through increased generalization. This generalization helps to abstract mechanisms so that they can be elevated to enterprise level, which essentially requires a set of composite AI applications.

Composite AI has been used in aerospace to predict and assess vibrational frequencies in wing structures of different materials, including the use of composites. Shallow neural networks were used using a Python script in combination with a MATLAB design tool.[2] Aircraft manufacturer Airbus also highlights the importance of using multi–disciplinary artificial intelligence in aircraft design and operations. It uses composite AI to optimize

166　*Artificial Intelligence and Organization*

solutions for complex constrained problems to enable decision making. In the maintenance area alone, the following technologies and applications are used in combination[3]:

- Knowledge extraction: Extracting value from unstructured documents (notes).
- Computer vision: Transforming images and video into objects and activities based on deep-learning detection and decision-making.
- Anomaly detection: Finding hidden patterns in data.
- Conversational assistance: Designing natural language-interaction systems to query databases and pull up information that can be used in analytics.
- Autonomous flight: Enabling the next generation of aerial vehicles with new capabilities.

18.4　Airline Organization Design Using AI

Composite AI can help deliver toward the promise of enterprise AI. And given how enterprise AI is executed, it can help design new airline organizations. This is because the logic of workflow and business processes follow the logic of where human intelligence should enable but also assist AI applications. Chapter 20 discusses this field in more detail, which is called hybrid intelligence. It concentrates on maintaining and improving human-AI interaction.

So, how do we design an airline organization that can best execute its strategy and take advantage of Enterprise AI? By combining departmental processes and optimizing them around a common goal, to run faster and smarter. In other words, the solution lies in using Enterprise AI to guide organization design.

Enterprise AI stacks departmental AI 'problem solvers' (such as market analytics, trends, demand generation, ancillary, revenue management, fleet, finance, aircraft acquisition, and slot requests) on top of each other and compares this to a higher overall logic (the 'end model') that integrates all workflows along a common goal. It takes the customer's perspective of how airline products and services are received, perceived, and used, as well as where and when. Then there is room for further monetization of augmented data hubs.

18.5　Enterprise AI Use Case: The Digital Assistant for (Airline) Experiences

As mentioned, enterprise AI will enable new use cases that are complex to construct and execute from a technical point of view. They are very intuitive and easy to understand from a customer standpoint, which is how the end goals are envisioned. Creative innovation is about bridging the gap between novel use cases and identifying the practical mechanisms and tools that can make it happen. One such use case involves empowering the customer to design and use a digital assistant that interacts with an airline's set of digital assistants on top of a recommendations-based marketplace of experiences. It can inspire shoppers, grow airline profits, and solidify customer relationships and loyalty. Figure 18.1 provides a simplified illustration of how AI problem solvers can be stacked on Enterprise AI to drive the ultimate relevance, coherence, and consistent personalized offering based on real-time behavioral analytics and procurement of relevant offerings. The remainder of the chapter will explore this in the context of creative airline commercial innovation.

According to Expedia,[4] web browsers are looking at more sites than they used to. In 2015, the average person surfed through 38 sites for travel experience planning, compared with eight sites ten years ago. With the proliferation of further fragmentation, this number has likely gone up. To win a shopper's business, web retailing platforms need to be more compelling than ever to inspire the shopper to stick around and buy.

Unfortunately for airlines, their current Internet Booking Engines are mainly lackluster, based on legacy 'from > to' technology that does not represent the way people shop for travel in the real world. True retailing may require an experience marketplace with attractive window displays as well as well-stocked virtual shelves. An inspirational shop is full of exciting and interesting things to touch, experience, and buy, with more on offer than the owner's own products and more than just one shelf. Airlines who want to be real retailers may need to become lifestyle businesses and avoid being seen as merely selling seats in a plane and letting customers figure out what is included or important not to miss. The way airlines offer products could be based more on how people shop in the real world rather than stackable sequences that resemble how airline distribution was structured since the 1960s.

Building social proof into the retailing experience will be important too, as consumers gain confidence to buy when they see believable insights from

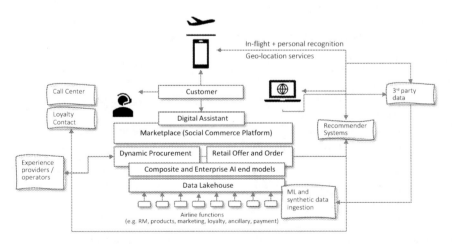

Figure 18.1 Enterprise AI application on marketplace with digital assistants. Illustrative

168   *Artificial Intelligence and Organization*

third-party influencers they trust. Hotel chains like Accor now include Trip Advisor ratings in their booking engines and airlines could show similar things, including passenger photos, tweets, videos, and trip reports, the list is limited only by their imagination. We can stream it live, as well.

Airlines creating such an experience marketplace will need to figure out how to play around with the options, trading off flight price against other travel spend and any commission earned from partners, a shopper's previous brand loyalty, and many other attributes.

18.5.1 Content and Control

Shoppers want more content than airlines offer today, and the shopping experience is not well aligned with how flights and the current ancillaries are sold. Airlines start with a schedule, constructing an origin–destination pair, departure time, and price from there. Travel or experience shoppers on the other hand start with why and where they want to be, and what they want to do. Some may have a specific experience in mind, but others choose either a beach, a mountain, or a city with the exact location a secondary decision. Other important things shoppers bear in mind are weather, distance, budget, and maximizing their time at the destination, which may be based more on arrival time rather than departure.

Shoppers also want more control over how content is delivered to them and to choose which third-party sources they trust. They need a digital assistant that automates the heavy lifting of search, profiling, and many recommendations into a simplified, customizable user interface. Nonetheless, the digital assistant will need to work in tandem with Enterprise AI applications that optimize the delivery and fulfilment of content to the screens where customers engage with the airline. And the experience has to be consistent based on the individual customer, their relationship and loyalty status, and other personal and location-based factors.

In essence, the Enterprise AI layer ensures and harmonizes how all offers and orders are presented to the customer along the business rules of

- Customer experience and intimacy and up to the latest technological standards.
- Consistency and recognition based on the goals of loyalty management.
- Marketing and branding.
- Commercial objectives of pricing and revenue management.
- Payment method and cost of content partners (commissions).

18.5.2 Creative Content Creation

Pushing airline approved content to shoppers is not the sole function of the marketplace. A good marketplace will make it worthwhile for shoppers and travelers to create their own content and stick around, and for retailers to join the marketplace without the airline telling them what to do. This does

Enterprise, Composite AI & The Real-Time Organization 169

not only give the social validation mentioned before to other shoppers, but it also increases the power of the marketplace at low cost by offering a more complete range of services without any high-cost centralized organization or the costs associated with centralizing content to build static products for sale.

Such content has a third benefit too, it generates deep data that modern machine and deep learning algorithms can use to find trends and patterns that airlines would not see otherwise. To address privacy and GDPR concerns, content creation can be an opt-in process. So, how will airline experience marketplaces work?

Experience marketplaces of the future will be like an Amazon of travel. On top of a well-designed selling platform, non-airline travel service providers will be able to make their own listings without any coordination with the airline. Virtual reality interfaces will be a given, too. AirAsia's super-app is a good example but is still more centralized yet fragmented from a browsing and shopping experience. The booking path is also pre-set, and not user defined. For full impact, the platform will be needed to work on modern aircraft. The A320neo, A330neo, and A350 families are ready to go with each having high-capacity technical backbones and communications capabilities able to handle the necessary data processing. The digital ecosystem announced by Airbus on 14 June 2022 is a good illustration of work in this area that will unlock new use cases, partnerships, and collaborative arrangements.[5]

At the back end, the platforms will need five components powered by AI to work:

- Input layers with airline's own, third-party, and live-streaming content.
- Output layers of recommendations relevant to a single shopper.
- Customer segmentation rules and filter engines using deep learning and composite AI.
- Optimization layers incorporating loyalty, pricing, revenue management, and other commercial (sub)rules, all cost factors, linked into a measurable and meaningful end metric like share of wallet, using composite AI and enterprise AI applications tapping into an enterprise data lakehouse.
- Integration with order and offer management systems, plus revenue accounting, using machine learning and AI.

If the experience marketplaces of the future are open-source, open-standard, and peer-to-peer they are likely to deliver better long-term results to airlines than high cost, highly centralized alternatives. It does require the big data preparation work and the development of enterprise AI applications described earlier in this chapter.

18.5.3 Three Startup Opportunities

Building websites, sourcing content through application programming interfaces (APIs) and selling plane tickets now have turn-key solutions. The

170 *Artificial Intelligence and Organization*

potential for startups in these spaces is low. But there are three high potential, high reward use case opportunities for truly transformational startups helping to build experience marketplaces:

- Finding a way to calculate what a flight should cost based on a shopper's journey and contribution margin they generate throughout the retail experience.
- Building an enterprise scale system for making multiple recommendations for shoppers, including all price components in real time.
- Developing a comprehensive airline commercial system that does not just price itineraries, hold reservations, check tickets, and accept passengers for travel but incorporates all shopper data, live-streamed traveler insights, third-party insights, and experiences content into recommendations for shoppers. These systems will create offers from sourced content in real time dynamically and manage orders independently of traditional airline fare classes. This would be powered by an enterprise application on enterprise AI platforms with live-streamed data and content.

In Chapter 11, I demonstrated how the airline marketplace of experiences could be an ultimate use case for personalized retailing. It described how the customer would have their own digital assistant as an additional value-added layer on the marketplace. This was, in fact, an illustration of an Enterprise AI application, bringing together the various products and services executed by different teams within an airline. It would also benefit from using data-driven organization design with its AI application, as discussed in the previous chapter.

18.6 Conclusions

Airlines can only become truly data-centric if they become goal-centric. This chapter described how Enterprise AI can help stack and harmonize the results of work people do when they are separated by departmental boundaries. It demonstrates how AI can overcome human challenges and that, when combined with data-driven organization design, airline customers and the company's bottom line will benefit. Building transformational roadmaps to simplify coherent customer delivery using Enterprise AI is needed. The chapter showcases a marketplace retail experience to make its point and lists other potential use cases.

Notes

1 C3 (2022) 'What is enterprise AI – AI suite model-driven architecture', pp. 8. https://c3.ai/what-is-enterprise-ai/c3-ai-suite-model-driven-architecture/.
2 Register, J., et al. (2021) 'Artificial intelligence based aerospace composite design', DOI: 10.13140/RG.2.2.21648.74248. https://www.researchgate.

net/publication/352478957_Artificial_Intelligence_based_Aerospace_Composite_Design.
3 Airbus (2022) 'Artificial intelligence – capitalising on the value of data'. https://www.airbus.com/en/innovation/industry-4-0/artificial-intelligence.
4 Travel Market Report (2015) 'Consumers visit 38 sites before booking, Expedia says'. https://www.travelmarketreport.com/articles/Consumers-Visit-38-Sites-Before-Booking-Expedia-Says.
5 Airbus (2022) 'Airbus launches Airspace Link HBCplus – the flexible high bandwidth connectivity solution for airlines'. https://aircraft.airbus.com/en/newsroom/press-releases/2022-06-airbus-launches-airspace-link-hbcplus-the-flexible-high-bandwidth.

Bibliography

Defined AI (2021) 'A guide to AI in enterprise: the what, the why, the who'. https://www.defined.ai/blog/ai-in-enterprise/

Deloitte Insights (2022) 'State of AI in the enterprise, 2nd edition'. https://www2.deloitte.com/content/dam/insights/us/articles/4780_State-of-AI-in-the-enterprise/DI_State-of-AI-in-the-enterprise-2nd-ed.pdf

Kerzel, U. (2020) 'Enterprise AI Canvas integrating artificial intelligence into business', *Applied Artificial Intelligence*, 35(1), pp. 1–12. https://www.tandfonline.com/doi/full/10.1080/08839514.2020.1826146

Siddique, S. (2018) 'The road to enterprise artificial intelligence: a case studies driven exploration'. MIT Thesis. Cambridge, MA: MIT Library.

Zdravković, M., et al. (2021) 'AI-enabled enterprise information systems for manufacturing', *Enterprise Information Systems*, 16(4), pp. 668–720. https://www.tandfonline.com/doi/abs/10.1080/17517575.2021.1941275

Part 4

Trends and Evolutions in AI

Part 4 of this book highlights and explores specific subfields within artificial intelligence (AI) to demonstrate the benefits they can bring to commercial aviation and the adoption of AI. It discusses things like Explainable AI (AIX), Hybrid Intelligence, and Ethical Intelligence and goes on to reveal trends and ongoing debates within the field of artificial intelligence. The second section of this final part of the book explores novel applications of AI on blockchain, how distributed AI on blockchain can help the travel industry, and what AI in the metaverse could bring.

As a unique round-up of the book itself, the last chapter shares insights into how applied psychology and how organizational psychologists can help increase the adoption of AI technology around humans and bring benefits to humans, organizations, and society.

Part 4 is structured as follows:

Chapter 19 addresses Explainable AI.
Chapter 20 delves into Hybrid Intelligence.
Chapter 21 explores the evolutions in Ethical or Responsible AI.
Chapter 22 reviews trends and debates in the AI field.
Chapter 23 concentrates on AI and distributed AI applications on blockchain.
Chapter 24 examines the applications and opportunities of AI in the metaverse.
Chapter 25 concludes the book by sharing how applied psychology can aid AI adoption.

DOI: 10.4324/9781003018810-23

19 Explainable AI

19.1 Explainable AI Described

ML models have recently gained a reputation that has made people and users skeptical. This predominantly happens in situations where the models and results are part of critical processes, such as facial recognition for security purposes or models used in the medical profession for detecting diseases. It could equally be envisioned in aviation when radar-observed weather is misinterpreted and guides an aircraft into a storm. Alternatively, models that predict better transportation flows in disrupted supply chains need to be carefully examined to not result in perishable cargo. Also, and in a more general sense, non-transparency of algorithms could potentially lead to unintended results such as bias, racism, or wrongful exploitation of vulnerable groups.

Revenues and customer satisfaction increase when trust in artificial intelligence (AI) is established. It helps improve commercial processes, build robust customer engagements, and shrinks time to market. This in turn improves competitive positioning. However, when this is overlooked, trust in the organization can erode and result in failed audits, and regulatory fines resulting in the loss of brand reputation and revenues.

The more complex the algorithm, the more difficult it is to understand how an AI/ML model has arrived at a decision. Explainable AI (XAI) tries to tackle the black-box nature of such systems and build trust and transparency. It is also abbreviated as XAI.

One of the key challenges in AI adoption is trust and transparency. The people working with models can often monitor prediction accuracy but automating decisions entirely requires a different level of trust. What if the outcomes are biased? For instance, a credit card company may use an AI algorithm that mildly reflects social bias to advertise their products, targeting less-educated people with offers featuring higher interest rates. What if the outcomes produce illegal actions? For example, based on accidental racial profiling, we are not providing equal opportunity for a traveler to redeem points for travel. There are many potential negative outcomes and ethical issues around allowing automation to be autonomous when its workings have not been probably explained. This is also the topic of Chapter 21.

DOI: 10.4324/9781003018810-24

Clearly, building and scaling AI requires trust and transparency, and the industry has found ways in which AI, and its performance, can be better explained as part of an overall end-to-end AI life cycle. Further, it can help to detect and correct model drift, which is where bias, unfair, or non-compliant behavior could occur. This is where XAI can help.

The goal of XAI is to gain confidence in the entire AI life cycle from the data and models to the processes involved. One of the ways to achieve this is through integrated governed data and AI technologies in a unified platform. It does require a complete view of all available and applied data throughout an organization to drive data operations and practices that will help identify and mitigate model drift. This also helps to increase the accuracy of insights obtained when working with the data and understand the predictions better, so that they can be explained better to users and stakeholders of the applications.

In its simplest description, XAI uses human language, charts, and images to explain back to people how the model came to its results. This logic is narrated and visualized and makes it very easy to monitor the models and control for fairness. In essence, XAI contrasts with the concept of the 'black box' in machine learning and enables transparency. For instance, airline marketers need to trust that recommender systems propose relevant hotel, excursions, or lifestyle items in the pursuit of personalization in ancillary products and services. They would like to understand how the models come to their predictions and to what extent they are logical, accurate, and hit their mark. This can be measured after the fact by measuring how many people engage and transact, but the damage may have been done by then. Hit-and-miss is not an acceptable tactic when digitizing shopping baskets as customers deliver their vote of confidence by clicking onwards. With a bad experience, they will remember not to return. Similarly, when using AI-powered models can predict when to power up jet engines during taxiing can spell the difference between being fuel-efficient or being wasteful. AI can predict time estimates for movement and other vehicular traffic and build in the required 4 minutes of engine running time prior to take-off.

Since the late 2010s, researchers have pushed to encourage XAI. Research was directed toward the development of tools, methods, and techniques, and although their use is practical, explaining them can still sound quite technical. In summary, the tools are intended to provide:

- Interactive visual interfaces meant to help visualize datasets and better understand how they calculate the output and came to accurate results.
- Views of the performance (accuracy of predictions or 'problem solving').
- What-if analyses to see where subsets of the data perform best or worst.

In essence, it is about using graphs, colors, and layers to link explainable pieces of information as they relate to how the model gets to its result. It

176 *Trends and Evolutions in AI*

is like putting together a puzzle with bigger and more obvious pieces that the eyes and people cognitively can follow and understand. It is about more logical steps, not complicated formulae. Companies like IBM were the first to offer XAI and conducted research with Forrester on the benefits of using XAI. They found that it would help overcome the following challenges in the journey to AI adoption by the late 2010s:

- The difficulty in ensuring fairness and minimizing bias.
- An insufficient number of models that make it to production.
- Inability to use more sophisticated (but opaque) algorithms.

In fact, when data scientists create models, the lack of explainability "erodes trust in the results and increases the risk of regulatory penalties and reputational risk", according to IBM. The more sophisticated the work gets, the more obscure the results, and the fewer business leaders trust the outcomes. This can lead to executives opting for reduced performance because it can be more easily explained. XAI addresses this.

Relying on data scientists to manually create explainability metrics, visualizations, or documentation only adds to their workload and does not work in practice. It is also not practical and very laborious. In fact, data scientists are generally more in tune with algorithms and have a higher tendency to trust models that indicate 98% prediction accuracy. But this is not the same in the business, and companies like IBM offer a solution to help address these challenges. IBM's solution is called Cloud Pak for Data, whereas other competing products include InRule, Google Cloud XAI, Rulex XAI, and VirtuousAI.

The benefits of these technologies are

1 Increased number of models and higher productivity.
2 Increased revenue/profit from getting more models in production due to higher trust.
3 Increased profits because of a higher level of model accuracy.

Clearly, data quality and its accessibility are two main challenges in building machine learning pipelines. The problems that can arise pertaining to the information that is ingested into a model become problematic when (1) an incorrect model gets pushed, (2) incoming data is corrupted, or when (3) incoming data changes and no longer resembles datasets used during training.[1] Even more recently, data scientists and developers started using deep learning within deep learning networks, to better understand the inner workings of a model. The objective there is to observe the influence of the model on layers above or below and back to the original data source.

There are illustrations of what XAI looks like, but it was not possible to obtain permission to publish images for the release of this book's first edition. AnalyticsMagazine.com will provide examples online showing comparisons of original models with a set of mathematical expressions tied together that

Explainable AI   177

represent the way inner layers of an algorithm or a neural network function. It compares them to others where the message is more lucid.

19.3 XAI in Aviation

On March 19, 2018, a self-driving Uber car struck and killed a woman in Tempe, Arizona, USA.[2] It demonstrated the serious safety concerns about autonomous vehicles and that it was crucial to understand what had gone wrong, and how the composite set of AI algorithms had not met their principal goal of safe operations. This placed more importance on the explainability techniques for AI techniques.

In civil aviation, the use of unmanned or autonomous aircraft carrying passengers has not occurred or has not been authorized, yet. However, aircraft are increasingly more sophisticated and autonomous take-offs with modern aircraft using computer vision are now possible. Also, airports are progressively looking into deploying autonomous vehicles that can operate on airport aprons for baggage transportation, ground handling, and ground service equipment. This requires situational awareness much like what is required in autonomous cars. And like with all moving vehicles and potential obstacles on airport aprons, unexpected situations are rampant and there is zero tolerance for incidents or accidents. It is in these areas where XAI will play a more important role before the adoption of more autonomous operations will be widely accepted.

But there are other areas where XAI will be very helpful. Consider the following use cases:

- Air navigation and fuel efficiency: Understanding how optimal routes are calculated and explained back to pilots so that recommendations can be followed.
- Conflict resolution: Understanding how recommended customer service actions will actually resolve specific customer complaints so that staff does not hesitate to accept them.
- Inflight retailing: Understanding how prices of food and beverages are calculated in real time based on inventory, perishability, and customer demand and be able to explain the logic to crew and passengers inflight.
- Network planning: Understanding how the model produces recommendations at schedule and fleet level to suggest which slots to apply for when negotiating with airports.
- Demand forecasting with ancillary: Understanding how a model ensures we are still controlling seat inventory well with new inputs based on other related potential revenue (such as baggage fees) and share of wallet potential.
- Personalization: Understanding how the model suggests the most relevant features or attributes that are in line with what passengers expect when they shop around.

178 *Trends and Evolutions in AI*

- Loyalty: Understanding how the model gets to recommending new tier levels and customer lifetime value appraisals without upsetting current loyalty members.
- Brand and social media: Understanding how the models manage and place content in key places, like social media, without undermining customer perceptions.
- Human resources and organizational analytics: Understanding how the model works to suggest moving people into other departments and what it considers to be sufficiently accurate.
- Cargo: Understanding how the model works to predict how to best build a pallet so that staff will accept the recommendations and not challenge it.

There are many more use cases for XAI and the factors that typically drive the need for this center around the following:

- There is a high reliance on hands-on experience and intuition (gut feel), like in cargo handling, payment fraud prevention, marketing, and advertising.
- There is a predominant process and procedures-driven work environment that includes manual intervention, like ramp handling.
- The use of richer data is relatively new, and the adoption of decision-support software is in its 2nd or 3rd generation (i.e., 20–30 years in evolution), such as pricing and revenue management.
- The use of decision intelligence and automation is in its infancy in professional disciplines, such as accounting but less so in finance.
- The provider proposing the automation is relatively new to the field or industry, such as startups proposing the optimization of route navigation or navigation fee predictions.

19.4 XAI – The Data Fabric

What is needed to reap the benefits of XAI? In order to build AI that people trust, they need to know that the desired outcomes are reliable and the method strong enough to mitigate risk. And to achieve that, this requires building trust in the data, the models, and the processes that AI can be well-planned, executed, and controlled.

According to specialists at IBM, trust in data strength is related to an accurate 'connection to data'.[3] It means that data should be abundant, of high quality, and ready to use by various stakeholders on a self-service basis. That requires the combination of structured and unstructured data from various sources, both internal and external, as well as from private or public clouds and on-premises data. This connection to data also involves 'data lineage', which essentially shows what happens to data and where it moves over time. Data lineage gives visibility while greatly simplifying the ability to trace errors back to the root cause in a data analytics process.[4]

Trust in models is built by concentrating on the integration of various data science tools. Individual models that are operationalized separately can perform well, but the risk of end model drift is in combining stacks of AI models. For example, revenue management and dynamic pricing may make seats available for $1,447 from Montreal to Paris non-stop whereas the loyalty program is offering the equivalent of $1,536 in points value (68,000 miles) plus $448 in additional fees for a Montreal to Paris itinerary with a detour stop in Toronto (e.g., YUL-YYZ-CDG). In this case, the value propositions are not aligned and undermine customer experience.

In some cases, using human input (supervised training) fairness, explainability and robustness can be infused into the AI model that is required for high-performance co-creation. This is discussed further in Chapter 20 on hybrid intelligence.

Trust in processes is the third component. IDC FutureScape in 2021 predicted that by 2025, 60% of enterprises will have operationalized their ML workflows through MLOps or ModelOps capabilities and AI-infused their IT infrastructure operations through AIOps capabilities.[5] But this trust in processes across the model lifecycle requires AI governance that provides confidence that automation can drive consistent, repeatable processes to increase model transparency and ensure traceability all the while also decreasing time to production at scale. And this is still an ambitious view as recently, it is still found that most organizations have increased their AI budgets to grow the number of data scientists but conversely the time required to deploy a model has gone up. TechTarget[6] reported that 83% of companies had increased their budgets and that the number of scientists employed grew by 76% but 64% of them report needing a month or longer to deploy a model.

The challenge in commercial aviation remains primarily the modernization of data and democracy across airlines, airports, and ground handlers and secondly finding the right level of automation at each stage of the AI lifecycle. Subsequently, there are a few key capabilities that will unlock this potential and should thus get priority focus. First, finding ways to integrate data of many types and sources across multiple deployments. Second, the ability to provide a more democratic and autonomous (self-service) access with privacy controls to appropriate data. Third, a way to track and map data lineage (also for learning purposes). Also, support to automate model building, operationalizing, deployment, scaling/training/monitoring. And finally, automated support to govern and help ensure data quality is up to standard and meets regulatory compliance.

To put the above components and moving parts together in a coherent manner for an enterprise like an airline means many silos and related organizational as well as data complexity challenges must be overcome. An architectural approach that was designed to address and simplify this is called the 'data fabric'. It was a concept created in the mid-2010s that is growing out as a practice and often touted by Gartner, DataWorld, IBM, and Hitachi Vantara as a value proposition at least 25% of data management vendors will provide

180 *Trends and Evolutions in AI*

a full framework for by 2024. Vendors include K2View, Talend, IBM (Cloud Pak for Data), Denodo, and Informatica.

Gartner refers to the new practice as follows: "A data fabric stitches together integrated data from many different sources and delivers it to various data consumers".[7] It essentially brings together capabilities into a unified architecture that avoids the cost and complexity of integrating an excess of point solutions. Instead of patching together fragmented groups of products or models together, the data fabric is an easier-to-use and more holistic solution built to work with enterprise data in a more frictionless fashion.

So, since a data fabric connects, governs, and also protects siloed data distributed across different landscapes (private/public clouds, on premises), it is helpful to see how this would serve airlines by drawing from lessons learned elsewhere. There are interesting use cases in healthcare, banking, and manufacturing and all provide insights into what applications have merit for airlines and airports. They can demonstrate how data-driven solutions around a data fabric help uncover hidden patterns in time series or deep learning data and provide valuable continuous predictions.

At Penn Medicine, a world-renowned academic medical center in Philadelphia, AI experts from IBM developed a machine learning model that allowed neurosurgeons to intervene and avoid intracranial hypertension (ICP) crises. It achieved this through better predictions that gave the surgeons a lead time of 20–30 minutes advance notice. They were able to achieve this by capitalizing on the benefits of a data fabric that utilized all data sources. We could achieve similar advance alerts for possible runway incursion risk or to improve situational awareness on airport aprons, but it could also help in improving aircraft and engine maintenance planning including in-shop safety around moving equipment and tools since data about physical objects, humans, and process-related insights can be combined. On the commercial side, using a data fabric to better combine insights about customers and their likely responses or preferences to service interruptions will significantly help service recovery and customer service.

Similarly, in manufacturing, the need for predictable manufacturing operations that are vulnerable to supply chain inefficiencies and labor shortages has increased. The same has hit aircraft manufacturers as well as airlines and airports, but in the case of cargo, it has represented immediate opportunities. But global firms, such as ABB, the robotics, power, electrical equipment, and automation technology firm, wanted to enrich their data pipeline to better mitigate labor shortage exposure. It worked with IBM to use a data fabric and build an enterprise-wide business process with advanced analytical capabilities to better predict sales engineer retirement and staff planning, which strengthened business continuity. During the post-COVID-19 recovery, airports could have gained significantly from similar data pipelines and operational models much before staffing issues at security and baggage handling would have become a stranglehold. In addition, the ongoing labor relation negotiations and pilot shortage related to changing aircraft fleets is a challenge that could merit from

Explainable AI   181

improved analytics and bringing to bear hidden insights around necessary talent pools and future operations to recommend mitigating solutions and practices.

Another example is the Royal Bank of Scotland (NatWest Group) which uses cognitive enterprise technology to support its agents that review customers' mortgage applications. It uses a data fabric architecture that brings rich insights together through machine learning models that are deployed to predict desired customer outcomes that are in line with the bank's acceptable risk levels. The digital mortgage support tool runs on an AI-powered, cloud-based platform provided by IBM, and helps agents with smart responses to the typing of keywords into a console. The digital assistant is literally at their fingertips and has improved customer NPS by 20%. The application of this for departments that are currently silos within airlines, such as customer service, revenue management, reservations, and loyalty could bring tremendous end-to-end benefits across disparate organizations.

19.5 Conclusions

This chapter discusses the tools available to explain the workings and accuracy of machine learning models better. Referred to as XAI, these solutions help increase AI adoption and push automation to more advanced levels. Modern tools explore data and build models (either visually or with code) that can be deployed with AI model lifecycle explainability and fairness. It further proposes that improved transparency, accuracy, and the removal of bias can significantly help airlines and airports to operationalize models that improve customer-facing processes including disruption management, staff and workload planning, and commercial processes to provide relevant products and services throughout the inspiration and shopping experience. XAI can be instrumental in ensuring that models remain impartial and do not hurt any person or group in society while we maintain the necessary integrity to make climate-neutral decisions.

Notes

1 Analytics India Magazine (2019) '8 Explainable AI frameworks driving a new paradigm for transparency in AI'. https://analyticsindiamag.com/8-explainable-ai-frameworks-driving-a-new-paradigm-for-transparency-in-ai/.
2 New York Times (2018) 'Self-driving Uber Car kills pedestrian in Arizona'. https://www.nytimes.com/2018/03/19/technology/uber-driverless-fatality.html.
3 IBM (2022) 'Trustworthy AI book'. https://aix360.mybluemix.net/videos.
4 Imperva (2022) 'Why is data lineage so important'. https://www.imperva.com/learn/data-security/data-lineage/.
5 IDC FutureScape (2022) 'Worldwide artificial intelligence and automation 2022 predictions'. https://www.idc.com/research/viewtoc.jsp?containerId=US48298421.
6 TechTarget (2022) 'Piloting machine learning projects through harsh headwinds'. https://www.techtarget.com/searchenterpriseai/feature/Piloting-machine-learning-projects-through-headwinds.

182 *Trends and Evolutions in AI*

7 Gartner (2022) 'Data fabric, top strategic technology trend for 2022'. https://www.gartner.com/en/information-technology/trends/top-strategic-technology-trends-data-fabric-gb-pd?

Bibliography

Capterra (2022) 'Comparing 2 master data management software products'. https://www.capterra.com/master-data-management-software/compare/118978-168312/Data-Integration-vs-Informatica-MDM

Cinchy (2022) 'The way data should work'. https://cinchy.com/platform

IBM (2022) 'Watson studio'. https://www.ibm.com/watson/explainable-ai

K2View (2022) 'Delivering data products in a data fabric & data mesh' https://www.k2view.com/

NetApp (2022) 'Your data fabric: 6 ingredients, 1 tasty result'. https://www.netapp.com/data-fabric/

Nexla (2022) 'Top 5 data fabric takeaways from 2021 Gartner D&A Summit'. https://www.nexla.com/top-5-data-fabric-takeaways/

20 Hybrid Intelligence – Addressing Deskilling, Upskilling, Reskilling

20.1 Human–Machine Context

Hybrid Intelligence combines human and artificial intelligence (AI) to collectively achieve superior results and learn from each other. It will be a dominant workplace model in the digital age. This is how Aleksandra Deric defined it when the first talk about hybrid intelligence appeared in early 2019.[1] Capgemini has since even created a center of excellence entitled hybrid intelligence within its organization to focus on this area. Yet, it is not a common concept nor practice in the aviation industry, which is still in its early stages of AI adoption. It is important, however, to delve into the background of this discipline as it has several interrelationships with applied organizational psychology and successful business transformation. In many respects, it is also the culmination of the greatest and most complex confrontation between automation and the labor market since the early days of industrialization. This is because we are no longer dealing with automating lower-skilled jobs but combining and automating some of the most complex tasks that humans do not have the capability to perform in real time. While AI can solve and automate problems at different levels, the latter significantly impacts on how even knowledge workers are potentially deskilled by relying on technology they may only understand the recommendations of. There is therefore a growing group of researchers and practitioners that is concerned with the loss of professional skills due to technological or work practice changes.

To illustrate the point, a driver can cede many levels of operational controls to modern cars, especially self-driving cars. If a young or new driver has no experience and relies completely on autonomous driving, that driver may not have trained skills to intervene and take over in unforeseen circumstances. What is worse, those situations are likely the most complex emergencies when even intelligent self-driving cars would not know how to react, such as avoiding multiple objects from different directions at different speeds while a tire blows up, causing erratic car movements. The driver would never have acquired these skills, or be deskilled due to lack of recent experience.

Another illustrative and pertinent case is Boeing and its automated Maneuvering Characteristics Augmentation System (MCAS) for the 737 MAX. Due

DOI: 10.4324/9781003018810-25

184 *Trends and Evolutions in AI*

to design changes and additional weight, the aircraft had different aerody-namical characteristics and needed more automation to regulate the angle of attack ('pitch') during take-off as well as during some stages in flight where the AI technology would automatically intervene and adjust pitch based on sensor readings without much interaction with pilots. This was not properly explained to (younger) pilots who had mostly been trained on flight simulators. Many pilots never had an opportunity to be briefed about MCAS or even know of its presence. The reliance on the overall systems had led to deskilling, with fatal results. On 10 March 2019, a Kenya Airways Boeing 737 MAX 8 aircraft crashed near the town of Bishoftu six minutes after take-off, killing all 157 people aboard. On October 29, a 737 MAX 8 operating Lion Air Flight 610 crashed after take-off from Jakarta. The plane was subsequently grounded around the world.

The implications of smart automation on the role of workers and their adoption of or engagement with AI technology are prevalent. But there are also implications beyond the individuals or organizations and society (Rafner et al., 2019). Much depends on the nature of the knowledge that is required to accomplish the work and the ways in which these types of knowledge are distributed between humans and technology.

To put this in perspective, we need to classify different types of skills within categories. Traditionally, we had the skilled worker and knowledge worker. The skilled worker had a role of a trained employee with individual craftsmanship. Often, this craftsmanship was in designing and producing materials, for instance making shoes. The knowledge worker (such as an experienced manager) had other sets of skills that were less based on learned procedures and more on cognitive tasks, such as reasoning, planning, assessing risk, and decision-making.

With automation around craftsmanship, such as the introduction of production line robotics and other advances in machine automation, also came standardization. We were able to produce higher volumes of cars using robotics even though they were often human-assisted. But the higher production rate was traded for more standardization. Therefore, to some extent, craftsmanship was lost (an early example of deskilling). Today, we have fewer people that can design and produce cars with their own hands. However, a divide was created between the people that used to assemble things by hand, or those that evolved and were able to work with robot-assisted technology (with upskilling, i.e. training), and the people that designed the machines that could replace the tedious or laborious manual work. In the past, it was found that industrialization did lead to technologically induced unemployment, but it was found to be temporary (Feldmann, 2013). In fact, work that was replaced by technology often moves to the producers of that technology within three years' time. But this was for technology that replaced manual tasks or the manipulation of physical objects. What about mental processes?

Putting this in a more modern context, the same principle of craft versus cognitive worker applies. However, our classification of the knowledge

Hybrid Intelligence 185

worker must become more refined, because almost all jobs today involve the use of technology as part of manipulating information, not physical objects. The principal distinction is in the extent to which the technology is using human knowledge input or creating its own knowledge to automate a task a human used to or may not be able to complete. For instance, do pilots still have skills to determine how to preserve fuel consumption during taxi, or will they need to rely completely on new technology? What about take-off and landing with 99.99% optimized fuel efficiency managed in real time faster than hands can move throttles? If it fails, do pilots have updated skills to do it themselves? The human–AI interaction and whether the AI output requires new skills from the professional to continue a loop spells the difference between deskilling or upskilling.

This is leading researchers to question whether AI-based technologies will defy historical observations about new employment being created by technological advancements or automation in cognitive skills.

20.2 Human in the Loop vs. Human Out of the Loop

In order to make better assessments about the impact of (potential) automation on people and skills, better classifications are needed. Therefore, there are four new categories that distinguish the different roles of human–AI interaction:

1   The AI system helps plan, execute, or evaluate a task with data.

    For example, an AI model shows with X% confidence that there is a strong link between the propensity of a specific segment of customers in the loyalty program to purchase travel insurance for connecting flights in Asia and the willingness to pay for ticket refundability. This information remains an insight if not actioned.

2   The human checks the outcome of the AI system and whether to use it.

    For example, a revenue management system shows the likelihood of generating 9.5% higher revenues on a flight for all Origin-Destination passengers by closing a fare class and driving demand to another fare at which there is a higher chance they will also purchase seat selection at a fee and check a piece of luggage at a charge. The incremental revenue is expected to be 9.5% higher than selling the marginally higher base fare in the other fare class.

3   The AI system acquires data, plans, executes, and evaluates a performed task to solve a problem without any human involvement.

    For example, the shopping engine, driven by an AI bot, generates pop-ups with recommendations of activities to sell to individual customers as well as price levels at which they are expected to purchase in a fully automated manner. There is no human included in the entire activation and sale process. Airline staff are not able to come up with these recommendations or optimize retail revenues themselves, and they do not know how it works.

186   *Trends and Evolutions in AI*

4   A combination of (1–3) where the human and the AI need each other for continuous improvement of the outcomes toward a goal.

For example, an airline retail scientist keeps reviewing the performance of the AI model and how it is optimizing revenue successfully at individual level by reviewing the performance of the machine learning model and to what extent customers engage and transact on the AI-generated recommendations. It adjusts (supervises) the model and introduces additional rules based on new insights from deep learning acquired by ingesting new data. The professional is also learning from the outcomes, which are generating new insights into creative use cases to script and test with emerging data.

The above classifications were named as Human-in-the-loop (HITL), Human-on-the-loop (HOTL), Human-out-of-the-loop (HOOTL), and Hybrid Intelligence by Rafner et al. (2019). If we extend on it, these classifications are helpful in looking at human–AI interactions for different types of knowledge, and how they can be managed before and after AI adoption. This will impact on how we manage (AI) project implementations and work with HR and organization design specialists.

20.3 Knowledge Management

It is becoming evident that traditional approaches of IT engagement models need to be revisited. Traditional IT was about enabling information systems (IS), where AI extends into the realm of automating knowledge management around individuals. The way people engaged with IS in the past is also different, as it was about using technology to generate an outcome. AI-based technology is about solving problems without first exposing the workings to humans, based on mutual learning. The implications on organization, IT governance, and project management are profound.

It is not the purpose of this chapter or book to create new practical frameworks as they would be stand-alone projects. But a new framework is needed to assess and adapt AI technology while safeguarding valuable skills and even facilitate upskilling. In order to do so, we need a combined view of the nature of knowledge, the types of knowledge, and the life cycle of knowledge before and after the adoption of AI technology.

The different dimensions to look at when we assess knowledge/skill management against AI capabilities are the following:

- Motoric (physical tasks).
- Task characteristic (analyzing numbers and understanding the numbers).
- Procedural (understanding the workflow).
- Rule-based (knowing about rules, or why they are necessary).
- Knowledge-based (new insights, new applications).

There is a life cycle of knowledge that loops from before, during, to after the adoption of AI technology. Skill analytics are necessary before automation takes over. And these are the questions to ask to determine whether a human should have an involvement in the evolution of the human-AI interaction, or whether we can resort to a full reliance on smart automation:

- How fundamental is this skill in today's business model?
- Will this skill remain important in changing business models?
- Can this skill be transferred to other departments during organization redesign?
- Did this skill require any formal education and depend on certification?
- Is this a common skill in the industry, or an internal skill?
- Has this skill been subject to influence and training on the job?
- Is there any risk of losing this skill as part of business continuity?
- Is this skill important in any day-to-day operation, or can it be recovered?
- Is there an opportunity for the skill to evolve outside the machine and be part of future automation?
- Is this skill necessary as part of future restructuring, mergers, or acquisition activity?

These are some examples of questions that help map how hybrid intelligence can combine human knowledge workers and AI agents to solve tasks that exceed the capabilities of either humans or AI alone. More specifically, as discussed in the chapter on Explainable AI as well as in the chapter on AI and Organization Design, it will help determine the design of user interfaces to the technology that is executing the smart automation.

20.4 Sociotechnical Future of Hybrid Intelligence

Automation at the expense of expertise is a short-sighted solution, as argued by many.[2] Therefore, in order to preserve employee engagement and enable upskilling, the social aspects of technical systems need to work in tandem so that human and AI skills, knowledge, and talents can grow together. This is very different than how we used to look at technology when we looked at the requirements of technical components first. Use cases were based on hard system requirements, but with AI, we have an opportunity to design along three critical dimensions:

1. Solving the end goal (results and confidence).
2. Guiding the employees along the logical journey (visualized workflow).
3. Mutual learning from human-AI interaction (upskilling based on performance).

188   *Trends and Evolutions in AI*

I see two parallel tracks for this happening in real life. One is the fully automated flow that uses the full capability of AI technology within the defined scope of the process, and one that exposes its workings to the employees so that the skills can be applied, improved, and preserved. They can then also be used to design new use cases for future AI-based solutions within commercial aviation. The applications of this are abundant such as in aircraft engine maintenance, metallurgic analytics (aircraft skin analysis), but also in commercial planning especially if we are to work with Customer Data Platforms (CDPs) that allow us to do more with all potential data we can source or generate around individual customers.

20.5 Conclusions

This chapter focused on the collaboration between humans and AI, called Hybrid Intelligence, with the aim to avoid the potential competition that undermines learning. Mutual learning is not only the goal but also the enabler of hybrid intelligence and is argued that this is the only practical way for the airline industry to foster more AI adoption across airline, airport, and aviation-related companies' processes. While there is potential for tasks and jobs to be replaced by AI technology, there are ample opportunities to generate new jobs and upskill those that are impacted by smart automation using hybrid intelligence. This chapter also stressed that hybrid intelligence underscores a human context as it emphasizes our human needs. It went on to explain that it will likely create new forms of interaction and synergies between humans and algorithms that encourage upskilling and even reskilling. This is expected to unlock new opportunities in commercial aviation.

Notes

1 Deric, A. (2019) 'The future of work is hybrid intelligence: How artificial intelligence and human intelligence support each other'. *CQ Net blog.* https://www.ckju.net/en/blog/future-work-hybrid-intelligence-how-artificial-intelligence-and-human-intelligence-support-each-other.
2 Sutton, S.G., et al. (2018) 'How much automation is too much? Keeping the human relevant in knowledge work'. *Journal of Emerging Technologies in Accounting*, 15, 2, pp. 15–25. https://doi.org/10.2308/jeta-52311 and Appelbaum, S. H. (1997) 'Socio-technical systems theory: an intervention strategy for organizational development'. *Management Decision*, 356, pp. 452–463.

Bibliography

Brugger, F., et al. (2018) 'Skilling and deskilling: technological change in classical economic theory and its empirical evidence', *Theory and Society*, 47(5), pp. 663–689. https://doi.org/10.1007/s11186-018-9325-7

Dellermann, D., et al. (2019) 'Hybrid intelligence', *Business & Information Systems Engineering*, 61(5), pp. 637–643. https://doi.org/10.1007/s12599-019-00595-2

Feldmann, H. (2013) 'Technological unemployment in industrial countries', *Journal of Evolutionary Economics*, 23(5), pp. 1099–1126.

Kafner, J., et al. (2021) 'Deskilling, upskilling, and reskilling: a case for hybrid intelligence', *Morals + Machines*, 2, pp. 22–39.

Knight, W. (2017) 'The dark secret at the heart of AI'. *MIT Technology Review*. https://www.technologyreview.com/2017/04/11/5113/the-dark-secret-at-the-heart-of-ai/

21 Ethical and Responsible AI (Security Privacy, Environment)

21.1 Ethical AI Described

Digital decisioning and automation take on a new meaning when personal information is used to provide recommendations to people. Good intentions can have unwanted side effects. So, in an era where trust has gained tremendous importance to customers, every organization has a responsibility to adhere to ethical, explainable artificial intelligence (AI), respecting individual rights, privacy, and non-discrimination. Ethical AI (also referred to as Responsible AI) is concerned with these aspects and the risk mitigation of ethical violations since they have become more common in companies and turning these anxieties into actionable conversations can be difficult. But the overriding goal of work in Ethical AI is to encourage a dialogue between those using the technology and those who are affected by it.

Gartner asserts that by 2025, 70% of all organizations will require a professional code of conduct regarding the ethical use of data and AI. This is to deal with making proper ethical choices in business concerning the implementation of AI with respect to fairness, bias mitigation, safety, privacy, accountability, and balanced risk regarding business and societal value. Responsible AI should respect emerging regulatory oversight and avoid all exploitation or violations of diversity, equality, and inclusion.

Governments, just like commercial enterprises, are concerned with ensuring that their processes, programs, and services are aligned with ethical considerations and values. They need to be seen as setting the standards. Even provincial governments such as Ontario[1] in Canada set out and publish their 'beta' principles followed by their Digital Service, drawing from best practices set out in New Zealand, the USA and the European Union (EU). Generally, these principles are to be

- Transparent and explainable
- Good and fair
- Safe
- Accountable and responsible
- Human centric
- Sensible and appropriate

DOI: 10.4324/9781003018810-26

With the complexities of machine learning, ethics, and all related aspects can seem abstract but the realities of getting it wrong can be felt by individuals and publicly in society. It can also exacerbate problems for historically disadvantaged people. Blackman et al. (2022), in their piece in Harvard Business Review, argue that companies must first decide who needs to be part of the ethics in AI dialogue.

They then forward that the key steps to make next include

1 Defining your organization's ethical standards for AI (specifically).
2 Identifying the gaps between where your organization is now and what the standards call for.
3 Understanding the complex sources of the problems and operationalizing solutions.

But before companies investigate ethical standards for AI, it is important to consider what counts as bias or discrimination, or unfairness. This is perhaps one of the more difficult questions to answer because it requires us to benchmark against something. Is the benchmark what humans do well or don't do well? What is 'well'? If humans discriminate when they hire people, what is the acceptable bias that a machine may have? If marketers send biased promotional campaigns to some customers, what is sufficiently unbiased when a machine automates campaigns? If software may produce recommendations that seem unfair to some people in the population or customer base, is the average bias acceptable as long as it is at least as good as how people avoid bias? These become difficult aspects to measure.

In the airline industry, there is arguably a disproportionate risk of bias and ethical risk due to the way the industry is structured and how seats are distributed. Moreover, personal identities and passport details are required for check-in purposes while we collect behavioral information from browsing to purchasing to detailed travel itineraries and spend from co-branded credit card merchandising partners. In pricing and revenue management, the industry applies point-of-sale (POS) control to optimize revenue generation based on directional differences in willingness to pay, so tickets sold in Paris on flights to Montreal are cheaper than tickets sold in Montreal for the same flights to Paris. With machine learning and improved audience segmentation, the potential for bias to discriminate against individuals exists when we start customizing unique bundles of offers and refine prices based on characteristics of people based on their identities. But apart from potential risk, it is essential to assess the current sources of ethics problems.

21.2 Sources of AI Ethics Problems, and Aviation

While many companies often jump to reviewing ethics standards and how they apply to digital decisioning solutions, it is often more practical and useful to unroot ethical risk by understanding how data is used and supports

192 *Trends and Evolutions in AI*

decision intelligence such as ML and AI. Explainable AI and Hybrid Intelligence, as discussed in Chapters 19 and 20, illustrate the point and their value in assessing for ethical violations, model drift, and social risk.

In more practical terms, consider a number of problems associated with information that is deployed into machine learning models such as

- An incorrect model gets pushed.
- Incoming data is corrupted.
- Incoming data changes and no longer resembles datasets used during training.

There are many illustrations of the above, and many surfaced during the COVID-19 pandemic or otherwise triggered a rethink of future models. In revenue management, historical data was no longer representative to control seat inventory because demand was not derived from economic activity but more related to health rules and travel restrictions that were not part of the models. Recommendations or offers created by MarTech using machine learning and campaigns automated through AI were inaccurate as they were pushing for destinations based on the wrong datasets and parameters. The travel that did take place was in many cases related to repatriation and shifts in locations that were more related to remote work or return to home and were essentially distorting historical views. But the ripple effects of such underlying effects are widespread. They can impact on network planning, scheduling, crewing, and aircraft serviceability due to deviating patterns of aircraft block hours, engine maintenance, staff shortage, and absenteeism, and before long, the entire value chain is out of sync. Chapter 18 has described the importance of Enterprise AI in aligning workflows and outputs toward end problem-solving to maintain relevance and customer satisfaction at the very end of the process. It also requires human input and calibration when contexts change.

Returning the discussion to ethics, incorrect data or incorrect models can push biased and discriminating results. Gender bias can occur when a model is using a subset of representative data that is incorrectly making linkages between behaviors and genders and using this for recommender systems going forward. Models could end up pushing unattractive mortgage offers to people of color or minority groups because corrupted data appears to suggest that there is higher associated risk, simply because the quality of the data is poor. A recommender system could ignore airplane upgrade offers to certain groups in society because the data implicitly suggests lower income or inability to pay and thus a low propensity to purchase simply because the wrong data was used to ingest it. But the results of these processes are felt by real people with real emotions. And no company wants to be the object of a lawsuit or regulatory investigation for violations of privacy. Also, regulation in this area is only in its infancy but will evolve quickly.

Operating in the dark has made AI less trustworthy as a solution. Providing a solution to any problem is the end of the story for any ML model. However,

Ethical and Responsible AI   193

for the practitioners, it is crucial to explain their results in the most intuitive way to their clients. And the need for explainability now has an additional dimension. Not only is Explainable AI necessary to improve adoption, but it will also become a requirement for ethics compliance.

21.3 AI Ethics Risk Exposure

Upcoming regulation is threatening how data and insights are generated and ingested in traditional ML and AI solutions that enable automated decisions. In 2018, the EU's General Data Protection Regulation (GDPR) went into effect.[2] It governs and insists on having high-level data protection for consumers and harmonizes data security regulations within the EU. As part of the regulation, companies must notify people when personal data is collected or will be processed and requires them to obtain consent. Moreover, article 14 of GDPR stipulates that companies must provide meaningful information about the logic of automated decision-making tools, including the significance and intended consequences of data processing on people.

Notwithstanding future regulation on ethics compliance, moral standards dictate that the use of AI should include exposing and mitigating risk areas by addressing the following areas:

- Do the results explain how transparent and fair they are, so that no hidden intentions surface?
- Does the data life cycle seem to consistently operate in a good and fair way, meaning there is no compromise to dignity, autonomy, privacy, protection, equality, and fairness at any stage?
- Is the automation safe from the standpoint of scaling and human interventions not interfering with how the model is working as intended? Is there a protection against amplifying undesirable patterns in data that was used? Can it prevent decisions that are not intended or considered unsafe?
- Is accountability sufficiently distributed such that regular audits can prevent model or bias creep? Are the models sufficiently transparent such that human oversight and peer-reviews are sufficiently effective and prevent problems before they occur?
- Is AI automation sufficiently closing the gap between humans using the technology and humans affected by the technology to avoid unsafe applications? How does bridging this gap ensure societal benefits and avoid adverse side effects?
- Is the level of automation sensible and appropriate for the context in question, and are the applications bringing benefits to people over benefits to private enterprises?

Airline or airport executives, like in any other vertical or business need to ensure that risk is reduced to a level that is acceptable to regulators and

194   *Trends and Evolutions in AI*

individuals. It may be impossible to mitigate away all risks to a 'zero risk' environment using AI, but unnecessary risk is a menace to society, people, and ultimately the bottom line. There are legal and compliance experts that specialize in aligning existing risk mitigation practices with those that are adapted to AI applications but more regulation is expected in this field. It is not certain what is coming down the pipeline of various governments so the importance of ensuring ethical and reputational safety of airlines and other firms lies in recognizing the relevance.

21.4 Ethical AI Solutions

As is also the objective of Hybrid Intelligence, a safer and more reliable inclusion of AI requires a unified blend of human and AI. It will lead to a practice that will more easily allow managers using AI to evaluate the quality of the decision rules in use and thereby reduce false positives.

The solutions to addressing ethical risk in AI therefore involve people with complementary views, roles, and technology. In the second step, ethical AI will build in risk mitigation from a process and compliance perspective. Technologists, ethicists, business managers, and legal or compliance experts need to gather around the problem the department/company is trying to solve with an AI application. Only a deep understanding of the problem and the types of data that will be used to solve the problem and the assumptions the automated solution will use (using advanced analytics) can unveil the risk. The questions that are raised include

- Which part of the system might impact human rights?
- Are any uses of information or application prohibited?
- Are any people indirectly affected including demographic groups (e.g. race, gender, age, disability, skin tone, or any intersections)
- What types of harm may exist in terms of stereotyping, denigration, over- and underrepresentation?
- Do the benefits of the system weigh up against potential harm?
- Do all stakeholders benefit, or only some?
- What type of personal information is required?
- What aspects of identity are revealed or potentially considered?
- What information is private and confidential?
- Which combinations of personal information elements would the customer consider invasive?
- What data can never be presented back to the customer?
- Is there historical bias in data that can be recognized and filtered out?
- Which information elements, when combined, would be unsafe to use in end models?

By exploring these types of questions in detail and from the perspective of customer rights protection will enable companies to develop appropriate

Ethical and Responsible AI 195

frameworks and mechanisms. These tools will allow managers to guide the technical teams that need to write code toward the algorithms that will automate decision intelligence. Reporting on this further helps explain the mechanisms to regulators. In addition, when the minimum ethical standards are adhered to, customers will ultimately also display trust in using a company's services.

From a more technical standpoint, developers today are starting to use deep learning technology to analyze deep learning networks. This allows them to understand the inner workings of a model by exposing the kinds of influence relationships between data flow to layers above or below the end model and ultimately back down to the original underlying data sources. This field is very sophisticated in that it uses layers of mathematics (deep learning) to understand the validity of complex insights and it seems very appropriate to do this from an ethics risk standpoint.

Vendors such as Microsoft also offer solutions in the area of Ethical AI, which the company refers to as Responsible AI. Microsoft offers workbooks, checklists, packages, and toolkits that empower developers and users to assess fairness and mitigate negative impacts for groups of people. The tools Microsoft offers can be used to build, improve, and implement AI systems. The technology tools it provides can then be used to build the properties of AI systems in companies. These properties can be fairness, privacy, security, and other responsible assets such as diversity, equality, and overall transparency.

Workbooks are tools for structuring conversations early in the process of building new products or for redesigning existing ones. They allow teams to look beyond the pure engineering parts and assess what impacts the entire system, including the user experiences (UX), the user interface (UI), the engineering, and the project management. The UX and UI, in combination with the engineering (coding) should foster a 'glassbox' approach, which goal is to avoid opaque or blackbox models that cannot be screened for responsible AI.

AI fairness checklists are also available, which help prioritize this aspect when developing AI. These checklists help structure processes by operationalizing what would otherwise remain conceptual, so that fairness can be put into practice. Such checklists will also probe for the identification of potential harm in all of the AI development phases of (1) envisioning, (2) definition, (3) prototyping, (4) building, (5) launching, and (6) evolving.

> Checklists in other domains, such as aviation, medicine, and structural engineering, have had well-documented success in saving lives and improving professional practices. But unless checklists are grounded in practitioners' needs, they may be misused or ignored.
>
> —Microsoft

But other than checklists and using deep learning, there are sociotechnical solutions in the form of algorithms that can be run on AI models to assess fairness. These packages, like Fairlearn, can be installed with pip from PyPi

196 *Trends and Evolutions in AI*

and onto the code (pip is the package manager to install code on Python). Fairlearn will then enable the use of mitigating algorithms, for instance, fairlearn.reductions.GridSearch or fairlearn.postprocessing.ThresholdOptimizer as described by Microsoft regarding their Fairlearn tool. These methods can validate metrics, such as

- False-positive rate difference (e.g. a customer is qualified for an offer whereas it does not fit with their profile or purchasing preferences).
- False-negative rate difference (e.g. a customer is declined a buy-now-pay-later product based on a demographic whereas the person should qualify based on other factors).
- Equalized-odds difference, which quantifies the disparity in accuracy experienced by different demographics.

As part of responsible development and deployment of AI systems, there are other tools that companies can use. They include InterpretML, Error Analysis, and Counterfit, all also Microsoft solutions. InterpretML is a toolkit to help understand models and enable responsible machine learning. Error Analysis helps identify cohorts with higher error rates and diagnose underlying causes, whereas CounterFit helps evaluate security risks.

Ethical AI is increasingly enabled by new techniques that are becoming available. For instance, companies can use synthetic data. This allows enterprises to train algorithms on datasets that are rendered anonymous and artificially generated. Second, the application of differential privacy allows data scientists to extract insights from datasets that include personal information that is protected by ingesting statistical noise. Another technique is FedML (federated machine learning), which uses machine learning models in a decentralized environment for local learning and does not require the sharing of local data in this remote environment. This is particularly useful for IoT devices and autonomous vehicles. Fourth, the use of 'glass box' or explainable (often visual) tools is now more commonplace and helps to solidify responsible AI.

21.5 Conclusions

This chapter dealt with the emerging field of Ethical AI. It described how the IoT has contributed to sources of ethics issues in aviation. This includes individual rights, privacy, non-discrimination, and any bias or compromise to dignity, equality, and fairness. In the second part of the chapter solutions for Ethical AI are explored to demonstrate how human actions and automation can function together to close the gap between commercial enterprise and societal benefits. Examples include software, such as Microsoft's Error Analysis that is designed to flag and remove unintended consequences of AI.

Notes

1 Government of Ontario (2022) 'Beta principles for the ethical use of AI and data enhanced technologies in Ontario'. https://www.ontario.ca/page/beta-principles-ethical-use-ai-and-data-enhanced-technologies-ontario.
2 European Union (2016) 'Regulation 2016/679 of the European Parliament and of the Council on the protection of natural persons with regard to the processing of personal data and on the free movement of such data, and repealing Directive 95/46/EC'. *Official Journal of the European Union.* https://eur-lex.europa.eu/legal-content/EN/TXT/PDF/?uri=CELEX:32016R0679.

Bibliography

Blackman, R., et al. (2022) 'Ethics and AI: 3 conversations companies need to have'. *Harvard Business Review.* https://hbr.org/2022/03/ethics-and-ai-3-conversations-companies-need-to-be-having
Gifthub (2022) 'Binary classification with the UCI credit-card default dataset'. https://github.com/fairlearn/fairlearn/
InterpretML, by Microsoft (2022) https://interpret.ml/
Microsoft (2022) 'Responsible AI resources'. https://www.microsoft.com/en-us/ai/responsible-ai-resources

22 Trends and Debates in AI

22.1 Introduction

Between 2012 and 2022, the domain of artificial intelligence (AI) has overcome its previous ups and downs to build a steady foundation for future advances. Gartner (2022) finds that five key factors have led to this as they converged to become strong enablers:

1　The rise of big data and parallel processing systems that can store and process data at a massive scale and do so more cost-effectively.
2　Advancements in computing and memory infrastructure, notably the emergence of powerful graphics processing units (GPUs) for complex computations.
3　The rise of new machine learning (ML) techniques, especially advancements in deep learning and reinforcement learning.
4　The emergence of cloud computing to experiment and operationalize AI faster with lower complexity.
5　The vibrant open-source ecosystem, which enabled mainstreaming of deep learning frameworks and resulted in an explosion of startups.

But there are important trends and debates in the field of AI to heed. This chapter describes some of the most important developments.

22.2 Trends in AI

The trends that shape the future of AI in enterprise have many facets and can be categorized in numerous ways. Broadly speaking, they range in different scopes and whether the AI applications are more centralized or in the periphery and closer to Internet of Things (IoT) connected devices. Gartner and McKinsey both refer to these trends as the most significant trends by 2025 and foreseeable future:

1　Responsible AI – The responsible, or ethical, use of AI.
2　Composite AI – The ability to implement a variety of AI techniques aligned with the right use cases.

DOI: 10.4324/9781003018810-27

Trends and Debates in AI 199

3 Democratized AI – The accessibility and making AI available to a wide set of users.
4 Generative AI – The use of AI to generate new artifacts and create ground-breaking products.
5 Edge AI – The harnessing of AI for real-time analytics closer to data sources.

Composite AI was addressed in Chapter 18 whereas responsible AI was discussed in Chapter 21. It is worth elaborating on democratized, generative AI and edge AI, as they open an array of new use cases, particularly in combination with blockchain and metaverse in web3.

22.2.1 Democratized AI

Democratization of AI is the idea that everyone gets the opportunities and benefits of a particular resource. In this case, AI. Democratized AI is about making it more available to a wider group of users and providing more access to tools, analytics, and automation throughout the enterprise. The goal of Democratized AI is also to reduce the burden on humans and the need for expert knowledge so that even AI expertise can be replaced by augmented AI functionality.

Democratized AI takes several forms and consists of sub-trends such as Everyday AI, Citizen AI, and Augmented AI. Everyday AI is about the integration of AI techniques within devices or software that people use daily in their work to increase productivity. Examples are automated calendars or meeting scheduling, or email sorting and filtering. Citizen AI is about making AI easier to use or embed into daily work so that limited coding is needed to develop and deploy highly accurate models. Automated ML (AutoML) is an example of helping people or new users along quickly. Augmented AI (also known as 'Intelligent X') is about an additional layer of intelligent automation between applications that render an enterprise business application more intelligent. In some cases, because AI to AI applications enhance the 'intelligence' of a process and accelerate the resulting automation. Technically, human-centered AI (HCAI) also falls under these trends, but this is yet another term for hybrid intelligence, as discussed in Chapter 20.

The importance of democratized AI in an enterprise is that adding intelligence into applications, instead of more procedural processes or features, allows applications to support decision-making processes alongside transactional processes. It is allowing people to be more empowered but, in a data-driven way to enable intelligent automation. Potential use cases for this would be in airline pricing, more comprehensive retailing, and optimizing offers while controlling the availability based on commercial guardrails.

22.2.2 Generative AI

Generative AI is an innovative technology that helps generate artifacts that formerly relied on humans. It produces inventive results without any biases

200 *Trends and Evolutions in AI*

resulting from human thoughts and experiences. This new technique in AI determines the original pattern entered in the input to generate creative, authentic pieces that display the training data features. The MIT Technology Review (2019) stated that Generative AI is a promising advancement in AI as it allows us to 'reinvent how we invent'. The technology can enhance creative workflows together with humans by developing artifacts using content preferences or guidelines in an automated manner. Humans provide parameters and rules but the results can be generated independently and will be unique.

In practice, generative AI becomes very useful in web3 or metaverse. Avatars can be produced with little effort and offer security to those that do not wish to be identified. Another benefit is that Generative AI strengthens ML models but also makes them less partial, while ingesting more abstract concepts that are imitated from the real world. In healthcare, this technique can allow better detection of disease because it will be able to generate images from different angles of an X-ray picture to expose the possibility of a tumor development or expansion. This is done through Generative Adversarial Networks (GANs), a specific application of Generative AI in healthcare.

Generative AI is used also in the art world. With the sales of non-fungible tokens (NFTs) already reaching $25 billion in 2021,[1] this sector promises to be a profitable market that is leveraging the power of AI and human imagination to produce 'AI-generative art', i.e. machine-based art images.

There are other applications of Generative AI, even in software development by automating coding. It can be used in audio synthesis to create voices that resemble humans to make video clips or audible clips easier to understand for people that are used to other languages or accents.

22.2.3 *Edge AI*

AI methods and capabilities in the context of edge computing are referred as Edge AI. Edge computing is the deployment of computing and storage resources at the location where data is produced. This ideally puts compute and storage at the same point as the data source at the network edge, also called the periphery. As an example, an aircraft manufacture might place a modest amount of compute and storage within the aircraft to collect and process myriad aircraft system and sensor data. The results of any such processing can then be sent back to a data center for human review, archiving and to be merged with other data results for broader analytics.

Sometimes, cloud computing is touted as highly scalable deployment of compute and storage resources at one of several distributed global locations. But even though cloud computing offers more than enough resources and services to tackle complex analytics, the closest regional cloud facility can still be hundreds of miles from the point where data is collected. This distance may be important in that connections rely on the same temperamental internet connectivity that supports traditional data centers. In fact and in practice, cloud computing is an alternative, or sometimes a complement, to traditional data centers. The cloud can get centralized computing much closer to a data source, but not at the network edge. This is where a fog layer is often introduced. This is when a cloud data center is too remote and the edge deployment too resource-limited, or physically scattered or distributed, to make strict edge computing practical. In this case, the notion of fog computing can help. Fog computing typically takes a step back and puts compute and storage resources 'within' the data, but not necessarily 'at' the data. There are many potential uses for this depending on geographical location, remote places, and the fact that aircraft are mobile and often remote. In the context of airports and passengers and aircraft moving about, fog computing and AI-powered retail apps could be powerful and feasible because of the technology.

With the proper infrastructure in place, Edge AI can collect data from cameras, microphones, or any IoT-connected devices to run analytics and deploy AI models. The more obvious examples are self-driving cars that need to read traffic lights and depend on intelligent traffic control signals. The cars and traffic controls need to produce, analyze, and exchange data in real time. Similarly, drones or other automated functions in aircraft in-flight will need to cope with dynamic contexts to respond to.

With regard to autonomous cars and drones, the data must be aggregated and analyzed in real time, while the vehicle is in motion. When each vehicle becomes an 'edge', this requires significant onboard computing. In retail, the use cases have similar implications. Stores and retail businesses can produce large data volumes from surveillance, traffic and shelf behavior, stock tracking and sales data or other real-time consumer behavior details. If this is analyzed at the most local data source point to drive actionable tactics from the merchant, edge computing can help develop effective campaigns and predict or optimize vendor ordering.

The benefits of Edge AI are thus in

- Addressing vital infrastructure challenges.
- Driving autonomy.
- Data sovereignty.

Edge AI is useful where connectivity is unreliable, or where bandwidth is restricted because of the site's environmental characteristics. Examples include oil rigs, ships at sea, remote farms, or other remote locations, such as a rainforest or desert. Since edge computing does the compute work on site, sometimes on the edge device itself, this can reduce/remove data transmissions or at least remove the need for real-time connectivity. As a case in point, this has been done in Zimbabwe with water quality sensors on water purifiers in remote villages. By processing data locally, the amount of data to be sent can be vastly reduced. This requires far less bandwidth or connectivity time than might otherwise be necessary.

22.3 Technology Trends and Applications

Bernard Marr is a well-known futurist, influencer, and thought leader in the field of business and technology and a good source for trends and developments in AI. Following Marr, McKinsey & Co., Gartner, and other well-known consulting companies such as BCG or academic institutions like Harvard, MIT, and Stanford help to gain insights into the research they do, what their client practices are, and what results their experimental work generate.

One such trend that experts have spoken about is synthetic media. This is about the world of digital experiences and objects generated with input from AI. An example is Metaphysic's hyperreal videos of actor Tom Cruise are deepfakes that are very sophisticated.[2] In the future, we may spend more time online using synthetic content interactions around real or regular people.

In their 2022 Tech Trends Outlook, McKinsey outlined 14 trends of which Applied AI recorded the highest innovation score, while clean energy is drawing the most interest and investment. The 14 trends are

- Advanced connectivity.
- Applied AI.
- Cloud and edge computing.
- Immersive-reality technology
- Industrializing ML.
- Next-generation software development.
- Quantum technologies.
- Trust architectures and digital identity.
- Web3.
- Future of bioengineering.
- Future of clean energy.
- Future of mobility.
- Future of space technologies.
- Future of sustainable consumption.

It is beyond the scope of this book to explore the trends in detail and discuss the implications on business by identifying or delving into potential use case. However, of these technology trends, those that are considered the most relevant in bringing about beneficial change to aviation are advanced connectivity, applied AI, cloud and edge computing, future of mobility, and future of sustainable consumption. Also, it is important to highlight quantum technology as a trend as it relates to aviation and logistics.

Advanced connectivity has many innovative use cases in commercial aviation. Enhanced connectivity is an enabler for other new technologies, such as IoT applications, mobile AR/VR, and edge computing. In the air transport business, track and trace products can provide data to help customers optimize supply chains using Low-Power Wide Area (LPWA) wireless technology, which will improve efficiency.

Chapter 24 discusses AI and the metaverse, and talks about immersive-reality technology. This is about blending technology into the world, to see a real world a bit differently (mixed reality) and augment it (AR), or to see a different world (VR), as McKinsey puts it. This technology supports several use cases related to product design and development, training, new service enablement, or process improvements. For the airline industry, the use cases in shopping and retailing were outlined, but in engineering and maintenance, this technology will improve maintenance-related inspections or cargo warehouse procedures, even remotely. Further, simply by means of viewing an operation, situation, or operational process using immersive-reality technology, staff in airline operations will imagine potential improvements or risk-mitigation actions. Technologies used now include on-body sensors, off-body sensors, haptics,[3] holography, and electromyography.[4] Boeing uses AR to improve manufacturing process efficiency and has achieved a 90% quality increase and 30% speed increase on its pilot projects, as reported by McKinsey (2022).

Quantum technology is a futuristic technology that aims to improve computing by modernizing the computational infrastructure, including network and sensory. It is based on the principles of quantum theory, which explains the nature and behavior of energy and matter on the quantum (atomic and subatomic) level.[5] Quantum computing uses a combination of bits to perform specific computational tasks. All at a much higher efficiency than traditional computing. The development of quantum computers represents a significant leap forward in computing capability, with substantial performance gains for specific use cases. The main advantage of quantum computing is that it is excellent at solving specific problems and overcomes the obstacle that classical computers cannot scale well. While many use cases can be thought of, quantum optimization in real time is a promising one. It can compress computation times from hours to seconds, making it appealing for air navigation, road traffic management, portfolio optimization, and perhaps scheduling large networks and fleets. Examples of companies that have already launched commercial services around quantum computing are Google, IBM, Amazon, and Alibaba. Also, BMW has started using quantum ML for autonomous vehicles by using it to train models with a high accuracy level using huge data sets. It applies to car fleet routing optimization. In the airline industry, these quantum technologies could support fraud-resistant communication systems as well as augmented navigation systems, mostly likely for air navigation service providers (ANSPs).

The future of clean energy and the future of mobility are important topics for commercial aviation. The industry has set the goal of zero-emissions by 2050 and targets renewable energy, sustainable fuels (including biofuels), and hydrogen-based fuels as energy sources for aircraft power plants as well as throughout the value chain for all air and ground-based operations. Energy storage, optimization, and distribution will deploy AI on smart grids. This will benefit electric vehicles (EVs) as well as short-range electric aircraft.

204　*Trends and Evolutions in AI*

22.4　Debates in AI

The field of AI is not without criticisms or heated debates, both from within as well as in general. AI is often still considered a buzzword and there are downsides to the recent hype. AI is often still misunderstood and researchers in fields from medicine to sociology are rushing to use techniques that they do not always understand. This causes false results.

Then there was the recent uproar on sentient machines. Blake Lemoine, a Google engineer claimed that the program he created was sentient. He recounted having had dialogues with his Language Model for Dialogue Applications (LaMDA). He considered the program to be his 'colleague' and a 'person', but he was later put on administrative leave.[6] While technical experts in the field dismiss these claims, it did ignite an existing debate. But humans have always shown the tendency toward attributing a soul to objects that either resemble human beings (animism) or that we are fond of because of the interactions we have with them. It is important to distinguish between machines that people design to appear like human and them becoming human or having feelings. Even if machines express feelings using our language (words), it is because they have learned to associate word use with other programmatic learnings. Having emotions is related to having a body.

A lot of the debates center on unresolved questions such as:

- How might companies better determine which AI application provides the most benefit?
- Will AI in immersive reality shift the new wave of (remote) work?
- How can AI mitigate virtual crimes?
- How does AI in cloud or edge evolve regarding sustainable IT?
- Do AI applications affect intellectual-property issues for code written by an AI application?
- How are the expectations of customers, employees, and communities changing regarding their data, data analytics, privacy, or toward diversity, equality, and inclusion goals?

There will unlikely be many more debates about the future of AI but the benefits it brings to people, companies, customers, and societies will likely continue to outweigh the concerns and negative applications governments will have to regulate and minimize.

22.5　Conclusions

This chapter discussed the most recent trends in the field of AI, including Democratized AI, Generative AI, and Edge AI. It also described a selection of topics that are debated within the field, as tensions continue to be high about the usefulness or potential harm of the application of AI in life as we evolve. In most fields, including the medical field and aviation sector, the benefits appear to outweigh the potential harm, although more regulation is expected to maintain safety standards.

Notes

1 IT Business Edge, 'What is generative AI', 15 February 2022. https://www.itbusinessedge.com/data-center/what-is-generative-ai/.
2 Metaphysic (2022) 'How I became the fake Tom Cruise'. https://metaphysic.ai/how-i-became-the-fake-tom-cruise/.
3 Haptic devices (e.g., haptic gloves or vests) convey the sense of touch to the user with vibrations to augment virtual experiences. McKinsey & Company 2022 Technology Trends Outlook.
4 EMG is a neuro technology that detects and records electrical activity from muscles to control movement and manipulate objects in virtual spaces and is being used in wearables to augment AR/VR headset devices. McKinsey & Company 2022 Technology Trends Outlook. https://www.mckinsey.com/~/media/mckinsey/.
5 TechTarget, 'What is quantum computing', June 2020. https://www.techtarget.com/whatis/definition/quantum-computing.
6 Scientific American (2020), 'Google engineer claims AI chatbot is sentient: why that matters', 12 July 2022. https://www.scientificamerican.com/article/google-engineer-claims-ai-chatbot-is-sentient-why-that-matters/.

Bibliography

Chui, M., Roberts, R., and Yee, L. (2022) *McKinsey Technology Trends Outlook 2022*. McKinsey&Company. https://www.mckinsey.com/capabilities/mckinsey-digital/our-insights/the-top-trends-in-tech

Gartner (2018) 'What edge computing means for infrastructure and operations leaders'. https://www.gartner.com/smarterwithgartner/what-edge-computing-means-for-infrastructure-and-operations-leaders

Harvard Business Review (2021) 'Why your business needs to treat your edge data as capital'. https://hbr.org/sponsored/2021/07/why-your-business-needs-to-treat-your-edge-data-as-capital

IBM (2021) 'What is edge computing'. https://www.ibm.com/cloud/what-is-edge-computing

McKinsey Global Institute (2015) 'The internet of things, mapping the value beyond the hype'. https://www.mckinsey.com/~/media/McKinsey/Industries/Technology

MIT Technology Review (2019) 'AI is reinventing the way we invent', 15 February 2019. https://www.technologyreview.com/2019/02/15/137023/ai-is-reinventing-the-way-we-invent

PWC (2022), 'PWC 2022 AI business survey'. https://www.pwc.com/AI2022

TechTarget (2022) 'What is edge computing', 23 July 2022. https://www.techtarget.com/searchdatacenter/definition/edge-computing#

23 AI on Blockchain, and Distributed AI with Blockchain

23.1 Introduction

Blockchain is much talked about as a secure and promising technology. It is also already used by British Airways, Singapore Airlines, and Lufthansa. But what exactly is blockchain, and which problems does it solve? Or, what opportunities does it represent in aviation and travel, for airlines, airports, and other supply chain stakeholders?

The aim of this chapter is to demystify the buzz word blockchain and most importantly to learn through examples and case studies how it applies to aviation and how it can be used in combination with artificial intelligence (AI) in aviation and travel.

23.1 Blockchain Described

One of the key drivers behind blockchain is that the internet itself is not secure enough. The world needed a new infrastructure that allows people and companies to run different types of transactions without old or unsecure obstacles. Blockchain was first created to enable cryptocurrency but has since been widely touted for its potential to transform entire industries. The technology is used by global companies like IBM, Walmart, VISA, and Siemens in many different ways, for various aspects and in multiple disciplines in business. It is used in

- Banking and finance for
  - International payments.
  - Capital markets, faster clearing, and settlement.
  - Trade finance, for cross-border imports and exports.
  - Finance accounting and auditing.
  - Money laundering protection.
  - Insurance.
  - Peer-to-peer transactions.
- International business:
  - Supply chain management and real-time tracking.

DOI: 10.4324/9781003018810-28

- Healthcare, connecting medical devices.
- Real estate and transaction transparency.
- Media, eliminate fraud, and protect intellectual property rights.
- Energy, and metering, billing, or even energy supply.
- In Government:
  - Record management, simplify record keeping and making is secure.
  - Identity management.
  - Voting.
  - Tax filings.
  - Compliance and regulation.
- Overall, across industries:
  - Record management.
  - Cyber security.
  - Big Data and storage.
  - IoT, for supply chains and asset tracking.

Blockchain is not just a database, it is a new technology stack with 'digital trust' that is revolutionizing the way we exchange value and information across the internet, by taking out the 'gatekeepers' from the process. In more formal terms, blockchain technology supports methods for a decentralized peer-to-peer system, a collective trust model, and a distributed indisputable ledger of records of transactions.

For the past few decades, we had the Internet of information. When we send somebody an email or a PowerPoint file, we are actually not sending the original; we are sending a copy. That is great, and it has democratized information and learning. But when it comes to assets, things like money, financial assets like stocks and bonds, loyalty points, intellectual property, music, art, a vote, an airline ticket or vacation package, sending somebody a copy is a really bad idea. If we send somebody $1,000, it is important that we do not have the money afterward.

Today, we rely entirely on big intermediaries, middlemen like banks, government, big social media companies, credit companies, and so on. This is to establish trust in our economy. These intermediaries perform all the business and transaction logic of every kind of commerce, from identification and authentication of people through clearing, settling, and record-keeping. They capture our data, which means we cannot monetize or use it to better manage our lives, and our privacy is being undermined. So, the blockchain is about the evolution from the internet of information to the internet of value. That is the essence of the revolution.

As mentioned earlier, blockchain is not a database, it is a new technology stack with digital trust that is radically changing the way we exchange value and information across the internet, by taking out the gatekeepers or traditional obstacles from the process. Unlike traditional methods, blockchain enables peer-to-peer transfer of digital assets without any intermediaries. These assets can be goods or services people exchange, like buying used aircraft

208 *Trends and Evolutions in AI*

engine parts overseas. It can also be information to solve problems. Let us look at this definition: "The blockchain is an immutable (unchangeable, meaning a transaction or file recorded cannot be changed) distributed digital ledger (digital record of transactions or data stored in multiple places on a computer network) with many use cases beyond cryptocurrencies" (MIT, 2021).

Blockchain was a technology originally created to support the famous cryptocurrency, Bitcoin. The blockchain by itself has taken a life of its own and spread through a broad range of applications across many industries as mentioned in the introduction. Each transaction or record on the ledger is stored in a 'block.' For example, blocks on the Bitcoin blockchain consist of an average of more than 500 Bitcoin transactions. The information contained in a block is dependent on and linked to the information in a previous block and, over time, forms a chain of transactions. Hence the word blockchain.

The blockchain will allow us to innovate and transform a wide range of things, including goods transfer, for example, across supply chains or for digital media transfer, for example, or the sale of art. That's also what TravelX and Air Europa did in April 2022, when they auctioned a digital art plane ticket from Paris to Miami.[1] These tickets were sold as the right to access a digital piece of art, called 'Non-Fungible Tokens' (NFTs) through blockchain. There are earlier examples as well. In 2018, to celebrate Latvia's centenary, airBaltic ran a competition asking entrants to vote for their favorite Latvian towns and cities, from which the company's Airbus A220–300 fleet would be named. NFTs were then created and issued by airBaltic of the most popular cities, starting with the city of Kuldīga. On launching the airBaltic NFT in 2021, Martin Gauss, CEO of airBaltic, said

> Blockchain technology has proven to be here long-term. After being the first airline to accept Bitcoin as a form of payment, it is the next step for us in blockchain technology to offer non-fungible tokens. NFTs are not only used for digital art transactions but may as well be expanded to tickets for concerts and other unique one-time pieces, including airline tickets. The issue of the limited collector NFTs will serve as a tourism campaign for Latvian cities, certainly still an undiscovered destination for many.[2]

23.2 How Blockchain Works in a Nutshell

Blockchains are essentially a modern way of creating ledgers to store information. It is an improved way of single or double-entry accounting. However, records stored using traditional ledgers are also easy to tamper with, meaning you can easily edit, remove, or add a record. As a result, you are less likely to trust that the information is accurate.

Public blockchains solve both these problems – and the way we trust – by evolving the traditional bookkeeping model to triple-entry bookkeeping. Transactions on a blockchain are cryptographically sealed by a third entry.

This creates a tamper-proof record of transactions stored in blocks and verified by a distributed consensus mechanism. These consensus mechanisms also ensure new blocks get added to any blockchain. An example of a consensus mechanism is proof-of-work (PoW), often referred to as 'mining.'

Mining is not universal to all blockchains, it is just one type of consensus mechanism currently used by Bitcoin and Ethereum, though Ethereum moved to another, proof-of-stake (PoS), in 2022.[3] The process with Bitcoin works as follows. When sending Bitcoin, you pay a small fee (in bitcoin) for a network of computers to confirm your transaction is valid. Your transaction is then bundled with other transactions pending in a queue to be added to a new block. The computers (nodes) then work to validate this list of transactions in the block by solving a complex mathematical problem to come up with a hash, which is a 64-digit hexadecimal number. Once solved, the block is added to the network and your fee, combined with all other transaction fees in that block, is the miner's reward. It is that simple.

Each new block added to the network is assigned a unique key (via cryptography). To obtain each new key, the previous block's key and information are input into a formula. As new blocks are continually added through the ongoing mining process, they become increasingly secure and harder to tamper with. Anyone caught trying to edit a record will simply be ignored. All future blocks then depend on information from prior blocks and this dependency from one block to the next forms a secure chain, that is the blockchain.

A public blockchain functions through consensus mechanisms, the process for validating transactions without a third party like a bank. PoW and PoS are two such mechanisms. While their goal, to reach a consensus that a transaction is valid, remains the same, how they get there is a little different.

PoW, the technical term for mining, is the original consensus mechanism. It is still used by Bitcoin and Ethereum but, as mentioned, Ethereum moved to PoS this year (2022). PoW is based on cryptography, which uses mathematical equations only computers can solve. The two big problems with PoW are that it uses a lot of electricity and can only process a limited number of transactions simultaneously (seven for Bitcoin). Transactions typically take at least ten minutes to complete, with this delay increasing when the network is congested. Though compared to the days-long wait required to wire money across the globe, or even to clear a check, Bitcoin's ten-minute delay is quite remarkable.

Other consensus mechanisms were created to solve these PoW problems, the most popular being PoS. PoS still uses cryptographic algorithms for validation, but transactions get validated by a chosen validator based on how many coins they hold, also known as their stake. Individuals are not technically mining, and there is no block reward. Instead, blocks are 'forged.' Those participating in this process lock a specific number of coins on the network. The bigger a person's stake, the more mining power they have, and the higher the chances they will be selected as the validator for the next block. To ensure those with the most coins are not always selected, other selection methods are used. These include randomized block selection (forgers with the highest

210 *Trends and Evolutions in AI*

stake and lowest hash value are chosen) and coin age selection (forgers are selected based on how long they have held their coins).

The results are faster transaction times and lower costs. The NEO and Dash cryptocurrencies, for example, can send and receive transactions in seconds.[4]

23.2 Benefits of Blockchain

There are several benefits to using blockchain in business. It does not require trust, it cannot be blocked, it cannot be tampered with, decisions are not centralized, it operates at a lower cost, is peer-to-peer, and fully transparent.

1 Trustless: The blockchain is immutable and automates trusted transactions between counterparties who do not need to know each other. Transactions are only executed when programmed conditions are met by both parties.
2 Unstoppable: Once the conditions programmed into a blockchain protocol are met, an initiated transaction cannot be undone, changed, or stopped. It is going to execute and nothing – no bank, government, or third party – can stop it.
3 Immutable: Records on a blockchain cannot be changed or tampered with – Bitcoin has never been hacked. A new block of transactions is only added after a complex mathematical problem is solved and verified by a consensus mechanism. Each new block has a unique cryptographic key resulting from the previous block's information and key being added into a formula.
4 Decentralized: No single entity maintains the network. Unlike centralized banks, decisions on the blockchain are made via consensus. Decentralization is essential because it ensures people can easily access and build on the platform, and there are multiple points of failure.
5 Lower Cost: In the traditional finance system, you pay third parties like banks to process transactions. The blockchain eliminates these intermediaries and reduces fees, with some systems returning fees to miners and stakers.
6 Peer-to-Peer: Cryptocurrencies like Bitcoin, let you send money directly to anyone, anywhere in the world, without an intermediary like a bank charging transactions or handling fees.
7 Transparent: Public blockchains are open-source software, so anyone can access them to view transactions and their source code. They can even use the code to build new applications and suggest improvements to the code. Suggestions are accepted or rejected via consensus.

23.3 Airlines and Blockchain Use Cases

Let us look at a few examples of initial use cases of blockchain by airlines. Air France trialed a blockchain-powered health passport in 2022, called ICC

AOKpass.[5] This app enables passengers to present their COVID-19 negative test on their mobile phones. The ICC AOKpass then confirms that the test presented is valid and complies with the regulations of the country of destination via a network secured by blockchain technology. British Airways has invested in and is working with Zamna,[6] a company that is using facial recognition with blockchain technology. Delta airlines is a member of the blockchain research institute, exploring various technologies to improve the flying experience for its customers.[7] Etihad Airways partnered with Winding Tree's blockchain travel platform in 2019 to bypass travel intermediaries, similar to programs initiated by Air France-KLM.[8] Lufthansa started the initiative Blockchain for Aviation (BC4A), which plans to include participants such as aircraft manufacturers, logistics providers, MRO service providers, software developers, and many more.[9] It will take exchanging value and important transactions to another level.

Singapore Airlines is using blockchain technology as part of its frequent flyer loyalty program using KrisPay, which offers promotions to customers.[10] Blockchain could also be used there to manage loyalty currency, the accrual and redemption of points across affiliate airline networks.

In Europe, it is hoped that SlotMachine will allow for more optimal use of airport resources and result in fewer passenger delays.[11] Notably, airlines will not be able to access any competitors' private data, such as what they are bidding on and how many slots the different airlines have released, but they will be able to see the slots available which best suit their incoming and outgoing flights.

23.4 Airports and Blockchain Uses Cases

There are many other use cases for blockchain in commercial aviation and travel. One important area is around security and personal identity. The world needs to maintain a tightly secure system to keep out threats. And this applies to airport terminal buildings, on planes, and clearly across country borders. Blockchain could be used to set up a centralized identity verification system that could make the world safer. We could also combine records of people on the safe lists with their biometric information. For instance, facial recognition. Or for those willing to get even speedier treatment, their retina or fingerprint can be scanned and verified when people opt-in. There are a few other use cases of blockchain for airports and the travel supply chain:

- Airlines are using blockchain technology to help manage take-off and landing slots. The EU-funded SlotMachine consortium is using blockchain technology to develop a cost-efficient solution that will enable airlines to swap take-off and landing slots more efficiently.
- Personal identity security: Traditional systems for storing identities are insecure and fragmented. Blockchain provides a unified, immutable,

212 *Trends and Evolutions in AI*

and interoperable infrastructure so you can store and manage records securely and efficiently.

- Identity is also important in managing loyalty status, or privileged access to airport lounges, perhaps incorporating smart documents and biometrics, like retina scans.
- Blockchain can be used for purchasing fuel contracts and payment settlement. KLM currently handles 85 local currencies for paying its fuel bills alone. It could save money in a more efficient blockchain system.[12]
- Maintenance and compliance are important areas. All parts and maintenance activities must be logged, combined with operating statistics of hours flown, cycles completed, and number of landings. Knowing the origins of all maintenance incidents is a crucial safety aspect.

If one looks at aviation in a linear way, there are many operational processes that are lined up. Parties exchanging information about bags, gates, jet bridges, de-icing operations, and baggage handling. Those operational processes can be digitized with the exchange of digital information and local applications. But from a planning perspective, these parties are all stakeholders in a supply chain. They all need supplies and contracts, even at duty-free. And if you include trains and urban mobility like electric vertical take-off and landings (eVTOLs), it is not unimaginable to foresee an aerotropolis exchanging value among its stakeholders on a large-scale blockchain. This requires contracts between all ecosystem partners for all the moving parts. It requires smart contracts in terms of how all the monies or value flows work and are triggered in real time based on deliverables, deadlines, or time stamps.

23.5 AI on Blockchain, and Distributed AI with Blockchain

AI and blockchain have become two of the most trending and disruptive technologies. As described before, blockchain technology can automate payment in cryptocurrency and provide access to a shared ledger of data, transactions, and keep a log in a decentralized, secure, and trusted manner. In addition, with smart contracts, blockchain can govern interactions among participants with no intermediary or a trusted third party. But AI, conversely, offers intelligence and decision-making capabilities for machines like humans and there are many emerging blockchain applications, platforms, and protocols specifically targeting AI areas.

The intersection and opportunity of AI on blockchain are twofold. It is about (1) using AI in blockchain applications and in (2) decentralizing AI itself using blockchain. The use of AI in blockchain applications concentrates mostly on predicting security issues and solving them ahead of time. Some consensus protocols (such as Proof of Stake) are not free of hacking threats and AI can help detect early signs. The decentralization of AI using blockchain is about completely different use cases.

The massive production and generation of data by sensing systems, IoT devices, social media, and web applications have contributed to the rise of AI. All this data can be used by various machine learning and deep learning techniques to perform analytics, including predictive analytics to solve problems. But AI is known to work with huge volumes of data and there are concerns about computational power and capacity in centralized AI. And that is not all.

Today, most of the machine learning and deep learning methods of AI rely on a centralized model for training. In that case, a group of servers run a specific model against training and validating datasets. This is how not only large organizations like Google, Amazon, Facebook, and Apple but also airlines manage big data volumes to make informed decisions.

However, the centralized nature of AI has limitations. Not only is the amount of data and the types of data sources limited, but it may also not be sufficiently rich to solve more complex problems. In addition, centralized AI may lead to the possibility of data tampering as it can be subject to hacking. The data provenance and authenticity of the sources generating the data are also not guaranteed. And this may all lead to AI decision outcomes that can be erroneous, risky, and dangerous.

Distributed AI is therefore a combination of decentralized AI and blockchain. It enables a company to process and perform analytics or decision-making on trusted, digitally signed (immutable), and secure shared data that has been transacted and stored on the blockchain. But that is not the most promising aspect of decentralized AI. The feature of blockchain that is beneficial for the application of AI is in governing problem-solving and transactions among more participants involved in generating, accessing, and using data to solve problems. Smart contract-based autonomous systems and machines can learn and adapt to changes over time, and AI techniques that utilize blockchain can offer decentralized learning to solve even bigger and more complex problems. This can facilitate trust and secure sharing of knowledge and decision outcomes across a large number of autonomous 'agents', which could be different stakeholders in a vertical, such as freight forwarders, cargo transportation firms, including airlines and ground handlers.

Conventional blockchain is a very expensive matter for storing large amounts of data. So decentralized mediums for storing data and hashes of the data can now be used and linked with blockchain blocks. For instance, some of the now popular decentralized storage technologies are the Interplanetary File System (IPFS), BigChainDB, Filecoin, and Swarm.

Many shortcomings of AI and blockchain can be addressed effectively by combining both technological ecosystems. AI algorithms rely on data to learn, infer, and make decisions based on predictions and the learning algorithms work better when data is reliable, secure, and trusted, but also potentially of higher quality because it can be enriched through additional data sources through blockchain. The consolidation of this can also create a haven for highly sensitive information that AI-driven systems must collect, store, and use, such as in the medical field for hospitals, complex surgeries, or

214 *Trends and Evolutions in AI*

airline passenger spending behavior, or freight tendering and payment flows in complex logistics supply chains.

In decentralized AI applications, the goals of autonomic computing, improved optimization, better planning, and rich knowledge discovery and sharing can be achieved. Machine learning can also be 'upgraded' to federated learning as more versioning of additional learning models can be maintained by provenance (more sources) as well as their historical data footprints.

As part of decentralized AI operations, data storage must be decentralized, and metadata must be maintained in a secure way by source (provenance). But modern AI applications also need to handle continuously evolving data streams, and this is where decentralized learning algorithms take the input datasets from relevant swarms and shards and produce highly personalized learning models for each client. One can think of social media and mobile commerce but also new data streams from augmented reality (AR) infused Apps people use, or even the metaverse, as Chapter 24 describes. In the travel industry, more marketplaces and data sources appear every year.

The types of these decentralized AI applications certainly include public blockchains, private blockchains, and consortium or 'federated' blockchains. The latter is operated by a group of organizations, usually formed based on mutual interests between participating organizations in a larger value chain or industry vertical. An example is the Dutch land registry department having consolidated AI and blockchain technology into the real estate industry. It aimed to improve legal dependence and asset investment in a more stable process. It used AI and self-learning to predict outcomes while capitalizing on blockchain to handle and manage the huge volumes of data resources saved and produced by the land registry department.

It is in this area where airports, airlines, immigration agencies, and ground handlers could potentially collaborate. Another application could be among ground transportation (trucks), cargo terminals and ground handling companies as well as airlines, with full transparency and logs on the other side (import). It could help stabilize a supply chain process, help optimize the use of resources, and deal with predictable service interruptions before they are likely to occur. It will eventually minimize interruptions.

Another AI application can be offering the above service by cloud service providers as part of 'Blockchain-as-a-Service' (BaaS) model. Vendors like Microsoft, IBM, and Amazon today enable environments for companies to test blockchain services.

Overall, decentralized optimization using AI on blockchain and through distributed AI combined with blockchain leads to increased system performance by processing highly relevant data. The decentralized optimization is also beneficial when multiple strategies with different optimization objectives need to be run simultaneously across applications and systems.

As more and more functions within airlines, airports, and cargo carriers are optimized with 'local' applications of AI, even across functions using Enterprise AI, airlines may venture out and capitalize on the opportunities presented by distributed AI on blockchain for the deployment of smart contracts underpinned by federated learning. The use cases are in procurement, stakeholder operation alignment within the value chain, complex logistics processes involving third parties and the open market as well as a democratization of product creation, offering, and retailing optimization.

23.6 Conclusions

This chapter described blockchain as a distributed and unchanged ledger that makes transaction recording and asset management over a network more accessible. Blockchain network is a type of infrastructure that gives applications access to smart contract services and ledger services. Payments, accounts, production, and orders can be tracked via a blockchain network.

In the airline, travel, and airport business, there are many exchanges of information, value, and contracts made and executed between the various parties. The chapter argued that all stakeholders interact to facilitate services and exchange goods, equipment, tools, and parts to operate. This is mostly transborder and increasingly executed digitally, so it makes sense to improve efficiency and cut costs from older, heavy, or centralized processes.

The chapter explored the benefits of blockchain, AI on blockchain, and distributed AI through blockchain to elevate machine learning to federated learning using universe and no longer enterprise big data. It concluded that there are numerous novel ways blockchain can improve different business areas and industries, including travel, air transport, and cargo or logistics. Some examples were provided.

Notes

1 TravelX, (2022) 'Air Europa to sell sustainable NFT flight tickets to Miami'. https://www.travelx.io/air-europa-to-sell-sustainable-nft-flight-tickets-to-miami/.
2 Cryptoslate.com (2021) 'airBaltic becomes the world's first airline to issue NFTs'. https://cryptoslate.com/airbaltic-becomes-the-worlds-first-airline-to-issue-nfts/.
3 Investopedia (2022) 'Ethereum 2.0 is on Horizon after passing another test'. https://www.investopedia.com/ethereum-testnet-goes-live-6452575#.
4 CoinSutra (2019) 'Top 10 cryptocurrencies with fast transaction speeds'. https://coinsutra.com/transaction-speeds.
5 Presse Groupe ADP (2021) 'Air France and Groupe ADP extend the "ICC AOKPASS" solution'. https://presse.groupeadp.fr/aokpass-experiment-cdg/?lang=en.
6 LedgerInsights (2019) 'Blockchain airport ID firm Zamna raises $5 million after deals with Emirates, BA'. https://www.ledgerinsights.com/blockchain-passenger-airline-identity-zamna-funding-emirates-british-airways/.
7 Centre for Aviation (2019) 'Delta Air Lines leveraging AI, sees blockchain opportunities'. https://centreforaviation.com/analysis/reports/delta-air-lines-leveraging-ai-sees-blockchain-opportunities-454071.
8 LedgerInsights (2019) 'Etihad Airways partners with blockchain platform winding tree'. https://www.ledgerinsights.com/etihad-airways-blockchain-winding-tree/.

216 *Trends and Evolutions in AI*

9 Lufthansa Pressroom (2022) 'Generating more transparency in aviation with blockchain technology'. https://www.lufthansa-industry-solutions.com/de-en/solutions-products/aviation/generating-more-transparency-in-aviation-with-blockchain-technology.
10 Computer Weekly (2021) 'CW Innovation Awards: SIA taps blockchain for loyalty app', 29 March 2021. https://www.computerweekly.com/news/252497795/-CW-Innovation-Awards-SIA-taps-blockchain-for-loyalty-app#.
11 Frequentis (2022) 'EU funded project slotmachine to use blockchain technology for most cost-efficient flight slot allocation'. https://www.frequentis.com/en/pr/eu-funded-project-slotmachine-use-blockchain-technology-more-cost-efficient-flight-slot.
12 KLM (2019). Annual Report. https://ww.klm.com.

Bibliography

Burniske, C., and Tatar, J. (2019) *Cryptoassets*. New York: McGraw-Hill.

Champagne, P. (2014) *The book of Satoshi: the collected writings of bitcoin creator Satoshi Nakamoto*. Austin, TX: e53 Publishing LLC.

Elrom, E. (2019) *The blockchain developer: a practical guide for designing, implementing, publishing, testing, and securing distributed blockchain-based projects*. Berkeley, NC: Apress.

Lewi, A. (2018). *Understand bitcoin, blockchains, and cryptocurrency*. Miami, FL: Mango.

Mamoshina, P. *et al.* (2018) 'Converging blockchain and next-generation artificial intelligence technologies to decentralize and accelerate biomedical research and healthcare', *Oncotarget*, 9(5), pp. 5665–5690.

Marwala, T. *et al.* (2018) 'Blockchain and artificial intelligence'. https://arxiv.org/abs/1802.04451

Najafabadi, M.M. *et al.* (2015) 'Deep learning applications and challenges in big data analytics', *Journal of Big Data*, 2, p. 1.

Salah, K. *et al.* (2018) 'Blockchain for AI: review and open research challenges'. *IEEE*, 7, pp. 10127–10149.

Tapscott, D. *et al.* (2018) *Blockchain revolution*. London: Portfolio (Penguin).

24 AI and Metaverse, Web3

24.1 Introduction

Metaverse is one of the more recent buzzwords that have attracted much attention, in particular when Facebook changed the name of its main brand and holding company to Meta in October 2021. On 9 June 2022, it officially changed its stock market ticker symbol to META from FB.[1] It was timely and indicative of the future of experiences using electronic communication, notably as the metaverse is often referred to as the successor to mobile internet.

The rise of the metaverse is driven by four underlying factors. It is propelled by the evolution of retailing and IoT, social media, human psychological needs, and advances in technology. They blend in perfectly for what consumers and people want and believe they need to feel better. However, many people do not know or cannot envision what metaverse is. And the problem is that people cannot accurately judge the shape and boundary of the future metaverse. For instance, there is the 'tiny metaverse', like a potential Facebook/Meta metaverse, and the potential macro metaverse where companies and governments collaborate.

What consumers know, however, is that they increasingly want better and inspirational experiences. And as people shop and purchase more online, the metaverse offers opportunities to create engaging experiences when brands cannot meet their customers face-to-face, or when they believe a virtual experience can aid or otherwise improve an in-store experience. Forbes found that by 2021, metaverse was already valued at $14.8 trillion globally.[2]

So, as more people talk about it and more existing research is now getting more attention as it explores a promising technology with interesting use cases, airlines and other consumer-driven service companies have started to look at metaverse as well. Qatar Airways already experimented with a micro-metaverse in June 2022. Qatar is hosting the Middle East's first metaverse FIFA gaming tournament to let fans across the globe see the top FIFA players compete for the EA Sports FIFA 22 Champions Cup.[3] The metaverse concept comes in where viewers will get multiple opportunities to interact with one another and the players throughout the tournament. It will also offer viewers free non-fungible tokens (NFTs) that they can exchange for

DOI: 10.4324/9781003018810-29

218 Trends and Evolutions in AI

merchandise, and chances to meet players and influencers. Viewers can also purchase the NFTs as investments.

Metaverse and web3 go hand in hand. Metaverse is enabled by the next generation of internet and referred to as web3, or 'Web3.0'. It has become a term for the vision of a new, better internet that offers applications to run on blockchain, decentralized networks of many peer-to-peer nodes. It has also been called "the internet owned by the builders and users, orchestrated with tokens" by Packy McCormick, an investor behind the technology.[4]

But what is metaverse and what is it in relation to web3? What will these technologies enable, and which opportunities do they create in air travel, transportation, or for airports and other stakeholders? The aim of this chapter is to clarify the buzz around metaverse and most importantly to learn through examples and case studies how it applies to aviation. I will then look at how the fusion of artificial intelligence (AI) on blockchain in metaverse can bring about promising use cases and commercial opportunities for companies in aviation, travel, and logistics.

24.1 Metaverse Described

Web3 will convert the internet we are familiar today to an intermediary-free digital economy. Web3 also unlocks the use of blockchain and other technologies as well as applications that combine the underlying infrastructure with virtual reality (VR), augmented reality, and the growing interest in connecting devices that measure behaviors (IoT). So, while web3 is a process engine that utilizes blockchain advancements, the metaverse is an added creative dimension. This dimension is experiential much like what we are used to in video games ('gaming'), entertainment, and film. But metaverse is expansive, immersive, and its applications go further and deeper into health, social platforms, education, and virtual training approaches to achieve the intended goals.

What is driving the metaverse is not only a saturation of current technology adoption or the digital platforms' need to carve out future revenue pockets but also the fact that there is a perceived need to enhance shopping and entertainment experiences in a blended world. Brands want more and competition online is fierce. Social media have also promoted and enabled people to take on additional identities online or to represent themselves in ways they cannot in a physical world. In addition, technologies like VR and augmented reality are becoming more common, essentially paving the way for consumers envisioning other practical uses of it.

In the early days, people thought of metaverse in terms of artificial worlds with characters and made-up avatars and early adopters were either young or already favorable toward video games. Blending in physical and artificial with sophisticated technology, however, brings about use cases and complex applications that can have far-reaching consequences. Emotional systems also play a role in how adoption journeys and roadmaps look like, such as the fear of missing out, or the fear of loss of autonomy in a world one cannot control. This explains some of the strong resistance that can be found when people online argue that the world does not need metaverse, that life is not a video game, and that there are no business cases for its development. Yet, metaverse is there and it is growing in scope from 'local' to industrial development and deployment.

So, metaverse has many features, ranging from VR, non-NFT, gaming, geo-enabled virtual locations, virtual commerce, and community and sharing experiences. Fundamentally, though, metaverse encompasses the digital economy, from digital creation of product to digital consumption. The four components of this digital economy are:

1   Digital creation.
     This requires an authoring tool that can make the creation easy and personalized. For instance, this is how a hotel or vacation experience and location could be created.
2   Digital asset.
     This has the hidden property, which is the precondition of trade. For example, assets can be attributes of a rain forest, like waterfalls or different colors of unique costumes people can trade.
3   Digital market.
     This is the fundamental place in which avatars can trade to have income. For instance, this is the environment and digital appearance and digital 'touch and feel' of the marketplace.
4   Digital currency.
     This is the media in metaverse with which the avatars can finish the trade and exchange. For example, these are the different cryptocurrencies the marketplace accepts. What makes metaverse appealing also has a Zeitgeist element. Recent generations from Y, X, and Z have shown people to become more expressive, assertive, and diverse. The diversity, inclusion, and equality movement has also propelled openness. Conversely, the individuals in the metaverse are selfless and illogical. These individuals prefer to emphasize their personal feelings such as happiness and a sense of accomplishment and there are no limitations to ways of expressing it or the number of avatars used to do it. In the traditional physical world, there exists an industrial structure. In the metaverse, these boundaries are non-existent and the conceptual, digital, economy is the basic form of economic activity.

The differences between the economy of the metaverse and the conventional economy can therefore be described as follows:

•   In the metaverse, identity determines value instead of undifferentiated labor in the conventional economy.
•   There are unlimited resources, and the marginal benefits will increase in metaverse instead of diminishing marginal benefits of production in the physical world.

220   *Trends and Evolutions in AI*

- With the lack of scarcity and increasing scale, the marginal costs of products will decrease, compared with the physical world.
- Transaction costs in metaverse tend to be zero, which will incur frequent transactions.

24.2 Physical vs. Metaverse Behaviors

This is how Forbes (2021) describes the metaverse:

> In the metaverse, consumers can access a hyper-personalized experience that mimics leaving their home for a grand adventure—all from the comfort of their couch. Again, while it's still in its early stages, you may one day be able to work, play, shop and game in the metaverse. You'll be free to be yourself, or you can create an avatar to navigate the metaverse.

Brands want to improve digital commerce and create engaging experiences. The metaverse matters for retailers because it has many benefits, such as

- It enables conversational marketing, such as ongoing two-way dialogue with individual customers as well as the entire customer base simultaneously.
- It is trackable and can be analyzed, like all observed behaviors quality as first-party data.
- It is immersive, for instance, it is easier to keep a customer's attention while they are trying your product (like choosing a color of shirt on them).

Big brands are experimenting with metaverse and find meaningful results. IKEA, L'Oreal, Bolle have all trialled metaverse. Adidas, Burberry, Gucci, Tommy Hilfiger, Nike, Samsung, Louis Vuitton, and even banks HSBC and JP Morgan have deployed applications.[5] The combination of highly personalized products (e.g. Nike) and high-touch virtual engagements is the recipe for stickiness. This has important implications for airlines and possibly airport operators as well. New technology, that is not ready for release yet, will even allow people to wear gloves that provide real sensations, for instance, when you shake hands with somebody in the metaverse (BBC, 2022). Early users of the metaverse access it by wearing VR goggles, but there are other ways of entering and being in the virtual environment, like using your phone or other personal device.

Early adopters of metaverse are also curious to explore opportunities in identity, expression, and creativity. As mentioned earlier, online behaviors differ from those adopted in a real world. Yet, there are many ways in which the multiple identities people adopt on digital platforms reflect and impact on behaviors in the metaverse as well as the physical world. Ironically, there is evidence that consumption in metaverse has affected the physical world and even changed the behaviors of people in the physical world.

What forms the bridge between the physical and digital world is not only the people or consumers. In the world of the Internet of Things (IoT), objects and connected devices in the physical world interact with the metaverse. They represent the structure, behaviors, and context of physical assets (human, or process) in the virtual world. This becomes relevant in the context of the trend to build digital twins (DTs) with the goal of using them throughout the whole asset life cycle with real-time data. The DT is not only used to exist or take part in metaverse applications, but physical behaviors can be transferred into metaverse where they interact in another universe. A universe, that also creates new behaviors, which can be analyzed as metaverse analytics. They in turn provide insights into how we can also improve experiences in the physical world with applications for shopping, playing, meeting, or entertaining using VR and augmented reality with wearables or through projections, such as holograms.

The consequence of people adopting multiple identities in metaverse for retailers is threefold:

- First, companies will be able to market to avatars, and indirectly to the consumers that create them. The technology exists to create photorealistic 3-D models of products using algorithms based on scans of physical merchandise and it can be done at scale at low cost.
- Second, they need to master new skills of marketing, but it does require knowing your shoppers' platforms, gaming preferences, and VR/AR/3-D hardware.
- Finally, retailers must choose a location. Much like the physical world, location, location, location matters, and choosing a provider within the worlds of metaverse will be key. By 2022, there were already over 50 such metaverse worlds, with popular ones like Decentraland, Somnium Space, Meta's Horizon Worlds, and The Sandbox.

Similar to social media, there is a risk in choosing the platform. Some social media did not succeed, and it will be the same in the metaverse space. Some niche metaverses will succeed and some will not. What makes a metaverse world location powerful is its network effect, which again depends on multipliers we find behind other platforms.

24.3 AI and Metaverse

Artificial intelligence can be used for digital (object) and marketplace (exchange) creation. AI could also be used to provide intelligence to authoring tools and reach or exceed the level of human learning. These tools, which will accelerate how objects are created, will greatly affect the operational efficiency and intelligence of metaverse.

We can create metaworlds by programming in web3, but as suggested above we can jumpstart the process by using photorealistic 3-D models that can be

222 *Trends and Evolutions in AI*

generated and enhanced using AI. But once we participate in the metaverse, metaverse analytics can be used to monitor, track, and digest all avatar and other behaviors. The virtual world of metaverse generates a huge amount, variety, and velocity of data, such as structured data, and unstructured data.

The use of DTs is essential to populate the metaverse but also paramount in propelling a new level of analytics. Deep learning–based digital twins generate new insights in the metaverse that can be applied not only in the metaverse but also in real life. As avatars shop, meet, or attend training sessions, so will the physical world learn from experiments that can be duplicated in the real world. In fact, it can provide a better understanding of the underlying mechanics to all the stakeholders by the fusion of the virtual world with data sciences. Examples of active use of this technology where it is applied today are not only in fire evacuation drills but also in military training. Trainees are placed in different remote physical locations with real-time supervision, but they learn to put out fires in digitally-created environments to learn from. The experiences and level of training can exceed what can be replicated in the real world, which enhances skill levels. Evidently, similar applications could be found in flight attendant training to simulate situations that would be rare and very costly to create in real life.

AI-based activities in the metaverse can be created and offered by a new marketplace or a participating merchant in the marketplace. AI can be used to create these offerings, but distributed AI could also lead to value creation through collaboration when companies join forces and create bundles of personalized offers. The smart contract on blockchain approach could benefit from decentralized AI and solve bigger problems with higher security. For instance, airlines could work with concert organizers and destination management companies to create unique travel and entertainment experiences and allow avatars to have personalized sensations in their metaverse marketplace. They could rent out VIP space and allow other products to be marketed to them. They could use centralized AI using customer data platforms combined with distributed AI for personalized products and consumption in metaverse. Depending on how the avatars behave and what they purchase, this metaverse-based AI can be used to improve offers, products, and customer service in real life.

However, scattered ownership of data is a barrier since companies do not want to share commercially sensitive information, nor do governments. To address this issue, federated learning (FL) has emerged as a kind of collaborative learning paradigm, allowing participants to train the shared model locally by transferring the training parameters instead of raw data. This was described earlier in Chapter 23 on decentralized AI, i.e., distributed AI on blockchain. The federated learning paradigm can protect the data privacy and reduce the communication overhead, especially for the large-scale scenarios with large models and massive data.

The development of an intelligent metaverse is still a challenge, such as integrating big and fast or real-time streaming data analytics, big dataset shortage, and on-device intelligence. But the practice will become more widespread and improve products, services, and customer engagement in the physical world.

Metaverse differs from video games because it involves many activities that are not necessarily only for fun. Examples are:

- Users can attend events (concerts, virtual exhibitions, remote education, and meeting collaboration without having to travel.
- Metaverse is virtual and real symbiosis, meaning it can evolve in parallel even if people leave the virtual world anytime.

There are some other important characteristic aspects, particularly regarding avatar and non-player characters:

- Avatars are not only used in games but also as users' representations in eCommerce applications, virtual social environments, and geographically separated workplace meetings.
- There can be behavior transfer from a virtual demonstration to a physical robot through training.
- There can be behavior transfer from a physical person to a virtual avatar or twin.

24.4 Distributed AI in Metaverse Uses Cases

Artificial intelligence task in metaverse, as it is elsewhere, is to solve problems and find optimal solutions toward a well-defined goal using data. In the metaverse and given the many players and stakeholders, the technology stack involved is potentially overwhelming. And some of the goals between digital co-creators and providers using distributed AI in metaverse may conflict. By sharing rich behavioral data, service providers will be competing for customer engagement and attachments.

There are a few categories of promising use cases, both from a travel industry, provider, as well as customer perspective. First, there is an opportunity for vertical integration to experience and bundle experiences that are (so far) difficult to combine in real life. In addition, the metaverse enables a democratization of service creation among consumers and providers. Further, customer empowerment and immersion allow the industrialization of new capital goods markets. And fourth, metaverse marketplaces offer retail techniques that are unique and ultra-personalized.

From a vertical integration standpoint, airlines, hotels, venues, and experience providers can offer related services in the metaverse, with options of adding them to the metaverse experience or transfer them to physical or augmented reality services. Either on the plane, on the beach, while shopping with rich context-driven information. Other examples are in-journey offer and order management (AR-based) or previews and even metaverse trials of in-flight service and seat comfort.

224 *Trends and Evolutions in AI*

There is also the democratization of service product design. The metaverse enables airlines and cabin manufacturers to allow customers to design their onboard seat, features in the cabin or add cabin assets. How customers interact with the product they design and play with online will provide useful insights to both airlines and cabin and seat manufacturers.

Besides, the empowering of customers to co-create or influence new products will spur the development of marketplaces, trade, and even capital-intensive products such as planes and equipment, because it helps inspire and evolve future uses of new physical products.

Moreover, the marketplaces and retailing evolution unlocked by metaverse experiences will help evolve these and more experiences on the ground eventually:

- Airline and airport collaboration for improving buildings, passenger processing, and promotional campaigns for shopping as well as the shopping itself.
- Democratized the design of products and services in airport terminals or aircraft cabins through collaboration with end customers using avatars and metaverse analytics.
- Duty-free-on-arrival, from the comfort of the customer's seat at home, or in the plane, or upon arrival including navigating through buildings, stores, and aisles.
- Travel planning, bundling, and booking and reviewing of playlists through metaverse to experience previews and reserve options, attributes, or features.
- Trading tickets or options for travel in metaverse using tokens depending on other variables, such as experiences online or in person, or both.

Within organizations, there are many other useful applications of metaverse. For instance, think about all the contexts for blending in physical with (augmented) virtual environments for people to learn, exchange, and even visualize and understand complex situations:

- Visualizing value stream and workflows across departments.
- Viewing customer touchpoints holistically.
- HR talent recruitment for interviews, and onboarding.
- Electronic library category and reference material search.
- Remote training and immersive coaching or counseling.
- Instructional assistance with tools, equipment, and machinery.
- Logistics, warehouse management, inventory, and remote management.
- Navigating through buildings, such as airports, duty-free shops.
- B2B sales and negotiations.

24.5 Conclusions

This chapter talked about the metaverse. It explained the concepts and principles of metaverse and highlights the benefits it can bring to aviation, travel, and customers, especially in combination with AI. It will drive hyper-personalized experiences and new opportunities to market to avatars that allow customers to express themselves differently. The chapter further high-lights that, as the next generation of the internet using web3, the metaverse will enable a paradigm shift in the evolution of services such as retailing by layering on an experiential immersive feel that the metaverse can bring. As the centerpiece of the digital economy, products, and services will be created and consumed digitally while enhancing new propositions in the physical world. This will result in insights beyond 'Big Data' with metaverse analytics. A list of use cases for airline and travel companies is provided ranging from geo-enabled virtual retailing, travel experiences, virtual commerce, community and sharing, as well as remote training and democratized product and service design.

Notes

1 Forbes (2022) 'Facebook changes Ticker to META from FB'. https://www.forbes.com/advisor/investing/facebook-ticker-change-meta-fb/.
2 Forbes (2022) 'How the Metaverse is shaping consumer behavior'. https://www.forbes.com/sites/forbesbusinessdevelopmentcouncil/2022/07/05/how-the-metaverse-is-shaping-consumer-behavior/?sh=1ccc0bd13079.
3 Cryptoslate (2022) 'Qatar hosts the first metaverse FIFA gaming tournament'. https://cryptoslate.com/qatar-hosts-the-first-metaverse-fifa-gaming-tournament/.
4 New York Times (2022) 'What is Web 3.0'. https://www.nytimes.com/interactive/2022/03/18/technology/web3-definition-internet.html.
5 BBC (2022) 'The retailers setting up shop in the metaverse'. .https://www.bbc.com/news/business-61979150.0

Bibliography

BBC (2022) 'The retailers setting up shop in the metaverse'. https://www.bbc.com/news/business-61979150
Burniske, C. *et al.* (2019) *Cryptoassets*. New York: McGraw-Hill.

25 Applied Psychology and AI Adoption

25.1 Introduction

Psychology is still one of the youngest sciences, but it has evolved rapidly since its inception in 1886. And that is predominantly due to globalization and the internet. While retail specialists worked with psychologists to improve in-store experiences and stimulate sales in the past, the internet has led to a new field and numerous new studies of consumer behavior and factors influencing purchasing decisions for online shopping.

Nonetheless, with the first laboratories founded in 1886 in Germany, research quickly went from studying dreams (1900) to behaviorism, and to cognitive psychology, the scientific study of mental processes, problem-solving, and memory by 1956. Around the same time, the origins of artificial intelligence (AI) began. And of course, it is no coincidence. Technologists and psychologists started to work on using machines to mimic how people solve problems.

AI has had one big 'winter' (when credibility, funding, and enthusiasm falls) before. This happened between the 1970s and 1990s, and some say we are hitting another one. The first one happened because machines did not have enough capacity for memory. Today, it is more related to ethics (bias and DEI) and the fears created by unfounded talk about sentient machines that go overboard or can think, perceive, and feel like humans and thus have emotions. But that is not true. AI goals are defined by humans, and Ethical AI is a practice even regulators are looking at as discussed in Chapter 21. Also, there are many successful AI applications in flight operations where AI is helping to optimize routes (Eurocontrol) and even reduce fuel burn in-flight (offered by companies like OpenAirlines), as described in Chapters 1 and 2. But AI is also helping to accelerate recruitment, the review of CV content in HR and furthermore staff planning in airline maintenance and overhaul as we saw in Chapter 16.

There are many more applications on the way, but none of them include goals of feeling emotions like humans or disrupting society. It's not the problem-solving role of AI. Yet, psychologists are increasingly involved and brought into airlines, specifically to help with the adoption of AI. In their

DOI: 10.4324/9781003018810-30

Applied Psychology and AI Adoption   227

work to update change management practices, experienced psychologists stumble upon new challenges.

This chapter explores the reasons why and how successful bridges are built to modernize organizations consisting of people that interact with machines.

25.2 AI Adoptability Issue

Recently, an airline in the USA developed the perfect AI model to detect payment fraud. It was ready to be deployed but failed, like the 55% of AI projects that stall in the industry. Yet, the typical promises were all there – great value, efficiencies, fewer boring tasks, and more time to think strategically and experiment. The training sessions were well attended; everybody says it worked.

Often, the assumption airlines take is that an AI tool that is cool, cutting-edge and delivers value will motivate people to adopt it. But this only worked in conversational chatbots and automation in call centers, such as DigitalGenius deployed at KLM. Aircraft and jet engines are also full of hidden AI, until the Boeing 737MAX demonstrated that we had not explained it well to pilots, which led to disastrous results.

Yet, AI is everywhere; consumers are at the end of it in all sorts of Apps. They love it. At work, it is different. How come the tried-and-tested change management principles that worked so well before failed? It is for one specific reason.

Unlike other technologies before, AI impacts the human psyche of staff differently. While other technologies impact the work itself, AI impacts and triggers emotions related to personal identity. More specifically, it raises questions in people about how good they do their jobs, if they do it fast enough, if their experience is not good enough, or whether they are good at solving problems, to begin with.

It often leads people to doubt their skills or creates feelings of incompetence. And thus, triggers fears of being redundant. AI itself cannot reason or communicate this part with people, not even a conversational AI bot that is already proposed for automated therapy sessions in the field of psychotherapy. But these things matter because in an era of IoT and connected devices, more decisions must be made with higher volumes of data in real time to interact with customers. There is no escaping from automation of some tasks. Staff cannot cope. And customers won't wait, as described often throughout this book.

25.3 How AI Should Be Approached

So, what do applied psychologists do in AI application development and deployment? Psychologists start looking at the seven emotional systems and how they are triggered when intelligent work requiring experience is (partly) done by machines. They include fear, rage (anger), lust (pleasure), care, grief

228   *Trends and Evolutions in AI*

(panic), play (fun), and seeking (exploring). These emotional systems trigger hormonal changes, so the approach is to enable positive ones and avoid triggering negative emotions. That is caring about people and colleagues.

So, the primary ingredient in AI is people. The glue in the approach is the combination of actions that (1) positively balance the emotional systems, (2) psychological needs, and (3) recognize personality traits. Applied psychologists on AI projects then remove fears, enable play, and instill curiosity. They also boost feelings of autonomy, safety, and achievement around what the AI-powered tools do to lift people. But they recognize that the approach will be a mix of tactics depending on personality types. Much like leadership, that is an art that works best with authenticity.

Psychologists also help create the future role of staff before the AI tool is deployed. Staff further have a role in designing how they want to interact with the decision intelligence tool. This is also the focus of hybrid intelligence, which makes the best of human-AI interaction.

You may ask, why does this matter? The answer lies in the fact that 'local' AI applications within departments will be part of a layer that supersedes departments to create automated workflows across departments. This is necessary to service end customers better, and in real time. That is the Enterprise AI level discussed in Chapter 18. Applied psychologists are preparing for this level of facilitation, too.

In the meantime, as an overall tactic, AI can be used to upskill people in their work environment and it helps them feel more appreciated by doing more strategic work, toward measurable objectives they can be proud of. It is therefore important that airline staff have a hands-on role in improving the quality and effectiveness of AI models, which is done by providing 'glass box' technology that is visual, such as Explainable AI (Chapter 19).

In practice, airline managers can follow these steps that often work well:

- Define the goal of the AI model (application) in human terms (how it will help them feel better about their role and tasks).
- Develop the model around people (where their unique skills will be required).
- Ensure that the model's results show the people's contribution (demonstrate how their input has added value).
- Make sure that the interfaces to the applications are intuitive, easy to use, and appealing to the eyes, so that people feel it is an extension of how they logically think and work.

25.4 Dopamine and AI

Taking applied psychology one step further, psychologists can tap into neuroscience. Regarding AI, it is already linked to how humans solve problems by mimicking neural systems. But neuroscientists also deal with the structure or function of the nervous system and brain and how it impacts on behavior

Applied Psychology and AI Adoption 229

and cognitive functions. The relevance of neuroscience in AI is related to hormone levels, particularly hormonal changes that waver in relation to the adoption and expected results from predictive analytics powered by artificial neural networks (AI), which is essentially algorithms that design algorithms. In short, people that get too bogged down in their own AI bubble tend to display hormonal imbalances that either depress them or give them a high. The result is that AI for the sake of AI becomes self-fulfilling but not goal-centric to the enterprise. That is, algorithmic problem-solving can become detached from the end model that was to serve a business objective. A practical example of this would be predicting a passenger's favorite color based on data available in the loyalty system as part of a recommender system that is to propose personalized vacations to a top-tier customer. The models are not aligned. In fact, there is no relevance or pertinence. But a data scientist may be very proud of the predictive accuracy of what they deployed. The very reason data scientists sometimes get carried away is related to the technological capabilities and possibilities and their personalities as it concerns reward systems.

It is for this reason that psychologists investigate the hormonal impact that working with or in AI can have to ensure the appropriate level of motivation, focus, and goal-centric results. Understanding hormonal changes in the context of intrinsic and extrinsic rewards in a field as mission-critical as AI is important for airlines and helps to design better teams and workstreams that integrate across inter-disciplinary teams in a pragmatic enterprise that needs to deliver every day. Therefore, most attention within the hormonal household goes to dopamine, a neurotransmitter (chemical) that makes you feel good. Dopamine release can reduce oxytocin (hormone related to stress and anxiety) and can also increase energy levels, motivation, and the ability to focus, concentrate and solve problems. Too much of it results in the opposite.

Learning and motivation depend on internal and external rewards. As a result, what drives our behaviors at work is guided by predicting, or at least anticipating, whether a certain action we take will have a positive ('rewarding') or negative outcome. Placed in a work context, people also assess whether the outcomes are rewarding at a personal level or how it compares to a perceived expectation of (minimum) standards of others, like superiors. This reliance on reward prediction is related directly to the hormone dopamine. Dopamine is, for instance, released not only when people shop online and wait anxiously in anticipation to have it delivered to their doorstep but also when we grab items as impulse buys at the cash register in a store.

Having learned from studies with people and in laboratories related to shopping, substance abuse, or addictions, applied psychologists have turned to working with people's emotional systems and hormonal changes as it pertains to their professional lives when working with AI. In those instances, the goal is to capitalize on dopamine generation from working with AI while putting guardrails on the potential negative effects that self-induced runaway dopamine can cause when models and predictions become the goal and not

230   *Trends and Evolutions in AI*

the means to an end. Similarly, herein lies the risk of chasing a 'data–driven' approach that selects data to push an argument but is not goal-centric, and thus manipulative.

This is where the researchers thought of drawing parallels between distributed reinforcement learning algorithms and dopamine-related activities. Just as reinforcement learning works in algorithms (by layering on improved insights and better predictions), so does dopamine function as people see improvements in their AI models. The dopamine release has a multiplier effect and the motivation to solve more complex problems grows. But one must be aware of the law of diminishing returns, also when efforts overshoot and are not aligned with the business. This can lead to boredom, mental fatigue, lack of interest, and depression. Finding the right balance between personality and reward system for tasks that need to be well defined and aligned with business objectives is therefore now part of organization design.

The practitioners in this field believe that this work raises a bunch of important questions like[1]:

- What are the effects of optimistic and pessimistic dopamine neurons on the brain with regard to expected results from AI model design and deployment?
- What is the relation between representations done in brain and distribution learning across an AI team and all its members?
- How does the distribution of rewards work downstream and how well does it continue to deliver?
- How well do the reward systems protect against unethical practices?

In a recent case, an airline consulted psychologists to help select a team to work on new use cases for AI model deployment by focusing on how individuals receive rewards while they are completing a task. The psychologists stressed that, in the real world, the amount of future reward that will result from a particular action is not a perfectly known quantity and instead involves some randomness due to other work and personal conditions. But by understanding reward systems, the psychologists were able to map personality types to the kinds of problems to solve.

They then take this to a next level and focused on identifying rewards for AI specialists that would help create models that could accelerate and automate workflows across an airline to an Enterprise AI level. Particularly, how a loyalty management logic could supersede a general revenue management business rule. The use case was around optimizing a business rule that would take customer lifetime value, current loyalty tier status, as well as the expected marginal seat revenue from selling a seat in the market into consideration to allow the seat to be redeemed for points. The extrinsic reward for the AI scientists was that they could potentially create their own and more autonomous enterprise AI team, provided they successfully collaborated on a new deep learning model that would deliver accurate predictions.

25.5 Conclusions

This chapter is about applied psychology regarding the adoption and use of AI in commercial aviation. It argues that adoption is related to staff's reward system and fluctuates as a psychobiological influence. It furthers that the primary ingredient in AI is people and that solutions should be designed and deployed using Hybrid AI with humans in the loop. An approach and practical steps are provided to help airlines and travel companies be more successful in the adoption of their AI applications and roadmap.

Note

1 ScienceDirect (2021) 'Natural and artificial intelligence: a brief introduction to the interplay between AI and neuroscience', *Neural Networks*, 144, pp. 603–613. https://www.sciencedirect.com/science/article/pii/S0893608021003683.

Bibliography

360learning (2022) 'The link between dopamine and learning outcomes: what does it mean for business?' https://360learning.com/blog/dopamine-and-learning/

AIM, Analytics India Magazine (2020) 'Coding dopamine: how DeepMind brought AI To the footsteps of neuroscience'. https://analyticsindiamag.com/deepmind-neuroscience-reinforcement-learning-dopamine-temporal-difference/

DeepMind (2022) 'Dopamine and temporal difference learning: a fruitful relationship between neuroscience and AI'. https://www.deepmind.com/blog/dopamine-and-temporal-difference-learning-a-fruitful-relationship-between-neuroscience-and-ai

Larsen, R., et al. (2017) *Personality psychology – domains of knowledge about human nature.* London: McGraw-Hill.

Morrison, R. (2015) *Data-driven organization design – sustaining the competitive edge through organizational analytics.* London: KoganPage.

Reeve, J. (2018) *Understanding motivation and emotion.* Hoboken, NJ: John Wiley & Sons.

Rothmann, I. *et al.* (2015) *Work and organizational psychology.* New York: Routledge.

Watson, S. (2021) 'Dopamine: the pathway to pleasure', 20 July 2021, Harvard Health Publishing, Harvard Medical School, 2021. https://www.health.harvard.edu/mind-and-mood/dopamine-the-pathway-to-pleasure

Index

Note: **Bold** page numbers refer to tables; *italic* page numbers refer to figures and page numbers followed by "n" denote endnotes.

Accelya 73, 126
Accenture 139
acceptance, air cargo handling 129–131
Accor 103, 168
actionable insights 17
Adams, D. 89n4
Adidas 220
adoption of AI 226; aggressive 138;
  challenges 116, 174, 176; hybrid
  intelligence 187; issue 227; Metaverse
  218; Scandinavian Airlines 88
Aer Lingus 158
Aeroplan (Air Canada) 83, 112
Aerospace Vehicle Systems Institute
  (AVSI) 45, 50n6
Agoda 151
AI *see* artificial intelligence (AI)
Aimia 83
Air Asia 110; BIG 83
airBaltic 208
Airbnb 101
Airbus 45, 46, 50n5, 111, 165, 171n3,
  171n5
Airbus A220 67
Airbus A220–300 208
Airbus A320 50n9, 67
Airbus A330 57, 67
Airbus A350 67, 70
Airbus A350–1000 117
Airbus A380–800 44
Air Canada 36, 57–58, 74, 77, 85, 88,
  124, 134, 142, 143, 147, 152, 158, 165;
  Aeroplan 41, 83, 112; Air Canada's
  Signature Class 107
air cargo 137, 144; commercial
  management (*see* commercial cargo

management); explainable AI 178;
  handling 125–134 (*see also* cargo
  warehouse and handling); sales
  professionals 143, 144
Air Cargo Community System (ACCS)
  130–133, 140
aircraft: assignment process 57–58;
  business *vs.* economy class 57–58; and
  engine maintenance 23; finance 69–71;
  in-flight 201; on Montreal-Paris route
  58; revenue-generating capabilities of
  66, 70
aircraft cabin environment sensor (ACES)
  48, 50n9
Aircraft Interiors International 50n8
Aircraft IT 24n5
aircraft-on-ground (AOG) 23, 57, 133
aircraft operations 16; aircraft and
  engine maintenance 23; benefits 16;
  crew management 21–23; emissions
  reduction 17–19; fuel optimization
  17–19; operations control center 23,
  24; payload optimization 19–21; trim
  and fuel efficiency 19–21; weight and
  balance management systems 19–21
Air Europa 115, 208
Air France 17, 19, 24n1, 24n3, 107, 137,
  143, 210
Air France-KLM 67, 83, 211
Air France KLM Cargo 143
airline: and blockchain 210–211; fleet
  planning 150; managers 37, 228;
  operators factors 65–66; solutions to
  key challenges 75; USA 227
Airline Experience Marketplace (AEM)
  107–109

234   *Index*

Airline Retailing Maturity (ARM) index 101
Airline Weekly 80n3
air navigation 10–11; artificial intelligence in 11–13; explainable AI 177
air navigation service providers (ANSPs) 10–12, 14, 58, 203
Air New Zealand 46, 124, 143
Airport City 40
airport operations control center (AOCC) 12
Airportr 101
airports: and blockchain 211–212; slot and fleet planning 66, 68, *69*; truck congestion at 130
Airspace Intelligence 13
airspace management 11, 12
Air Traffic Control 12
Air Traffic Management sector 11
Air Transat 40
air transport management (ATM) 11–13
Air Waybill (AWB) 126
Alaska Airlines 13–14, 102, 109n4
algorithmic problem-solving 229
Alibaba 203
Al Jazeera channels 119
'all-inclusive' model 79
allotment management, in cargo 140–141
Alphabet 109n8
AltexSoft 124n4
Amadeus 20, 62, 64n2, 73, 75, 92; evidence-based research 63; retailing and digital assistants 103; sales and distribution 91; SkySuite 61, 67
Amazon 1, 109, 109n8, 134, 165, 203, 213, 214
American Airlines 85, 93, 122
American Express 112
Amsterdam Airport Schiphol 40, 75
Analytics India Magazine 24n2, 181n1
AnalyticsInsight 34n6
AnalyticsMagazine.com 176
ancillary products and fees 76–77
ANSPs *see* air navigation service providers (ANSPs)
APEX 50n7
APG 20
APIs *see* application programming interfaces (APIs)
App-2-App (A2A) interfaces 46
Apple 109n8, 213

application programming interfaces (APIs) 78, 102, 169
applied AI 112, 152, 202
applied psychologists 226–231
artificial intelligence (AI) 1–3; advanced analytic technique 7; AI-backed predictive technologies 120; in aircraft operations 16–24; air navigation 11–13; application of 4, 202–203; applied psychologists on 228; benefits of 5, **5**; blockchain technology 8, 206–215; brand management 120–123; cabin services 35–41; categories of 1, *2*; in corporate sales 93–96, *95*; debates in 204; digital cabin (*see* digital cabin); end model 3; fairness checklists 195; in finance world 69–71; fleet acquisition 69–71; in fleet planning 67–69; fraud prevention and 87–89; goal of 3, 226; hormonal changes 228, 229; inflight services 35–41; local application 78; loyalty management 86–87; *vs.* machine learning 4, 6–8; metallurgic analytics 23; metaverse 217–225; need for 3–5; in network planning 59–64, *61*; neuroscience 228–229; prediction models 13; primary ingredient in 228; revenue management (*see* revenue management (RM)); sensory applications 47–48; technologies of **29**; technology trends 202–203; trends in 198–203; types of 1, **2**; use cases of **29**; within-system applications 23; working of 5–7; *see also specific artificial intelligences*
artificial neural network (ANN) 117
Ash Cloud 28
Atkinson, J. 33n11
ATM *see* air transport management (ATM)
augmented AI 199
augmented network optimization process *61*
augmented reality (AR) 129, 218, 221; infused Apps 214
automated machine learning (AutoML) 88, 89, 199
automated storage and retrieval systems (AS/RS) 128
automation: in air cargo handling 126–127; human resources management 148–151
autonomous flight 166

Avianca 85
aviation: aspects of 55; carbon footprint
10; civil 177; commercial 101–103,
119, 145, 156, 179, 202, 203;
environmental impact 11; ethical AI
191–193, 196; human resources in 153;
self-service in 30; strategies in 156;
XAI in 177–178
Avionica 20
AWS IoT 165
Azure Machine Learning (AzureML)
88, 165

balanced score method 66
BBC 119, 225n5
BCG 201
Benjuya, D. 89n6
Ben Vinod 74
beverages provisioning process, inflight
services 36–38, **37**
bid price approach 140, 142
BIG (Air Asia) 83
BigChainDB 213
Big Data 225
Birst 93
Bitcoin 208–210
'black box' approach, in cargo 137
Blackman, R. 191
blending technology 203
blockchain 8, 206–208; airlines and 210–
211; airports and 211–212; benefits
of 210; distributed AI with 212–215;
feature of 213; intersection and
opportunity of 212; loyalty program
87; in metaverse 218; smart contract
on 222; use cases 210–212, 215; works
in nutshell 208–210
Blockchain-as-a-Service (BaaS)
model 214
Blockchain for Aviation (BC4A) 211
Block Sale Agreements (BSA) 140
Bloomberg 40, 42n8, 148, 153n4
BlueBiz 92
BlueBot (BB) 28
BMW 203
BNN Bloomberg 89n1, 89n2
Boeing 46, 50n1, 50n10, 111, 183, 203;
Boeing 737 67; Boeing 737 MAX 67;
Boeing 747 67; Boeing 767 58; Boeing
777 43, 58, 143; Boeing 777-300ER
aircraft 142; Boeing 787 55, 70, 72, 114
Bolle 220
Bond Brand Report 87–88

Booking 105
Boston Consulting Group (BCG) 24,
24n7
branded changes 77
branded fares 74, 77, 110
brand management 119–120; AI 120–
123; applications in 121; explainable AI
178; objectives 119; use cases 123
Brauer, B. 33n1
Brightplan 153n7; 2021 Wellness
Barometer 148
British Airways 27, 41, 67, 71n1, 76, 85,
88, 158, 164, 206, 211
Buckendorf, P. 13
buckets 73
Burberry 220
Business Extra 93
Business Intelligence (BI) tools 6
business level optimization: in cargo
142–143; profit 114–116
business rule 31, 37, 92, 94; enterprise
AI 164, 168; goal-centric 164; revenue
management 230
Butterfly seating 102

C3 170n1
cabin depressurization 102
cabin services 35–41
Caeli Nova 102, 109n1
Caffe 165
call centers **29**
Capgemini 183
Caravelo 102
CargoAI 136
cargo handling *see* air cargo
Cargolux 139
CARGO MIND 131
cargo.one 136
cargo warehouse and handling 125–134;
acceptance, truck docks and (un)
loading 129–131; applications 134;
automation in 126–127; COVID-19
127–128, 130; last-mile delivery 133–
134; management system 134; pallet
build-up 132; rule-based management
127; screening 131–132; service
recovery 132–133; staff planning 133;
storage 128–129; ULD planning 133;
use cases for 127–134; *see also* air cargo
Cassandra 165
catchment areas 54, 73
Cathay Pacific 27, 41, 88, 139, 158
CB Insights 146n3

236 Index

Cebu Pacific 17
center of gravity (CG) rules 20
centralized AI 201, 213, 222
Centre for Aviation 215n7
CHAMP Cargosystems 20
Channel News Asia 33n3
chatbot 27
check-in process 30, 31, 33, 37, 76, 191
Chief Solutions Officer 11
churn rate 87
Cision PR Newswire 33n5
Citizen AI 199
cleansheet approach 57, 58
cloud computing 200–201
Cloudera 165
Cloud Pak for Data 176
cloud service providers 214
CNN channels 119
CodeSignal 152
cognitive enterprise technology 181
CoinSutra 215n4
collective trust model 207
Collins Aerospace 20
commercial aviation 119, 203; blockchain
    in 211; challenge in 179; component
    145; future 188; innovative cases in 202;
    startups in 101–103; transformational
    business models in 156
commercial cargo management 136;
    allotment management 140–141;
    benefit 141; 'black box' approach 137;
    business level optimization 142–143;
    capability gaps 137–138; changing
    role 138–139; COVID-19 138; digital
    distribution platforms 136; focal
    shift to smart sales steering 143–145;
    modernization of *144*; network
    optimization 141–142; revenue
    optimization 137–145; use cases 145
Comnica 26
competitive market 55
competitive rate monitoring tools 76
composite AI 165–166, 198, 199;
    organization design 166; technologies
    and applications 166
computer vision 166
Computer Weekly 215n10
conflict resolution, explainable AI 177
connecting flights 39, 73, 185
constant engagement 33
consumer packaged goods (CPG) 86
content: creation 168–169; retailing
    104–105

continuous integration and continuous
    deployment (CI/CD) development
    model 89
conventional blockchain 213
conversational assistance 166
convolution algorithms 61, 70, 113
convolutional neural networks (CNN) 117
corporate sales 93–96, *95*
Counterfit 196
COVID-19 11, 18, 40, 43, 67, 130, 148,
    192; air cargo handling 127, 128, 130;
    blockchain technology 211; brand
    management 122; cargo commercial
    management 138; cargo organizations
    128; ethical AI 192; facial recognition
    31; fallout in travel 40; ICC AOKpass
    211; impact of 58–59; KLM 158; on
    loyalty management 84–86; preighters
    during 138; principal challenges
    122; recruitment 151; on revenue
    management 74–75, 78, 110
creative content creation 168–169
creative dimension, metaverse 218
creativity 114
credit decisions 70
crew management 21–23
CRMs 93
Cruise, Tom 202
Cryptoslate 225n3
Cryptoslate.com 215n2
CSFs 164
customer data platform (CDP) 33, 188
customer engagement 81
customer intimacy 48, 101, 122
customer journey 32–33
customer loyalty programs 81; *see also*
    loyalty management
customer revenue management *78,*
    113–114
customer service 26, 28, 31, 84; conflict
    resolution 177; incremental fuel
    savings 43; passenger, inflight 38–39;
    use cases 46

Dash cryptocurrency 210
data analytics process, explainable AI
    178–181
Databricks 165
data-driven approach 102, 230;
    automation, loyalty management 84;
    organization design 160–161
data fabric 179; enterprise AI 108;
    explainable AI 178–181

Index 237

Dataiku 148
data quality firms 19
DataStax 165
DataWorld 179
Decaire, A. 62
decentralized AI 213; applications 214; blockchain 210; optimization 214; peer-to-peer system 207
decision-making 7, 93, 96, 139; automated tools 193; meals and beverages provisioning 37–38; proactive 23; problem-solving and 76
deep learning 7, 8, 14, 33, 47, 113, 198, 230; algorithms 61; based digital twins 222; cargo commercial management 143–144; centralized model 213; convolutional neural network 117; corporate sales 94; ethical AI 195; explainable AI 176; integrate with digital assistant 144; MarTech 61, 113; metaverse 222; to perform analytics 213; sales and distribution 94, 99; scripts 143
Deloitte 147, 153n2
Delta Airlines 31, 33n10, 85, 86, 88, 115, 158, 211
demand forecasting, explainable AI 177
democratized AI 199; retailing with digital assistants *104,* 108
Denodo 180
Departure Control System (DCS) 20
Deric, A. 183, 188n1
DevOps 33, 89, 150
differential pricing 72
digital assistants: for airline experiences 103–108; deep learning with 144; enterprise AI 166–170, *167*; and marketplace 48–49; retailing and 101–109
digital cabin 43–46, *49,* 79; cameras and sensors 48; facial emotion 47–48; and physical assets revenue management *49*
digital distribution platforms, cargo 136
digital economy 218, 219, 225
DigitalGenius 28, 227
digital marketing and targeting 121–122
digital marketplace 103, 127
digital media, brand management 123
Digital Service 190
Digital Towers 11
digital trust 207
digital twins (DTs) 221, 222
digitization 4, 40, 41, 127, 132, 133, 140

DIGITS 165
discretionary fuel 19
distributed AI 8, 213, 222; with blockchain 212–215; consensus mechanism 209; function 91–93; on market penetration and margin goals 99; in metaverse 223–224; use cases in 96–99, *97–98*
distributed ledger technology (DLT) 8
dopamine 228–230
Drone Delivery Canada 134
Dutch flag carrier's organization 158
duty-free shopping 40–41
dynamic pricing 76, 110, 139–140, 145

easyJet 72, 158
eBay 4
eCommerce 127, 134, 138
Ed Bastian 158
edge AI 49, 199–201
elastic distributed processing 165
electric vehicles (EVs) 203
electric vertical take-off and landings (eVTOLs) 11, 49, 212
embedded RM 108–109
EMG 205n4
Emirates 40, 46, 85, 124
emissions reduction, aircraft operations 17–19
emotional systems, metaverse 218
employee engagement 149–150
Engberg, D. 88
enhanced connectivity 202
enterprise AI 63, 102, 113, 163–165, 214; applications 163; corporate sales 94, *95*; data fabric 108; goal-centric business rules 164; integrating planned changes 160; on marketplace with digital assistants 166–170, *167*; model-driven architecture 165; organization design 157, 162, 166; stacks 161; strategic sales 144; use cases 166–170
enterprise RM 78; *see also* revenue management (RM)
environmental, societal, and governance (ESG) 115
Error Analysis, Microsoft 196
Ethereum 209
ethical AI 190–191, 198, 199; aviation 191–193; COVID-19 192; development phases 195; glassbox approach 195, 196; MarTech 192; problems 191–193; provincial

238   *Index*

government 190; risk exposure
193–194; solutions 194–196; zero risk
environment 194
Etihad 36, 83, 211
Etihad Guest (Etihad Airways) 83
EuroBonus 88–89
Eurocontrol 12, 14n3
European Commission 10, 12
European Union 193, 197n2
EVA Air 41, 46
Everyday AI 199
eVTOL *see* electric vertical take-off and
landings (eVTOLs)
Expected Marginal Seat Revenue
(EMSR) 110
Expedia 105, 167
experience marketplaces 105–106, 168,
170; case study of 106–108; digital
assistants for 103–108; of future 169;
three startup opportunities 106; true
retailing 167
explainable AI (XAI) 88, 164; in aviation
177–178; benefits of 176, 178;
challenges in 174; civil aviation 177;
commercial aviation, challenge in 179;
data fabric 178–181; deep learning
176; facial recognition 174; goal of
175; hit-and-miss 175; tools 175; use
cases for 178

FAA 64n3
FAAAM 105
Facebook 26, 102, 109n8, 119, 151, 152,
213, 217
facial emotion, digital cabin 47–48
facial recognition 31, 174, 211;
blockchain technology 211; cargo
warehouse and handling 130;
explainable AI 174
Fairlearn 195–196
fare bundles 74
fatigue risk, crew management 22–23
federated learning (FL) 214, 215, 222
federated machine learning (FedML) 196
FIFA 22 Champions Cup 217
FIFA gaming 217
Filecoin 213
financial advisory services 70
financing commercial aircraft 69
fine-tune network planning 56
Finnair 41, 165
First and Business Class: halo effect of
119; meals in 44

fit for purpose 114
fleet acquisition models 67, 69–71
fleet planning 65–67; airport slot and 66,
68, *69*; artificial intelligence in 67–69;
financial and capital market, changes
in 67; integrated and automated 68;
political/legal aspects 66, 68, *69*
Flight Management System (FMS) 18
flight planning system 18
flyer loyalty program 211
FlyerTalk 158
Flying Blue 83, 92
FLYR Labs 82, 111
Flyways 13–14
fog computing 201
food and beverage (F&B) planning
37–38, **38,** 41
Forbes 148, 153n1, 217, 220, 225n1,
225n2
Forrester 176
Fox, L. 33n7
fraud: detection 70; fraud-resistant
communication systems 203;
prevention 70, 87–89; types of 8
fraud-resistant communication systems 203
freight forwarders 213; cargo commercial
management 138–141; cargo
warehouse and handling 125–129, 131
Freightwaves 145n1
frequent flier program (FFP) 39, 81–83,
89, 112; *see also* loyalty management
Frequentis 215n11
fuel costs 17, 19
fuel efficiency 17; air navigation and 177;
explainable AI 177; optimization 185;
programs 17–19; trim and 19–21

Gallup 149, 154n9
Gantt chart 22
Garner, C. 92, 100n1
Gartner 151, 154n10, 179, 180, 181n7,
190, 198, 202
Garuda Indonesia Airlines 44
Gauss, M. 208
General Data Protection Regulation
(GDPR) 105, 193
General Motors 91
Generative Adversarial Networks
(GANs) 200
generative AI 199–200
geo-fencing 130
geo-targeting, brand management 122
GetYourGuide 107

Index 239

glassbox approach, ethical AI 195, 196
global distribution systems (GDS) 61,
91–92, 96, 103
Global Human Capital Survey 147
Global Positioning Systems (GPS)
10, 130
Go Air 17
golf enthusiasts 112
Google 1, 103, 152, 203, 204, 213
Google Ads 119
Google Cloud XAI 176
Google Home 28
Google Maps 1, 13
Government of Ontario 197n1
Grab in Singapore 49
graphics processing units (GPUs) 198
Great Resignation 148
green lake approach 108
ground handling (GHA) 131
Gucci 220
Gulati, Nittin 18
Gunjan Kumar 86, 87
Gustavsson, P. 89

Hadoop 165
HALO filters 48
haptic devices 205n3
harmonize business model 94
Harvard Business Review 191, 202
Harvard Business School 26, 31
haul flight 142
Herbert Smith Freehills 71n3
hiring process 147; *see also* human
resources management
Hitachi Vantara 179
home-grown analytics systems 137
Hong Kong Airlines 41
Hopper Research 80n4
hormonal changes, artificial intelligence
228, 229
HSBC 220
human–AI interaction 185–187, 228
human capital management (HCM)
systems 151
human-centered AI (HCAI) 199
human interaction 12, 30
human-in-the-loop (HITL) 185–186
human-machine context 183–185
human-out-of-the-loop (HOOTL)
185–186
human resources management 147;
analytics and automation 148–151;
basic functions 148; challenges in

147–148; COVID-19 148; explainable
AI 178; recruitment 147–148, 151–
152; technologies **149**; use cases in 148,
149, 152–153; workforce analytics
148–149
human service agent 28
human touch 29–30
hybrid intelligence 150, 166, 188;
human-in-the-loop 185–186; human-
machine context 183–185; human-
out-of-the-loop 185–186; knowledge
management 186–187; sociotechnical
future of 187–188
hyper-personalization 86

IAG Cargo 136, 139
IATA *see* International Air Transport
Association (IATA)
Iberia 158
IBM 93, 176, 178–181, 181n3, 203,
206, 214
IBS 126, 136, 143, 144
ICAO 50n2
iCargo 136
ICC AOKpass 210–211
IDC FutureScape 179, 181n5
IFE screen 164
IKEA 220
image recognition, CNN 117
immersive-reality technology 203
immutable blockchain 210
Imperva 181n4
incremental costs 72
inference techniques 82
inflight entertainment (IFE) systems 32,
35, 43, 46–47
inflight retailing 177; *see also* retailing
inflight services 35–41; duty-free
shopping 40–41; meals and beverages
provisioning 36–38, **37**; passenger
customer service inflight 38–39
Infogain 21, 24n6
Informatica 180
Information Builders 93
information systems (IS) 186
InRule 176
Insider 122
Instagram 26
instrument flight rules (IFR) 10
integrated system, fleet planning 68
intelligent listening technology 150
intent-to-purchase analysis 78
interactive voice recognition (IVR) 26

240 *Index*

International Air Transport Association (IATA) 10, 11, 14n1, 89n7, 125, 132, 135n1, 136, 158; New Distribution Capability 78
Internet Booking Engines 167
Internet bulletin board 158
Internet of Everything (IoE) 4, 47, 157
Internet of Things (IoT) 23, 157, 198, 221, 227
Interplanetary File System (IPFS) 213
InterpretML 88, 196
inventory management function 73
Investopedia 215n3
iPhone 43
irregular operations (IRROPS) 12, 23, 133, 142
IT Business Edge 205n1
ITnews 33n2

Jakarta-Singapore-Amsterdam 139
Japan Airlines 46
Jeppesen 20, 21
JetBlue 85
Jobvite 152
Johnson & Johnson 91
Journal of Commerce 135n6
Joyce, Alan 158
JP Morgan 220
Jupyter Notebooks 165

Kale Logistics 135n7
Kayak 105
Kelly, J. 153n3
Kenya Airways 184
Key, N. 28
key performance indicators (KPIs) 68, 74, 150, 164; cargo commercial management 139, 142; loyalty program 87; total revenue optimization 116, 118
kiosk technology, self-service 30–33, 85
KLM Royal Dutch Airlines 46, 67, 76, 85, 122, 124, 137; applied psychology 227; blockchain 212, 215n12; customer, contact and self-service 24, 27, 28, 30, 33n8; inflight and cabin services 38, 39, 41, 42n5; organization design 157–159; sales and distribution 92, 93
knowledge extraction 166
knowledge management 186–187
Koenig, D. 153n5
Korean Air cargo 144
Kotler, P. 120

KrisFlyer 83
KrisPay 211
K2View 180

Lahlou, M. 107
Language Model for Dialogue Applications (LaMDA) 204
lantern consciousness 108
last-mile delivery, cargo warehouse 133–134
LATAM 85
LedgerInsights 215n6, 215n8
legal professionals, machine learning 69
Lemoine, B. 204
LG 47
Li-Fi 43, 50, 50n3
linear programming (LP) 76
LinkedIn 92
Lion Air Flight 610 184
Load Master 20
long-term network planning 55–56, 62
L'Oreal 220
Louis Vuitton 220
lower cost, blockchain 210
Low-Power Wide Area (LPWA) wireless technology 202
loyalty management 38, 81–84; artificial intelligence 86–87; based revenue management 112–113; campaign modules 84; competency within 81; complexity of 84; COVID-19 impact on 84–86; data-driven automation 84; explainable AI 178, 179; fraud prevention 87–89; logics 230; regular patterns 88; service-oriented architecture 83
LoyaltyPlus 144
Lufthansa Airlines 27, 82, 92, 158, 206, 211
Lufthansa Cargo 139
Lufthansa Pressroom 215n9
Lufthansa Systems 20, 21
Lufthansa Technik 47

machine learning (ML) 1–2, 12, 29, 94, 198; advanced campaign management platforms 86; Air Cargo Community System 131; aircraft finance 69–70; Alaska Airlines 13–14; applications **29,** 139–140; artificial intelligence *vs.* 4, 6–8; for autonomous vehicles 203; blockchain 214; brand management 121; centralized model 213; component 38, 60; continuous model

Index 241

retraining 89; crux in 128; digital cabin 44; digitization of information 132; in ethics (*see* ethical AI); functional-level process 68; goals 93–94; legal professionals 69; mathematical statistical 6; network planning (*see* network planning process); organization design 159; performance 18, 186; predictive and prescriptive analytics 165; revenue management 76; separate group of 3; training 152; use cases of **29**

madrid-based IAG 158

Malaysia Airlines 17, 41

Mandarin Oriental hotel 107

Maneuvering Characteristics Augmentation System (MCAS) 183

marketing technology (MarTech) 61, 78, 86, 99, 113; brand management 122; ethical AI 192; organization design, airline 157

marketplace: digital 103, 127; digital assistant and 48–49; experience (*see* experience marketplaces)

MarketWatch 89n5

Marr, B. 202

Marriott Hotels 151

MarTech *see* marketing technology (MarTech)

Martinair Cargo 137

MATLAB design tool 165

maximum take-off weight (MTOW) 142

McCormick, P. 218

McDonald's 151

McKinsey & Company 128, 135n3, 135n4, 148, 153n8, 198, 202, 203, 205n4

meal provisioning process, inflight services 36–38, **37**

medium term, network planning 56

Meister, J. 153n6

Mentionlytics in London 123

merchandising programs 83

mergers and acquisition (M&A) assessments 69

Merritt, B. 31

META 217

Meta metaverse 217

Metaphysic 202, 205n2

metaverse 217–220; adopters of 220; blockchain in 218; concept 217; deep learning 222; digital economy, components 219; distributed AI in 223–224; economy of 219; emotional systems 218; experiences 224; identities in 221; physical *vs.* 220–221; rise of 217; uses cases, distributed AI 223–224

Meyer, S. 89n8

MHI 128, 135n5

MI Airline 39

Microsoft 89n9, 93, 109n8, 195–196, 214; Azure Machine Learning 88; Error Analysis 196; Microsoft® Teams 151

Microstrategy 93

MileagePlus loyalty program 83

Miles and More (Lufthansa) 83

mining process, blockchains 209

MIT 202

MIT Technology Review 200

ML *see* machine learning (ML)

MLOps 179

Mobile Passport Control (MPC) 32

model-driven architecture, enterprise AI 165

ModelOps 179

modern scheduling solution 63

Montreal-Paris route, aircraft on 58

Morrison, R. 160

mortgage application process, digital cabin 48

motivation 30, **149,** 229, 230

Mulesoft Anypoint Platform 29

multi-disciplinary artificial intelligence 165

mutual learning, explainable AI 186–188

MyFuelCoach 19

MyInterview 151–152, 154n11

National Air Traffic Services (NATS) 11

National Geographic 119

Natural Language Processing (NLP) 1–2, 152, 160

NatWest Group 181

NDC 101, 102; NDC Smart Offer 92

NEO 210

network optimization, in cargo 141–142

network planning process 54–57; artificial intelligence in 59–64, *61*; benefits 59–60; building model 56; COVID-19 impact 58–59, *59*; explainable AI 177; fleet planning 67; integrated and automated 68; opportunities 55; and schedule development cycle 59–60; stages 55–57

neural networks 87; artificial 229; convolutional (*see* convolutional neural

242 *Index*

networks (CNN)); recurrent 116; shallow 165
neuroscience, artificial intelligence 228–229
Nevans, J. 14n2
New Distribution Capability (NDC) 78, 91–92, 96, 97
Newswire 135n9
New York Times 181n2, 225n4
Nike 220
non-fungible tokens (NFTs) 200, 208, 217
Norse Atlantic Airways 114
Norwegian 46
NVIDIA Developer 135n8

One Order certification 101
Online Travel Agents (OTAs) 99
OpenAirlines 17
open-source ecosystem 198
operational flight-based approach 48
operational rules, cargo handling 129, 132
operations control center (OCC) 23, 24
operations research (OR) 67, 76
optimization process 39; augmented network 61; business level optimization 142–143; decentralized AI 214; fuel efficiency 185; network optimization 141–142; payload 19–21; revenue optimization 137–145
Oracle 93, 147
organization design, airline 156–157; analytics 149–150, 159–160, 178; application of 160; challenges 157–158; composite and enterprise AI 166; data-driven 160–161; principles 157; progress 158–159; use cases 160–161
Ouzoud falls 107

pacific flights 143
pallet build-up, cargo handling 132
pallet moving robots 128
Panasonic 47
passenger communications 26; automation in 26; and social service 26–29
passenger customer service inflight 38–39
passenger engagement 32–33
passenger service systems (PSSs) 93
pattern recognition 117
payload optimization 19–21
Penn Medicine 180

personal identity 191, 211, 227
personalization: explainable AI 177; hyper-personalization 86
Philips 91, 158
PhocusWire 42n4
PhocusWright 81, 89n3
photorealistic 3-D models 221
pilot training programs 68
Plusgrade 102, 109n3
point-of-sale (POS) control 191
post-COVID-19 159, 180
PowerBI 93
PowerPoint 207
predictive analytics 16, 93, 142, 165, 213, 229
Premium Economy on Air Canada 107
prescriptive analytics 100, 118, 159, 165
Presse Groupe ADP 215n5
pricing in airline industry 72–73, 76, 77, 79
profit load factor 116–117
Profit & Loss (P&L) Account 70
proof-of-stake (PoS) 209
proof-of-work (PoW) 209
PROS 73
psychologists, applied 226–231
public blockchains 208–210
Python 165

Qantas Airways 27, 40, 42n7, 46, 85, 143, 158
Qatar Airways 85, 127, 139, 217
QualtricsXM 33n4
quantum computing 203

R 165
Radio Frequency Identification Device (RFID) 126
re:config 159, 162n2
recruitment 149, **149**; challenges 147–148; COVID-19 151; outsourcing process 152; video calls and video in 151–152
redeem points 41, 86, 174
Register, J. 170n2
reinforcement learning 230
Relay42 120, 122, 124n2
remote user-testing software 47
responsible AI *see* ethical AI
retailing 101, 114; and digital assistants 101–109; embedded RM 108–109; experience marketplaces 167; startups in commercial 101–103

Index 243

retention 26; customer 164; human resources management 149, **149**
Return on Ad Spend (ROAS) 120
revenue-generating capabilities, of aircraft 66, 70
revenue management (RM) 60, 72–74; ancillary products and fees 76–77; artificial intelligence 75–76; branded fares and changes 77; business rule 230; cargo 139–145; components 73; COVID-19 74–75, 110; customer 78, 113–114; digital cabin and physical assets 49; embedded 108–109; loyalty based 112–113; modernizing with wider scope 77–79; modifying during crises 75; role of 74; and yield management 72; *see also* total revenue management
reverse planning 132
RevFine 118n1
ripple effect 57, 63, 192
risk exposure, ethical AI 193–194
RM *see* revenue management (RM)
robot-assisted technology 184
Rolls-Royce 24
route planning 54
Rovinescu, Calin 158
Royal Bank of Scotland 181
Royal Dutch Airlines 38, 39, 42n5, 122
RTS 73
Rulex XAI 176
Ryanair 72, 158

Sabre 20, 36, 41n1, 41n3, 74, 91, 92
safety laws 10
sales: corporate 93–96, 95; function 91–93
SalesForce Service Cloud 29
SalesTech 78, 79
Samsung 91, 220
Santa Monica 111
SAP 93
Saudi Arabian Airlines 41
Scala 165
Scandinavian Airlines (SAS) 88, 89, 91–93, 96
schedule planning 59–61
ScienceDirect 231
Scientific American 205n6
screening equipment, air cargo handling 131–132
Seabury 138
search engines 1, 61

self-check-in 30–31, 85
self-fulfilling prophecy 150
self-guided industrial vehicles 128, 129, 132
self-learning 214
self-service technologies (SSTs) 30–32, 43
Semuels, A. 14n4
sensory applications 47–48
service agents 29
service product 125
service recovery, cargo management system 132
Setiaputr, I. 44
shallow neural networks 165
Shannon Airport 40
Shoppair 42n9
short-term network planning 57
Siemens 91, 206
Siemens Logistics 127, 135n2
Silicon Valley 13
SimpleFlying 40, 42n6
Singapore Airlines 82, 85, 139; blockchain 206, 211; brand management 122, 124, 124n3; customer, contact and self-service 27, 29, 33n9; KrisFlyer 83; KrisShop 40
Single European Sky (SES) 10, 11
SiSense 93
Six Sigma 159
Six Sigma Daily 162n1
Skift Webinar 80n3
skill management 186–187
SkyBonus 93
SkyBreathe 17, 19
SkyMiles program 86
SkySuite 61, 67
SkyTeam alliances 93
Sky tower 101
Skywards (Emirates) 83
Slack 151
SlotMachine 211
SMartech 78
SmartKargo 126
SMartTech 79
Smit, T. 30
Snowflake 165
social media 26, 33, 86, 178, 214, 218, 221; brand management 119, 120, 122, 123; human resources management 151; loyalty management 85; retailing and digital assistants 107; service agents 28
social service 28
sociotechnical future, of hybrid intelligence 187–188

244 *Index*

Southwest Airlines 62, 67, 72, 85;
  SWABIZ 93
Spark Hire 152
SPEEDCARGO 131
SpiceJet 17–19
Spirit 76
Spotify 101, 119
SP's Aviation 23
staff planning: air cargo handling 133;
  human resources management **149**
standard operating procedures
  (SOPs) 13
Stanford 202
STAR Alliance 82
Stattimes 146n3
StatusMatch 109n2
Statusmatch.com 102
strategic skillset 114
Suez Canal 136
SuperApps 33, 49
supervised learning 7
supply chain 4, 55, 202, 208, 211, 212,
  214; cargo commercial management
  136, 140, 142, 144; cargo warehouse
  and handling 127, 128, 130;
  explainable AI 174, 180
Sustainable Aviation Fuel (SAF) 111
Sutton, S.G. 188n2
SWABIZ 93
Swarm 213

Talend 180
talent management 150
Taneja, H. 109n5
TAP Air Portugal 47
TechTarget 179, 181n6, 205n5
Tech Trends Outlook 202
Teledyne Technologies 50n9
TensorFlow 165
Tesla 101
Tesseras, L. 124n1
TestGorilla 152
three-dimensional (3D) scanners 131
TikTok 85
time series analyses 76
tiny metaverse 217
TMCs *see* travel management companies
  (TMCs)
Tommy Hilfiger 220
Torch 165
Toronto Dominion (TD) 112
total mission optimization (TMO)
  approach 16

total revenue management 110–112;
  benefits of 112; business level profit
  optimization 114–116; convolutional
  neural networks 117; profit load factor
  116–117; *see also* revenue management
  (RM)
Touchdynamic.com 33n12
transformational business models 156
Travel Daily Media 41n2
travel distributors 91
travel management companies (TMCs)
  91, 93, 99
Travel Market Report 171n4
Travelport 91
TravelSky 91
TravelX 208, 215n1
trim and fuel efficiency 19–21
Tripadvisor 103, 107, 123, 168
T2RL 92, 100n2
truck docks and loading/unloading
  129–131
Trusted Reviews 50n4
trustless blockchain 210
TSA PreCheck customers 31
Turkish Airlines 85
Twitter 26, 27

Uber 49, 101, 177
Ukraine International Airlines 17
ULD planning 126, 132, 133
United Airlines 76, 83, 85, 86
unmanned aerial vehicles (UAVs) 13
unstoppable blockchain 210
unsupervised learning 7
UPS 134
upselling 32
USA 13, 39; airline in 227
use cases: for air cargo handling 127–134;
  blockchain 210–212, 215; brand
  management 123; cargo commercial
  management 145; customer service
  46; in distribution 96–99, *97–98*;
  enterprise AI 166–170; for explainable
  AI 178, 187; in human resources
  management 148, **149,** 150, 152–153;
  retailing and embedded RM 108–109
user experiences (UX) 195
user interface (UI) 195
US Federal Aviation Administration 63

value-distracting 37
Value Pack fare 110
VentureBeat 146n2

venture capital (VC) market 138
Vietnam Airlines 36
Vinod, B. 80n2
Virgin Atlantic Airways 24, 41, 46, 85
virtual reality (VR) 218, 220, 221
VirtuousAI 176
VISA 206
visual flight rules (VFR) 10
Vorneweg, L. 80n5, 109n7
Vueling 158

Walmart 91, 206
Walsh, W. 158
waypoints 10
webcargo 136
web3/Web3.0 111, 218, 221, 225
weight and balance (W&B) management systems 19–21
WestJet 72
WhatsApp 26, 27
Wi-Fi 77
Willingness to Pay (WTP) 138
Winding Tree's blockchain 211
Wingborn 64n1

Wireless Avionics Intra-Communications (WAIC) 43–45, **45,** 50
wireless sensor networks *see* Wireless Avionics Intra-Communications (WAIC)
Wizz Air 85
Wizz Jet 72
Workable 152
Workday Peakon Employee Voice 150
workforce analytics, human resources management 148–152
World Airline News 118n2
World Traveller 119

XAI *see* explainable AI (XAI)

Yahoo 1
yield management 72
YouTube 85

Zamna 211
Zeitgeist element 219
zero risk environment, ethical AI 194
Zimbabwe 201
Zuckerberg, M. 102

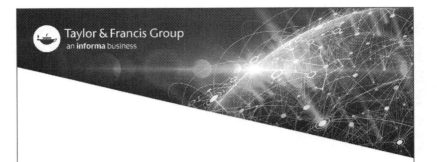

Printed in the United States
by Baker & Taylor Publisher Services